BEST-LOVED SONGS

OF THE AMERICAN PEOPLE

BEST-LOVED

 ## SONGS

OF THE

AMERICAN PEOPLE

DENES AGAY

Illustrations by Reisie Lonette

GUILDAMERICA
B O O K S

BOOKSPAN
GARDEN CITY, NEW YORK

To Mary and Susie

Published by GuildAmerica® Books, an imprint and registered
trademark of BOOKSPAN, Department GB, 401
Franklin Avenue, Garden City, New York 11530

ISBN: 0-7394-0381-8

ACKNOWLEDGMENT

It would be impossible to list the countless sources which were consulted in the compilation and editing of this volume. The following publications, however, were especially helpful and should be noted here:

Rudy Blesh and Harriet Janis. *They All Played Ragtime*. New York: Alfred A. Knopf, 1950.

D. Duane Braun. *The Sociology and History of American Music and Dance*. Ann Arbor, Michigan: Ann Arbor Publishers, 1969.

Ann Charters. *The Ragtime Songbook*. New York: Oak Publications, 1965.

Gilbert Chase. *America's Music*. New York: McGraw-Hill Book Company, Inc., 1955.

David Ewen. *Great Men of American Popular Song*. Englewood Cliffs, N.J.: Prentice-Hall, Inc., 1970, 1972.

William Arms Fisher. *Notes on Music in Old Boston*. Boston: Oliver Ditson Company, 1918.

Isaac Goldberg. *Tin Pan Alley—A Chronicle of American Popular Music*. New York: Frederick Ungar Publishing Co., Inc., 1930, 1961.

H. Wiley Hitchcock. *Music in the United States*. Englewood Cliffs, N.J.: Prentice-Hall, Inc., 1969.

John Tasker Howard. *Our American Music*. New York: Thomas Y. Crowell Company, 1929, 1939.

Philip D. Jordan and Lillian Kessler. *Songs of Yesterday*. Garden City, N.Y.: Doubleday, Doran & Co., Inc., 1941.

John A. Lomax and Alan Lomax. *Folk Song U.S.A.* New York: Duell, Sloan and Pearce, 1947.

Irving Lowens. *Music and Musicians in Early America*. New York: W. W. Norton & Co., Inc., 1964.

Maxwell F. Marcuse. *Tin Pan Alley in Gaslight*. Watkins Glen, N.Y.: Century House, 1959.

Myron Matlaw. *The Black Crook and Other Nineteenth-Century American Plays*. New York: E. P. Dutton & Co., Inc., 1967.

Hazel Meyer. *The Gold in Tin Pan Alley*. Philadelphia: J. B. Lippincott Company, 1958.

John W. Molnar. *Songs from the Williamsburg Theatre*. Williamsburg, Virginia: The Colonial Williamsburg Foundation, 1972.

John Rublowsky. *Music in America*. New York: Crowell-Collier Press, 1967.

Irving L. Sablosky. *American Music*. Chicago: The University of Chicago Press, 1969.

Irwin Silber. *Songs of the Civil War*. New York: Columbia University Press, 1960.

Eileen Southern. *The Music of Black Americans*. New York: W. W. Norton & Co., 1971.

Sigmund Spaeth. *A History of Popular Music in America*. New York: Random House, 1948.

Alec Wilder. *American Popular Song—The Great Innovators 1900–1950*. New York: Oxford University Press, 1972.

I want to express my gratitude to the following music publishing firms, which were kind enough to grant me permission to reprint outstanding songs from their catalogues:

Belwin-Mills Publishing Corp.; Irving Berlin Music Corporation; Boston Music Company; Chappell and Co., Inc.; The John Church Company; Sam Fox Publishing Company; Frank Music Corp.; Rinimer Corporation; Handy Bros. Music Co., Inc.; Harms, Inc.; T. B. Harms Company; MCA Music; Edward B. Marks Music Corporation; Edwin H. Morris & Co., Inc.; New World Music Corporation; Theodore Presser Company; G. Schirmer, Inc.; Shawnee Press, Inc.; Warner Bros. Publications, Inc.

A special word of appreciation goes to Mr. William G. Thompson, of Doubleday, for his inestimable guidance and assistance in all aspects of the preparation of this book. Finally, my loving thanks to my wife, Mary, and to our daughter, Susan, who have given me so much tangible help with research, typing, and proofreading, as well as sympathetic support from inception to completion of this volume.

DENES AGAY

CONTENTS

III BATTLE CRIES, HEART-THROBS AND HIGH-JINKS
VAUDEVILLE TUNES—SPIRITUALS—RAGS

IV FROM TIN PAN ALLEY TO MAIN STREET
"EVEN POP CAN PLAY THE PIANOLA"

V THE HEYDAY OF AMERICAN MELODY

THE GREAT WHITE WAY—THE AIRWAVES—FOLKWAYS

INTRODUCTION

THE aim of this book is entertainment: musical entertainment—with a perspective. These songs—loved and sung by the American people from colonial days to our time—are presented here in approximately chronological sequence. Inevitably, one is not only entertained but also made aware of the unfolding panorama of two hundred years of American life with its sounds, images, thoughts and sentiments.

It has been said many times that the songs of a nation are also a record of its history, and that the melodies a nation sings closely reflect its struggles and aspirations, its changing moods, manners and morals. This is especially true in America, where freedom of expression and the pursuit of happiness are constitutionally guaranteed. Here people could sing unrestrained; and sing they did, with heart and gusto, under all circumstances and on all conceivable subjects: noble and inspiring, playful and humorous, sentimental and nostalgic, boisterous and zestful. Farmers, city dwellers, soldiers, sailors, cowboys, lumberjacks, slaves, prisoners—rich and poor, young and old—they all sang, from the Atlantic to the Pacific, from Bunker Hill to Broadway.

The catalogue of American songs is unparalleled in its rich variety. The reasons for this are numerous:
–the many contributing nationalistic and racial traits resulting from immigration, often forced immigration, from Europe, Africa, Latin America;
–the essentially homogeneous, middle-class nature of American society, forming a vast audience and a receptive public eager for musical diversions;
–the expanding American frontier and the resulting mobility of the populace, constantly exposed to new experiences and challenges;
–and last, but not least, the many-faceted, dynamic, never-a-dull-moment quality of American life in general, which, it seems, had an innate need for song.

In spite of the enormous quantity and amazing variety of our song repertory, it has been maintained for a long time, indeed until relatively recently, that America's popular songs had no national characteristics and that we had no "national people's music." This superficial and by now largely refuted stand was nurtured by a coterie of rather pedantic, Europe-oriented surveyors of the American musical scene, who were either unaware of our rich, indigenous musical lore, or were so deeply steeped in and blinded by the "genteel tradition" of our nineteenth-century song culture, that they were unable to recognize the sturdy native characteristics in the body of our national music. These were the scholars who described minstrel songs as the "lowest dregs of music." They so strongly influenced prevailing musical opinion that Stephen Foster was willing to let his "Old Folks at Home" be published as "written and composed by E. P. Christy," the famous minstrel, so that his (Foster's) name might not be associated with what, in those days, were called "Ethiopian melodies." Similarly, ragtime, in the opinion of experts in 1913, was music which "exalts noise, rush and street vulgarity."

All this, of course, is history now. During the last few decades a more thorough research of our folklore, an unbiased evaluation of the tremendous, indeed decisive, contributions of black Americans toward the emergence of a distinctive American idiom, and a clearer view of the shaping forces of American history—political, social, artistic—enable us to evaluate the ingredients of our musical heritage with more understanding. Minstrel tunes, "Ethiopian melodies," ragtime, together with the nineteenth-century gospel songs and sentiment-laden ballads, often scorned by critics, all have their proper, much-appreciated role in our traditional song repertory.

It is true that a large portion of this repertory was imported, especially before 1800 and for a good many years after that. It is also a fact that many of our popular tunes written in the nineteenth century were patterned after European models. But we know now that typical American traits surfaced very early, as early as the 1820s, and by the 1840s a large crop of such songs was in full bloom. Could "Dixie" or "Oh! Susanna" have been written in any other part of the world? Could the rugged camp-meeting songs, the spirituals, the tunes of the westward expansion be part of any other nation's folklore? By the end of the century, with the cakewalk and ragtime, and a little later with blues and jazz, a typically indigenous American musical expression was at hand which not only provided a unique catalogue of popular tunes, but also profoundly influenced our writers of light music—uncommonly gifted writers, one should add, whose creative efforts during the past half century have made the melodies of Broadway and the American theater "best loved" not only in this country but the world over.

Selecting songs for this volume from the vast storehouse of American melody was an arduous and often agonizing task. What to include and what to omit, how to balance the contents so that there would be a fair representation from all periods of our history and from all the various song categories, became a matter of careful scrutiny at every step and in each instance. To qualify for inclusion, songs had to be characteristic of and widely known in their time. If by today they have been forgotten, they had to possess certain qualities and earmarks which, in the editor's judgment, were worth rediscovering. It also should be noted here that the main guiding factor in the selections was popularity and not artistic merit, polish or originality. Esthetic considerations were, however, operative when choice could be made between songs which in other respects were equally qualified.

Selections from the song repertory of our time require a further brief comment. Nearly all songs written in the twentieth century are protected by copyright and can be reprinted only by special agreements. It has been a source of great personal gratification that, with the exception of only one or two, all music publishers approached on this matter have granted the requested licenses. Only with their co-operation was it possible to make the contents of this collection so wide-ranging and all-encompassing.

Every song herein is presented in full, with verse and chorus complete, with no abridgments whatsoever. Where certain songs are known in differing versions, as is often the case with folk songs, decisions were made in favor of the more pleasing, or more popular, variant. Similar editorial procedure was applied to folks songs with many, often dozens, of varying lyric stanzas. To print all the verses of these songs would have been impossible, impractical, and often undesirable. In these instances selections were made on the basis of logical meaning, poetic sense and a better match of words and music ("singability").

Included are certain songs the words of which may be offensive for our society today insofar as they present the stereotyped caricature of the black man, as in some of the minstrel tunes and "coon" songs of the ragtime era. It was felt that the omission of these songs would misrepresent the continuity of American musical history and make this song panorama deficient. In addition, the omission would have deprived us of the presentation of song materials which were important building blocks of that uniquely American musical idiom, jazz. The existence of these songs is an historic-musical fact. They were written by both black and white Americans, and it was felt that their inclusion within the context of this survey of American melody is both justified and necessary.

Minor adjustments of spelling were made in the lyrics of those minstrel tunes, spirituals and other similar songs of the last century which, originally, had the words printed phonetically in the idiomatic speech of the southern Negro. This was retained only where it was deemed necessary for the preservation of the style, character and mood of the song. In all other instances words are printed with standard spelling. It was felt that the specific quality and genre of the song is not damaged; indeed, its general appeal is enhanced, if today we can sing:

> *Way down upon the Swanee River,*
> *Far, far away,*
> *There's where my heart is turning ever,*
> *There's where the old folks stay.*

instead of the 1851 version:

> *Way down upon de Swanee Ribber,*
> *Far, far away,*
> *Dere's wha my heart is turning ebber,*
> *Dere's wha de old folks stay.*

All songs are presented in new arrangements, comfortable to sing and easy to play. Original editions were consulted whenever possible, but had to be rearranged in most cases because of their archaic notation methods and often clumsy, primitive harmonizations which do not satisfy today's somewhat more sophisticated tastes and publishing standards. It should be emphasized that these new arrangements do not try to "modernize" or in any way alter the fundamental styles of the songs. On the contrary, they try to underline their generic character and utilize only the harmonic vocabularies of their respective eras. In playing and singing popular songs, freedom and spontaneity are vital elements. These new piano settings are kept simple and uncluttered in texture to leave way for occasional embellishments and improvisational touches on the part of the performer.

These, then, are the thoughts and principles that have guided the work on this volume. In addition to the objective criteria listed, the final selection of songs does, of course, reflect the personal taste and predilections of the editor. It is hoped that most people will agree with these choices, but it is also realized that there cannot be complete consensus on such a matter, involving, as it does, so many factors—regional, social and personal—which are apt to influence individual preferences. To help in the forming of a proper perspective on the collection as a whole, it was divided into five chronological segments with an introductory description for each period. In addition, a separate section, *Notes on the Songs*, furnishes some factual information and pertinent data of interest on both the songs and their writers.

Our journey through the colorful paths of American melody begins with a still popular psalm tune brought over by the Pilgrims on the *Mayflower*, and a group of eighteenth-century airs widely sung in colonial homes, theaters and taverns. The latest entries, bringing the contents up to date, are best-loved melodies from recent Broadway shows and from the large reservoir of modern folk-based hits. Between these two eras, spanning some two and a half centuries, unfolds a fascinating sequence of tuneful Americana, which is both an historic record and an uncommonly rich source of musical entertainment.

DENES AGAY

I

OLD COLONY TIMES
AND THE NEW NATION

AMONG the meager belongings each family brought to the New World on the *Mayflower* was a small book of psalm tunes prepared for them in Holland a few years before their departure by a fellow separatist theologian, Henry Ainsworth. In this book, known since as *The Ainsworth Psalter*, the original Hebrew texts of the Psalms were translated into versified English and adapted to well-known traditional hymns of European churches. The Reverend Ainsworth felt that, since the ancient Hebrew chants of the Psalms—"God's musick," as he called them—were not known, he was justified in combining the sacred words with "man-made tunes." His work in fusing text and music was singularly successful and a few of the original thirty-nine tunes are still widely sung, especially the sturdy, imperishable OLD HUNDREDTH, an adaptation of the one-hundredth Psalm, which, with a different text, is the "Doxology" of modern Protestant churches.

Not for long was *The Ainsworth Psalter* the only hymnal serving the Pilgrims' devotional needs. In 1640, just twenty years after their arrival, another, equally historic, collection, *The Bay Psalm Book*, was published in Cambridge, Massachusetts. This is the first English-language book printed in New England. Of the many sources nourishing the wide stream of American song, influencing its course and character, these two books are the oldest and among the most important.

There have been, of course, a great many other sources. America's music had many roots, taking hold and beginning to grow almost simultaneously in several widely dispersed areas of the continent where the first immigrants landed. The early settlers, who came first from the British Isles and later from Holland, France, Germany, Sweden, Italy and other parts of Europe, brought with them a vast heritage of songs in all categories of musical expression: faith, romance, patriotism, merriment. In time, all of these songs underwent changes. They were, by purely oral transmission and tradition, transformed to fit local circumstances and conditions. The colonists had to face a new life in a strange new world; they were confronted with new challenges and had to adapt to new ways of living. And the songs changed with the people. With every new ship docking in the harbors, new immigrants and new songs arrived. Slowly and inevitably, this ever-growing large body of songs underwent a process of assimilation—through many subtle changes in text, melody, rhythm, emphasis—to become part of the American experience and form a musical background characteristic of the life styles in the various colonies.

What were these factors influencing the evolution of American popular song? Faith and religion were among the earliest and strongest. For this reason the story of America's best-loved songs must begin with the aforementioned *Ainsworth Psalter* and *The Bay Psalm Book*. In order properly to gauge their long-range influence and importance we must recognize the unique role of psalm singing in the life of the Puritans. Their church was not only a house of worship, but also a school, a court of law, a meeting place of government—a focus of community life both spiritual and secular. Concomitantly, the psalm was not only a church song, but also a song for the home, for the workshop, for outdoors. In other words, the religious and the secular aspects of Puritan life closely intertwined. This is the reason that *The Bay Psalm Book* went through seventy editions and provided the keynote for the musical life of New England for over a century.

It should be noted here that the first edition of this book (1640) did not contain any musical notation. Only the words of the psalm verses were printed. The Puritan congregations knew well by heart the melodies to be sung with the psalm texts. Gradually, however, as memories weakened, as new generations of worshipers grew up, and as new immigrants arrived, not always familiar with the traditional tunes, the collective sounds of the congregations became somewhat less than pleasing, indeed quite chaotic at times. An anonymous critic scratched the following epigram on a pew of a Salem church:

> *Could poor King David, but for once*
> *To Salem Church repair,*
> *And hear the Psalms thus warbled out*
> *Good Lord how he would swear!*

The church fathers tried to remedy this situation by the use of a method called "deaconing" or "lining out." This was a kind of responsive singing: The deacon or another elder would chant a line of the psalm and the congregation would repeat it line after line. This practice created as many problems as it solved. The rendition of the originally sprightly and vigorous tunes soon became sluggish, dismembered and often drawn out beyond recognition. New remedies for this state of affairs had to be devised. Among them was the idea, quite revolutionary for the time, to print in the psalm books not only the text but the music as well. Beginning with the ninth edition of *The Bay Psalm Book* (1698), the custom of printing the psalm books with the proper musical notation began to take hold. This does not mean that the old ways of "deaconing" were quickly abandoned; indeed, for some time quite a controversy raged about this new way of "singing by note," which was regarded, especially by the older generation, with deep suspicion. A writer in *The New England Chronicle* in 1723 put it this way: "Truly I have a great jealousy that if we once begin to sing by rule, the next thing will be to pray by rule, and preach by rule; and then comes popery."

In spite of the opposition, however, the ways of the reformers won out. Not only was singing by note accepted, but in order to help those who were not versed in reading notes, instruction books which taught the rudiments of music and note reading began to appear. This was followed by an even more far-reaching development, the establishment of singing schools. These schools not only provided congregations with instruction in note reading and the proper way to sing the psalms; they also gave the youth of the community an opportunity for "innocent and profitable recreation." The first of these singing schools opened in Boston sometime before 1720; they multiplied quickly and were extremely popular throughout the eighteenth century. Ultimately, it was through these schools and the itinerant singing teachers traveling with their pitch pipes and music books far and wide, from place to place, that secular music and secular musical activities in New England received their imprimatur and began to flourish, independent of the church. In other parts of Colonial America, all along the eastern seacoast from New York to the Carolinas, secular musical diversions were more unrestrained than in New England. Only the Quakers of Pennsylvania formed an island of abstention against such "frivolous amusements." But the trend toward secularization was inevitable. The rapidly increasing population, the growth of the cities, the brisk commerce, the affluence of the planters, all contributed to the increasing pulse rate of musical activities. America grew, prospered, and sang. The farm houses, the city taverns, the stately mansions and fields of the plantations echoed songs of all descriptions: long narrative ballads, love songs, songs for dancing, courting, working, and for playing games. Ever-present were, of course, the melodies of spiritual uplift, the psalms and hymns.

All these melodies were still mostly imported, but with increasing frequency certain colonial activities and happenings were recorded in the so-called "broadside ballads." These broadsides were a kind of singing newspaper in which noteworthy events, political comments, misfortunes and scandals were put in verse form and set to music. They were printed on sheets and sold on the streets for a penny. Benjamin Franklin, at the age of nine, wrote a few of these and later in his *Autobiography* described the circumstances: ". . . my brother . . . put me on composing occasional ballads. One was called Lighthouse Tragedy . . . and the other was a sailor's song on the taking of Blackbeard the pirate. They were wretched stuff . . . and when they were printed he sent me about the town to sell them. The first one sold wonderfully, the event being recent . . ." The broadsides, which for decades were the only indigenous musical products on these shores, were very important in stimulating the beginning of songwriting in the colonies.

There were several other media through which eighteenth-century Americans could partake of the joys of music, both vocal and instrumental. According to available records, the first "concert of music on sundry instruments" took place in Boston in 1731. Charles Town (renamed Charleston after the Revolution), South Carolina, went a step further. After concerts there were "country dances for the diversion of the ladies." New York and Philadelphia offered series of concerts by subscription. Neither was life outside the cities devoid of music and fun. *The Virginia Gazette* of 1737 announces a horse race and county fair with "handsome entertainment provided for the subscribers and their wives; and such of them as are not so happy as to have wives may treat any other lady . . . ballads [will] be sung for by a number of Songsters, all of them to have liquor sufficient to clear their wind pipes. That a pair of handsome silk stockings of one Pistol value be given to the handsomest Young country maid that appears in the field. With many other Whimsical and Comical Diversions too numerous to mention."

For some reason, not quite obvious today, the theater had to overcome much stronger resistance before it could establish itself as a proper place of entertainment in America. Williamsburg had a theater by 1716, but Boston banned it until almost the end of the century, and even in musical Philadelphia the Magistrates were urged, in 1754, "to take most effective measures for suppressing this disorder." What eventually succeeded in overcoming this moralistic antagonism was the seemingly irresistible appeal of a type of stage presentation imported from England, called the "ballad opera."

The first such play with music, *The Beggar's Opera*, was produced on the London stage in 1728. Its phenomenal success firmly established the genre, which in a short time became very popular in the colonies as well. The reasons for its appeal were obvious: the down-to-earth librettos performed in the vernacular, interspersed with familiar tunes or with light, easy-to-hum songs written for the occasion. All these factors contributed to making the ballad opera ideal stage entertainment for eighteenth-century Americans. It also was, of course, an important source of enrichment for our popular-song repertory. OVER THE HILLS AND FAR AWAY and SWEET IS THE BUDDING SPRING OF LOVE are still thoroughly enjoyable examples from this tuneful era. This body of songs was still mostly imported, but after the 1750s native composers also began to emerge. One of the first and best-known of these was Francis Hopkinson, a signer of the Declaration of Independence, lawyer, judge, poet and, as he claimed, "the first native of the United States who has produced a musical composition." One of his works was a volume of *Seven Songs for the Harpsichord or Forte Piano*, which he dedicated to George Washington. ENRAPTURED I GAZE, included in this volume, is from this work. Hopkinson was a highly erudite, well-trained amateur musician whose songs, although by no means displaying any marked originality, are well-constructed, tastefully harmonized, charming period pieces.

By about 1765 the colonies' dissatisfaction with and resentment against their treatment by England began to be widely felt; it soon ignited into patriotic fervor and found expression in their songs. The first rich harvest of our native American tunes coincides with the Revolution. It is somewhat ironic that, because there were no professional musicians and songwriters among the colonists, some of the stirring verses that exhorted Americans to revolt and fight (THE LIBERTY SONG, for instance) were, in fact, sung to melodies borrowed from England. On the other hand, CHESTER, the most stirring and widely sung air of the Revolution, was written and composed by the first native writer of truly American music, William Billings of Boston.

In contrast to Francis Hopkinson's dainty and polished rococo cadences, Billings' music is sturdy and rugged, with deep roots in the American soil. Billings was a tanner by trade, but devoted all his time and unbounded energies to composing, publishing and promoting his own brand of spirited tunes. He was largely self-taught and had more zeal and enthusiasm than compositional skill. However, the lack of academic training and craftsmanship did not inhibit him in the least. "For my own Part," he explained, "I don't think myself confined to any Rules for composition, laid down by any that went before me . . . I think it is best for every Composer to be his own Carver." He published altogether six books of his psalm tunes, anthems and "fuguing tunes," the latter being a kind of pseudopolyphonic choral song in which "the parts come after each other, with the same notes." It may be of interest that the plates of his first publication, *The New England Psalm Singer,* were engraved by Paul Revere. Billings was well-recognized by his contemporaries throughout the States, but he died in poverty, leaving a truly American—and in its primitive simplicity, often beautiful—legacy of tunes.

Remarkable in its durability, but following the more conventional paths of New England psalmody is the tune CORONATION ("All Hail the Power of Jesus' Name"), published in 1793 and still one of the best loved of devotional songs. It was written by Oliver Holden of Charlestown, Massachusetts. Holden abandoned carpentry to become a very successful composer, singing teacher and choir director of his time.

A unique place among the tunes of the Revolutionary days is assured for YANKEE DOODLE, the first all-American hit song; it has survived for over two hundred years. The origin of both words and music is still somewhat of a conjecture; it became known around 1755 and gained quick popularity, not only in its original form but also through countless variants and parodies. It can be said that the American Revolution began and ended to the strains of YANKEE DOODLE. The British Redcoats marched to Lexington in 1775 singing the sprightly, satirical stanzas to taunt the Yankees. The Colonials adopted the tune very quickly, and when Cornwallis surrendered at Yorktown, it was a lusty Yankee rendition of the song that provided the musical background. The tune is imperishable, probably because, as one of its innumerable verses states:

It suits for feasts, it suits for fun,
And just as well for fighting.

The upsurge of native creativity in songwriting during and after the Revolution did not entirely stem the influx of European songs. Faith and patriotism were the wellsprings of American writers' inspiration, and so they did not cover the entire spectrum of vocal expression. The love songs, the ballads, the humorous and convivial ditties of the day were still importations, mostly from the British Isles. DRINK TO ME ONLY WITH THINE EYES, SALLY IN OUR ALLEY, THE LASS OF RICHMOND HILL, and THE GIRL I LEFT BEHIND ME were popular and well-liked by everybody, including the Founding Fathers.

This remarkable breed of men, while guiding the political and military destinies of the new nation, also had lifelong interests in music and profoundly influenced its growth in eighteenth-century American society. Benjamin Franklin played the guitar and harp; he also invented an instrument called the *glass harmonica,* which aroused considerable attention both here and in Europe. Even Mozart was attracted by its unusual sound and wrote a set of pieces for it. Franklin was also a music critic of keen perception and independent thinking. He did not hesitate, for instance, to find flaws in some of the songs of the great Handel and, at the same time, analyze and praise the simple beauty of his favorite Scottish airs.

Jefferson referred to music as "this favorite passion of my soul." A proficient amateur violinist of discriminating taste, he seized every opportunity to participate in chamber music activities and frequently played duets with Patrick Henry. Throughout his life he was somewhat frustrated because, for reasons of economy, at Monticello he was unable to emulate the ways of the more affluent European aristocracy, who often were able to maintain groups of musicians as part of their households. "The bounds of an American fortune," he regretted, "will not admit the indulgence of a domestic band."

George Washington, from the moment he assumed leadership to the day of his death—and even well after—was the inspiration and subject for countless pieces of music of all kinds. A large volume could be filled with the songs, marches, sonatas, odes and toasts written in his honor. One of the best-known of these was THE PRESIDENT'S MARCH, which later, with words added, became the famous HAIL, COLUMBIA. The Father of our Country did not play a musical instrument, but he was an avid listener and seldom missed an opportunity to attend a concert or theater performance. Anyone playing the spinet at Mount Vernon found a frequent and appreciative listener in him.

"One good song is worth a dozen addresses and proclamations," wrote Joel Barlow, American poet and diplomat at the start of the Revolutionary War. The entire history of our national songs well bears out the truth of this statement; their stirring cadences not only exhorted to battle or gave vent to deeply felt national pride, but also were very effective in calling attention to internal problems, highlighting events of importance and influencing public sentiment in the process of selecting our leaders. In other words, songs were also very effective and powerful tools of politics. The election of our second President was helped by the song ADAMS AND LIBERTY; the campaign before our third presidential election employed the tune of a lively Irish jig, with special lyrics urging the young country to "join with heart and soul and voice for Jefferson and Liberty." One of the most popular songs of early nineteenth-century America, which also helped to put Andrew

Jackson in the White House, was THE HUNTERS OF KENTUCKY, celebrating Old Hickory Jackson's great victory over the British at the battle of New Orleans.

Two years later, a well-known episode during the same war, the British shelling of Fort McHenry in Chesapeake Bay, inspired the young Baltimore lawyer, Francis Scott Key, to write the words of THE STAR-SPANGLED BANNER. The song became popular immediately and was soon recognized as our national anthem. Our other, almost equally honored and best-loved national song, AMERICA, has a melody identical to the British national anthem, "God Save the King," with words written in 1832 by Boston clergyman Samuel Francis Smith.

The richness, diversity and overall secular spirit of our popular-song repertory were manifest as early as the beginning of the 1800s in a profusion of songbook publications. Some of these books, usually pocket-size, had a general content of various song categories, such as *The Columbian Songster*, published in Boston, boasting "a collection of the newest and most celebrated Sentimental, Convivial, Humorous, Satirical, Pastoral, Hunting, Sea and Masonic songs, being the largest and best collection ever published in America." There were also songsters to appeal to more specific interests: *The Amorous Songster, The Jovial Songster, The Theatrical Songster;* there were *Songs for the Amusement of Children, Songs for Winter Evening Amusement,* and hundreds more.

In addition to the ever-present obvious human emotions—faith, love, patriotism—there were many social, economic and ethnic factors and crosscurrents which influenced the growth and character of song literature in early America, in the colonies and in the new nation. In the nineteenth century two other powerful influences were added—those of the expanding frontiers, and the black Americans.

[7]

Old Hundredth

Words by
William Kethe

Music by
Louis Bourgeois

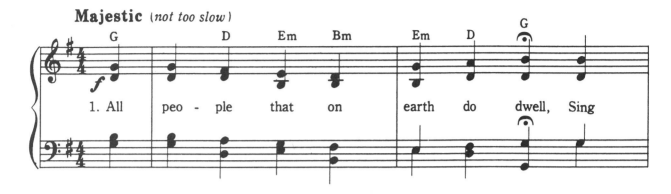

1. All peo - ple that on earth do dwell, Sing

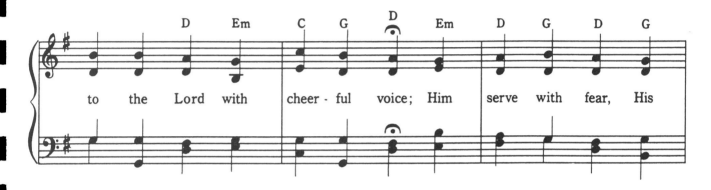

to the Lord with cheer - ful voice; Him serve with fear, His

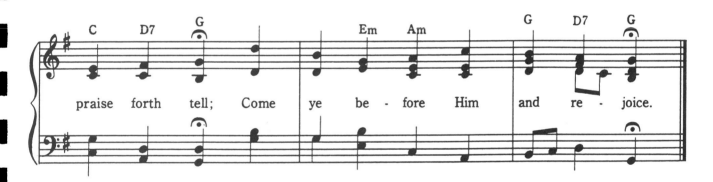

praise forth tell; Come ye be - fore Him and re - joice.

2. Know that the Lord is God indeed;
   Without our aid He did us make;
   We are His flock, He doth us feed,
   And for His sheep He doth us take.

3. O enter then His gates with praise,
   Approach with joy His courts unto:
   Praise, laud, and bless His name always,
   For it is seemly so to do.

4. For why? the Lord our God is good,
   His mercy is forever sure;
   His truth at all times firmly stood,
   And shall from age to age endure.

5. Praise God, from whom all blessings flow;
   Praise Him all creatures here below;
   Praise Him above, ye heav'nly host;
   Praise Father, Son and Holy Ghost.

Words of 5th stanza ("Doxology") by Thomas Ken

[9]

Greensleeves

Old Folk Ballad

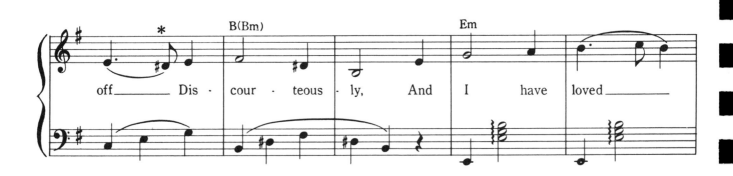

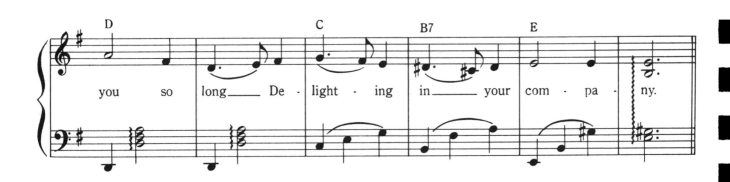

All sharps in small print are optional

2. I have been ready at your hand,
   To grant whatever you would crave;
   I have both waged life and land
   Your love and good-will for to have.
   Chorus

3. I bought thee kerchers to thy head,
   That were wrought fine and gallantly;
   I kept thee both at board and bed,
   Which cost my purse well favour'dly.
   Chorus

4. I bought thee petticoats of the best,
   The cloth so fine as might be;
   I gave thee jewels for thy chest,
   And all this cost I spent on thee.
   Chorus

5. My men were clothed all in green,
   And they did ever wait on thee;
   All this was gallant to be seen,
   And yet thou wouldst not love me.
   Chorus

6. They set thee up, they took thee down,
   They served thee with humility;
   Thy foot might not once thouch the ground,
   And yet thou wouldst not love me.
   Chorus

7. Well I will pray to God on high,
   That thou my constancy mayst see,
   And that yet once before I die
   Thou wilt vouchsafe to love me.
   Chorus

8. Greensleeves, now farewell, adieu!
   God I pray to prosper thee!
   For I am still thy lover true,
   Come once again and love me.
   Chorus

[11]

Froggie Went A-Courtin'

Very Old Tune for Children

With a lively, happy beat

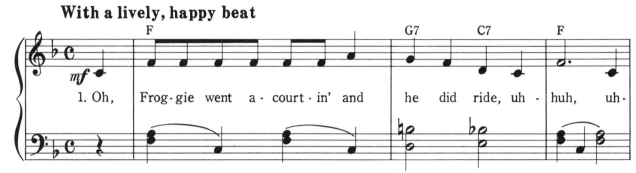

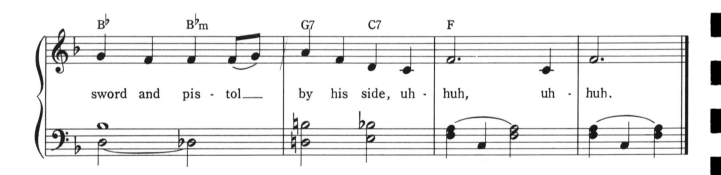

2. He rode up to Miss Mousie's door,
   Uh-huh, uh-huh.
He rode up to Miss Mousie's door,
Where he had often been before.
   Uh-huh, uh-huh.

3. He said, "Miss Mouse, are you within?"
   Uh-huh, uh-huh.
He said, "Miss Mouse, are you within?"
"Just lift the latch and please walk in."
   Uh-huh, uh-huh.

4. He took Miss Mousie on his knee,
   Uh-huh, uh-huh.
He took Miss Mousie on his knee,
And said, "Miss Mouse, will you marry me?"
   Uh-huh, uh-huh.

5. "Without my Uncle Rat's consent,"
   Uh-huh, uh-huh.
"Without my uncle Rat's consent,
I would not marry the president."
   Uh-huh, uh-huh.

6. When Uncle Rat gave his consent,
     Uh-huh, uh-huh.
   When Uncle Rat gave his consent,
   The weasel wrote the publishment.
     Uh-huh, uh-huh.

7. So, Uncle Rat, he went to town,
     Uh-huh, uh-huh.
   Uncle Rat, he went to town
   To buy his niece a wedding gown.
     Uh-huh, uh-huh.

8. Where will the wedding breakfast be?
     Uh-huh, uh-huh.
   Where will the wedding breakfast be?
   Away down yonder in the hollow tree.
     Uh-huh, uh-huh.

9. What will the wedding breakfast be?
     Uh-huh, uh-huh.
   What will the wedding breakfast be?
   Two green beans and a black-eyed pea.
     Uh-huh, uh-huh.

10. The first to come was the bumblebee,
      Uh-huh, uh-huh.
    The first to come was the bumblebee,
    He danced a jig with Miss Mousie.
      Uh-huh, uh-huh.

11. The next to come was Mister Drake,
      Uh-huh, uh-huh.
    The next to come was Mister Drake,
    He ate up all of the wedding cake.
      Uh-huh, uh-huh.

12. The owl did hoot, the birds they sang,
      Uh-huh, uh-huh.
    The owl did hoot, the birds they sang,
    And through the woods the music rang.
      Uh-huh, uh-huh.

13. They all went sailing on the lake,
      Uh-huh, uh-huh.
    They all went sailing on the lake,
    And they all got swallowed by a big black snake.
      Uh-huh, uh-huh.

14. There's bread and cheese upon the shelf,
      Uh-huh, uh-huh.
    There's bread and cheese upon the shelf,
    If you want any more just sing it yourself.
      Uh-huh, uh-huh.

Over The Hills And Far Away

from "The Beggar's Opera"

Words by
John Gay

Music
Anonymous

With spirited motion

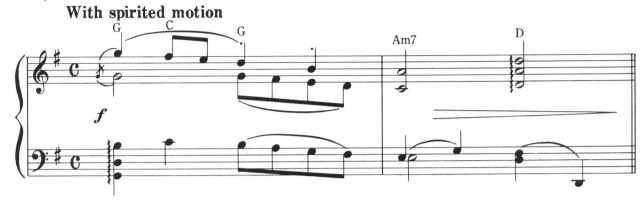

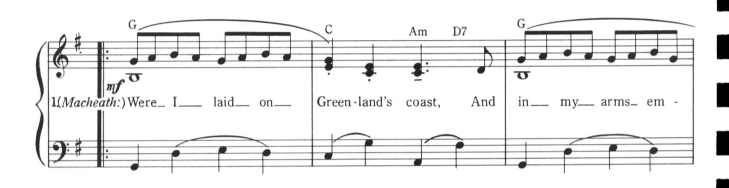

1.(*Macheath:*) Were I laid on Green-land's coast, And in my arms em -

brac'd my lass; Warm a - midst e - ter - nal frost, Too

soon the half year's night would pass. And I would love you

all the day, Ev - 'ry night would___ kiss and play,

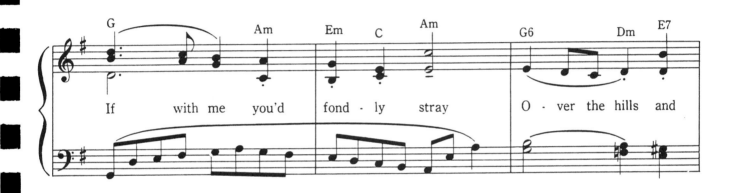

If with me you'd fond - ly stray O - ver the hills and

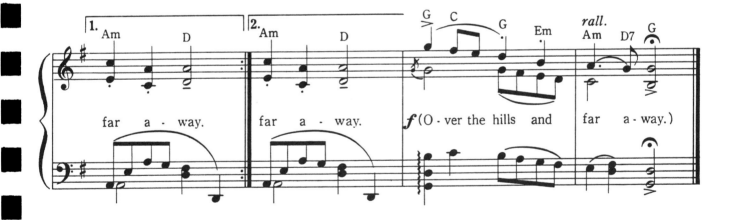

far a - way. far a - way. *f* (O - ver the hills and far a - way.)

2. (*Polly:*) Were I sold on Indian soil,
              Soon as the burning day was clos'd,
              I could mock the sultry toil
              When on my charmer's breast repos'd.

              Refrain

[15]

Sally In Our Alley

Words by
Henry Carey

Old English Air

2. Of all the days within the week,
   I dearly love but one day;
   And that's the day that comes betwixt
   The Saturday and Monday.
   Oh, then I'm dress'd all in my best,
   To walk abroad with Sally;
   She is the darling of my heart,
   And lives in our alley.

3. My master, and the neighbors all,
   Make game of me and Sally;
   And but for her I'd rather be
   A slave, and row a galley.
   But when my sev'n long years are out,
   Oh, then I'll marry Sally,
   And then how happily we'll live!
   But not in our alley.

[16]

Barb'ra Allen

Old English-American Folk Ballad

With an easy flow

1. In Scar-let town, where I was born, There was a fair maid dwel-lin',___ Made ev'-ry youth cry___ "Well-a-day", Her name was Bar-b'ra Al-len.

2. 'Twas in the merry month of May
When green buds they were swellin';
Sweet William on his deathbed lay
For love of Barb'ra Allen.

3. He sent his servant to the town,
The place where she was dwellin'
Cried, "Master bids you come to him,
If your name be Barb'ra Allen."

4. Well, slowly, slowly got she up
And slowly went she nigh him;
But all she said as she passed his bed,
"Young man, I think you're dying."

5. She walked out in the green, green fields,
She heard his death bells knellin'.
And every stroke they seemed to say,
"Hard-hearted Barb'ra Allen."

6. "Oh, father, father, dig my grave,
Go dig it deep and narrow.
Sweet William died for me today;
I'll die for him tomorrow."

7. They buried her in the old churchyard,
Sweet William's grave was nigh her,
And from his heart grew a red, red rose,
And from her heart a briar.

8. They grew and grew up the old church wall,
'Till they could grow no higher,
Until they tied a true lover's knot,
The red rose and the briar.

Sweet Is The Budding Spring of Love

from the ballad opera "Flora, or Hob In The Well"

Words by
John Hippisley

Music
Anonymous

cling 'til de - sires_ are_ lost, Suc - ceed - ed_ by_ e -

ter - nal Frost, Suc - ceed - ed_ by_ e - ter - nal Frost.

The Liberty Song

Words by
John Dickinson

Music by
William Boyce

With spirited motion

1. Come join hand in hand brave A - mer - i cans all, And rouse your bold hearts at fair Li - ber - ty's call; No ty - ran - nous acts shall sup - press your just claim, Or stain with dis - hon - our A - mer - i - ca's name

Chorus

In Free - dom we're born and in Free - dom we'll live, Our purs - es are ready. Stead - y, friends, stead - y, Not as slaves, but as Free - men our mon - ey we'll give.

2. Our worthy forefathers – Let's give them a cheer –
To climates unknown did courageously steer;
Thro' oceans, to deserts, for freedom they came,
And dying bequeath'd us their freedom and fame. *Chorus*

3. The free their own hands had to liberty rear'd;
They liv'd to behold growing strong and rever'd;
With transport they cry'd, "Now our wishes we gain,
For our children shall gather the fruits of our pain." *Chorus*

4. Swarms of placemen and pensioners soon will appear
Like locusts deforming the charms of the year;
Suns vainly will rise, showers vainly descend,
If we are to drudge for what others shall spend. *Chorus*

5. Then join hand in hand, brave Americans all,
By uniting we stand, by dividing we fall;
In so righteous a cause let us hope to succeed,
For Heaven approves of each generous deed. *Chorus*

6. All ages shall speak with amaze and applause,
Of the courage we'll show in support of our laws;
To die we can bear – but to serve we disdain,
For shame is to Freedom more dreadful than pain. *Chorus*

7. This bumper I crown for our Sovereign's health,
And this for Britannia's glory and wealth;
That wealth and that glory immortal may be,
If she is but just – and if we are but Free. *Chorus*

Yankee Doodle

Tradional
Early-American Tune

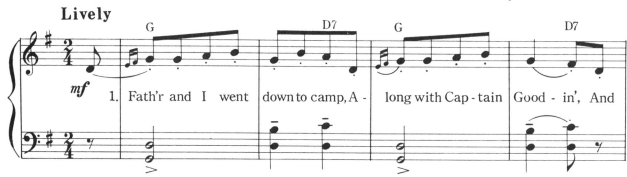

2. And there we saw a thousand men,
   As rich as Squire David;
   And what they wasted ev'ry day,
   I wish it could be saved.
   Chorus

3. And there was Captain Washington
   Upon a slapping stallion,
   A-giving orders to his men;
   I guess there was a million.
   Chorus

4. And then the feathers on his hat,
   They looked so 'tarnal fine, ah!
   I wanted peskily to get
   To give to my Jemima.
   Chorus

5. And there I saw a little keg,
   Its heads were made of leather,
   They knocked upon't with little sticks,
   To call the folks together.
   Chorus

6. And there they'd fife away like fun,
   And play on cornstalk fiddles,
   And some had ribbons red as blood,
   All bound about their middles.
   Chorus

7. The troopers, too, would gallop up
   And fire right in our faces;
   It scared me almost half to death
   To see them run such races.
   Chorus

8. Uncle Sam came there to change
   Some pancakes and some onions,
   For 'lasses cake to carry home
   To give his wife and young ones.
   Chorus

9. But I can't tell half I see,
   They kept up such a smother;
   So I took my hat off, made a bow,
   And scampered home to mother.
   Chorus

Another popular version

Oh, Yankee Doodle went to town,
A riding on a pony
He stuck a feather in his hat
And called it macaroni.

Yankee Doodle, doodle doo,
Yankee Doodle Dandy,
All the lads and lassies are
As sweet as sugar candy.

Bunker Hill

(The American Hero)

Words by
Nathaniel Niles

Music by
Andrew Law

2. Death will invade us by the Means appointed,
    And we must all bow to the King of Terrors;
    Nor am I anxious, nor am I anxious,
    If I am prepared, what shape he comes in.

3. Still shall the Banner of the King of Heaven
    Never advance where I'm afraid to follow:
    While that precedes me, while that precedes me
    With an open Bosom, War, I defy thee.

4. Life, for my Country and the Cause of Freedom,
    Is but a Trifle for a Worm to part with;
    And if preserved, and if preserved
    In so great a Contest, Life is redoubled.

Chester

Words and music by
William Billings

2. The foe comes on with haughty stride,
Our troops advance with martial noise;
Their vet'rans flee before our youth,
And gen'rals yield to beardless boys.

3. What grateful off'ring shall we bring?
What shall we render to this Lord?
Loud Hallelujah let us sing,
And praise His Name on ev'ry chord.

[25]

Enraptured I Gaze

Words and music by
Francis Hopkinson

With gentle motion

3. Beyond all expression my Delia I love,
My heart is so fix'd that it never can rove;
When I see her I think 'tis an angel I see,
And the charms of her mind are a heav'n to me.

The Women All Tell Me

Words and music anonymous

if you don't like them, why, let them a - lone.

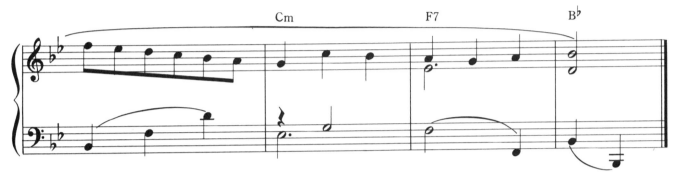

2. Although I have left her, the truth I'll declare;
   I believe she was good, and I'm sure she was fair;
   But goodness and charms in a bumper I see
   That make it as good and as charming as she.

3. My Chloe had dimples and smiles I must own;
   But, though she could smile, yet in truth she could frown;
   But tell me, ye lovers of liquor divine,
   Did you e'er see a frown in a bumper of wine?

4. Her lilies and roses were just in their prime;
   Yet lilies and roses are conquered by time;
   But in wine from its age, such benefit flows,
   That we like it the better the older it grows.

5. Let murders and battles and history prove
   The mischiefs that wait upon rivals in love;
   But in drinking, thank heaven, no rival contends,
   For the more we love liquor, the more we are friends.

6. We shorten our days when with love we engage,
   It brings on disease and hastens old age;
   But wine from grim death can its votaries save,
   And keep out th'other leg, when there's one in the grave.

7. She too might have poison'd the joy of my life,
   With nurses and babies and squalling and strife;
   But my wine neither nurses nor babies can bring,
   And a big-bellied bottle's a mighty good thing.

   Then let my dear Chloe no longer complain;
   She's rid of her lover, and I of my pain:
   For in wine, mighty wine, many comforts I spy
   Should you doubt what I say, take a bumper and try!

Drink To Me Only With Thine Eyes

Words by
Ben Jonson

Traditional Air

Rather slowly; tenderly

2. I sent thee late a rosy wreath,
   Not so much hon'ring thee
   As giving it a hope that there
   It could not withered be;
   But thou thereon did'st only breathe,
   And sent'st it back to me,
   Since when it grows and smells, I swear,
   Not of itself, but thee.

The Girl I Left Behind Me

Traditional Fife Tune

Briskly

1. I'm lone-some since I cross'd the hill, And o'er the moor and valley; Such heav-y thoughts my heart do fill, Since part-ing with my Sal-ly. I seek no more the fine and gay, For each does but re-mind me How swift the hours did pass a-way with the girl I've left be-hind me.

2. Oh, ne'er shall I forget the night,
The stars were bright above me,
And gently lent their silv'ry light,
When first she vow'd she loved me.

But now I'm bound to Brighton camp,
Kind Heav'n, may favor find me,
And send me safely back again
To the girl I've left behind me.

[31]

Hail, Columbia

(The President's March)

Words by
Joseph Hopkinson

Music by
Philip Phile

2. Immortal patriots, rise once more,
   Defend your rights, defend your shore,
   Let no rude foe with impious hand,
   Let no rude foe with impious hand,
   Invade the shrine where sacred lies
   Of toil and blood the well-earned prize.
   While off'ring peace, sincere and just,
   In heav'n we place a manly trust,
   That truth and justice may prevail,
   And ev'ry scheme of bondage fail. *Chorus*

3. Beloved the chief who now commands,
   Once more to serve his country stands,
   The rock on which the storm will beat,
   The rock on which the storm will beat,
   But arm'd in virtue firm and true,
   His hopes are fixed on Heav'n and you.
   When hope was sinking in dismay,
   When glooms obscured Columbia's day,
   His steady mind from changes free
   Resolv'd on Death or Liberty. *Chorus*

The Lass Of Richmond Hill

Words by
Leonard McNally

Music by
James Hook

Moderately lively

1. On Rich - mond Hill there lives_ a_ lass, More bright than May - day

morn,_____ Whose charms all oth - er maids'_ sur - pass, A

rose with - out a thorn. This lass so neat, with

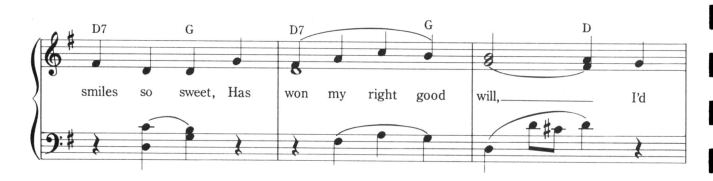

smiles so sweet, Has won my right good will,_____ I'd

2. Ye zephyrs gay that fan the air,
   And wanton thro' the grove,
   O whisper to my charming fair,
   "I die for her I love."
   This lass so neat, with smiles so sweet,
   Has won my right good will,
   I'd crowns resign to call her mine,
   Sweet Lass of Richmond Hill;
   Sweet Lass of Richmond Hill,
   Sweet Lass of Richmond Hill,
   I'd crowns resign to call thee mine,
   Sweet Lass of Richmond Hill.

Coronation
(All Hail The Power Of Jesus' Name)

Words by
Edward Perronet

Music by
Oliver Holden

Majestically

1. All hail the power of Je - sus' name, Let an - gels pros - trate fall; Bring forth the roy - al di - a - dem, And crown Him Lord of ____ all! Bring forth the roy - al di - a - dem, And crown Him Lord ____ of all.

2. Let every kindred, every tribe,
On this terrestrial ball,
To Him all majesty ascribe,
And crown Him Lord of all!
To Him all majesty ascribe,
And crown Him Lord of all.

3. Oh, that with yonder sacred throng
We at His feet may fall,
Join in the everlasting song,
And crown Him Lord of all!
Join in the everlasting song,
And crown Him Lord of all.

Auld Lang Syne

Words by
Robert Burns

Old Scottish Air

2. And here's a hand, my trusty frien',
    And gie's a hand o' thine;
    We'll tak' a cup o' kindness yet,
    For auld lang syne.
    Refrain

The Star Spangled Banner

Words by
Francis Scott Key

Music by
John Stafford Smith(?)

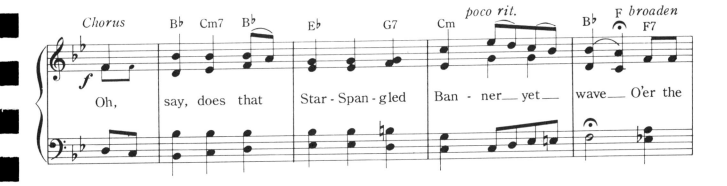

Oh, say, does that Star-Span-gled Ban-ner__ yet__ wave__ O'er the

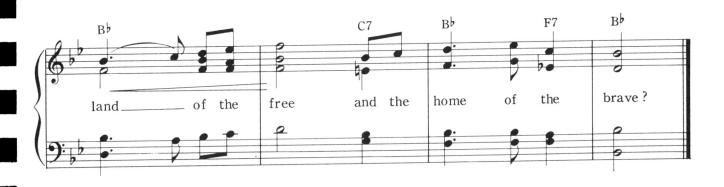

land_____ of the free and the home of the brave?

2. On the shore, dimly seen thro' the mists of the deep,
Where the foe's haughty host in dread silence reposes,
What is that which the breeze, o'er the towering steep,
As it fitfully blows half conceals, half discloses?
Now it catches the gleam of the morning's first beam,
In full glory reflected now shines on the stream;
'Tis the Star Spangled Banner, O long may it wave
O'er the land of the free and the home of the brave!

3. Oh, thus be it ever when freemen shall stand
Between their lov'd homes and the war's desolation!
Blest with vict'ry and peace, may the heav'n rescued land
Praise the Pow'r that hath made and preserved us a nation!
Then conquer we must, when our cause it is just,
And this be our motto, "In God is our trust."
And the Star Spangled Banner in triumph shall wave
O'er the land of the free and the home of the brave!

Old Colony Times

Traditional Early- American Song

In good old Col - o - ny times When we were un - der the

king, Three — ro - guish chaps fell in - to mis - haps, Be - cause they could not sing.

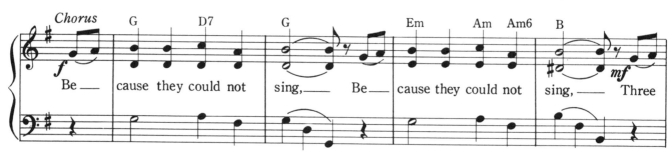

Be — cause they could not sing, — Be — cause they could not sing, — Three

ro - guish chaps fell in - to mis - haps, Be cause they could not sing. —

2. The first he was a miller,
And the second he was a weaver,
And the third he was a little tailor,
Three roguish chaps together.   *Chorus*

3. Now the miller he stole corn,
And the weaver he stole yarn,
And the little tailor stole broadcloth for
To keep these three rogues warm.   *Chorus*

4. The miller got drown'd in his dam,
The weaver got hung in his yarn,
And the devil clapp'd his claw on the little tailor,
With the broadcloth under his arm.   *Chorus*

America

(My Country 'Tis Of Thee)

Words by
Samuel Francis Smith

Old English Air

With spirit

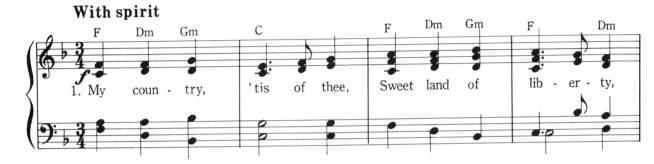

1. My coun - try, 'tis of thee, Sweet land of lib - er - ty,

Of thee I sing; Land where my fa - thers died, Land of the

pil - grims' pride, From ev - 'ry moun - tain - side Let free - dom ring.

2. My native country, thee,
Land of the noble free,
Thy name I love:
I love thy rocks and rills
Thy woods and templed hills;
My heart with rapture thrills
Like that above.

3. Let music swell the breeze,
And ring from all the trees
Sweet freedom's song;
Let mortal tongues awake,
Let all that breathe partake,
Let rocks their silence break,
The sound prolong.

4. Our fathers' God, to thee,
Author of liberty,
To thee we sing;
Long may our land be bright
With freedom's holy light;
Protect us by thy might,
Great God, our King.

[41]

The Hunters Of Kentucky

Words by
Samuel Woodworth

Traditional Tune

Chorus

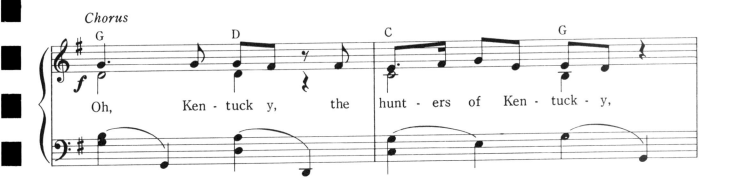

Oh, Ken - tuck - y, the hunt - ers of Ken - tuck - y,

Oh, Ken - tuck - y, the hunt - ers of Ken - tuck - y. _____

2. You've heard I s'pose how New Orleans is fam'd for wealth and beauty,
   There's girls of ev'ry hue it seems, from snowy white to sooty;
   So Packenham he made his brags, if he in fight was lucky,
   He'd have their girls and cotton bags, in spite of old Kentucky.   *Chorus*

3. But Jackson he was wide awake, and wasn't scar'd at trifles,
   For well he knew what aim we take with our Kentucky rifles;
   So he led us down to Cypress swamp, the ground was low and mucky,
   There stood John Bull in martial pomp, and here was old Kentucky.   *Chorus*

4. A bank was rais'd to hide our breast, not that we thought of dying,
   But that we always like to rest, unless the game is flying;
   Behind it stood our little force - none wished it to be greater,
   For ev'ry man was half a horse, and half an alligator.   *Chorus*

5. They found at last 'twas vain to fight, where lead was all their booty;
   And so they wisely took a flight, and left us all our beauty.
   And now if danger e'er annoys, remember what our trade is,
   Just send for us Kentucky boys, and we'll protect you, ladies.   *Chorus*

[43]

Last Week I Took A Wife

Cobbler's Song from "The Forty Thieves"

Words and music by
M. Kelly

1. Last week I took a wife, And when I first did woo her, I vow'd to stick thro' life, Like cob - bler's wax un - to her. But soon we went by

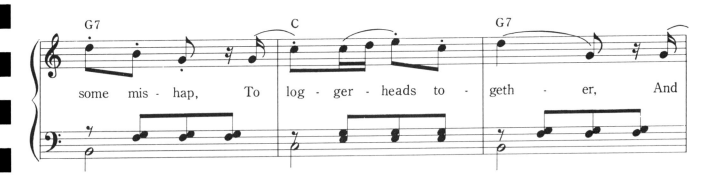

some mis - hap, To log - ger - heads to - geth - er, And

when my__ wife be - gan to strap, Why I be - gan to leath - er.

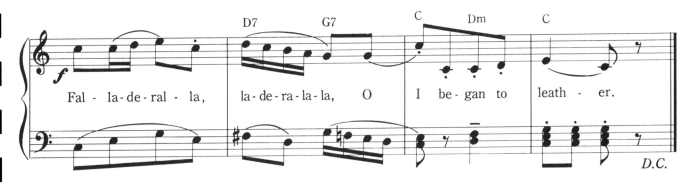

Fal - la - de - ral - la, la - de - ra - la - la, O I be - gan to leath - er.

D.C.

2. My wife without her shoes,
    Is hardly three feet seven,
    And I to all men's views,
    Am full five feet eleven.
    So when to take her down some pegs,
    I drubb'd her neat and clever,
    She made a bolt right thro' my legs,
    And ran away forever.
    Fal-la-de-ral-la, la-de-ra-la-la,
    She ran away forever.

3. When she was gone, good lack!
    My hair like hogs' hair bristled,
    I thought she'd ne'er come back,
    So went to work and whistled.
    Then let her go, I've got my stall,
    Which may no robber rifle,
    'Twould break my heart to lose my awl,
    To lose my wife's a trifle!
    Fal-la-de-ral-la, la-de-ra-la-la,
    To lose my wife? A trifle!

[45]

II
PIONEERS-MINSTRELS
-PARLOR PIANISTS

THE census of 1800 counted more than five million Americans, and the population was increasing rapidly. Immigrants arrived in a steady stream and the country was fast expanding in all directions. Although patriotism, politics, and current events were still frequent topics of our popular-song repertory, the early nineteenth century also began to yield a rich harvest of many other kinds of tunes, as varied in style and mood and form as the people and localities of this far-flung nation. The growing cities offered many opportunities for musical enrichment and enjoyment through their churches, their singing societies and theaters. However, the overwhelming majority of the American people were not city dwellers; they lived in small isolated communities or were on the move westward with their wagons piled high. For them, singing supplied the only release from the trials and rigors of frontier life; it was their main form, and often their only source of recreation, diversion and spiritual nourishment.

The songs of the frontier were overwhelmingly of folk origin. These were tunes of all description to fit all phases of the rigorous daily life of the pioneer. Songs to ease the work load while plowing, cutting timber, driving a wagon; songs for evening relaxation at the fireplace or around the campfire; tunes to play games by, to put baby to sleep, and songs to praise the Lord. Many of these melodies are still known today and some are even more popular than they were a century and a half ago. This is the reason why folk songs usually defy any attempt at chronological classification; like a mountain stream, they may refresh and delight a generation, then disappear just to surface again a decade or a century later, clearer and more enjoyable than

ever. POOR WAYFARING STRANGER, HUSH LITTLE BABY, BARB'RA ALLEN, PAPER OF PINS, CARELESS LOVE, to mention just a few, were part of the frontier lore, and they are also among the best-loved folk songs of our time.

The same is true of some of the religious songs of nineteenth-century America. Of particular importance and musical interest are those spiritual songs of the period which grew from that unique frontier phenomenon of mass worship, the camp meeting. These religious gatherings began on a small scale when people of a certain area came together to hear the circuit-riding preacher whose arrival was announced in advance. Within a short time these meetings developed into giant assemblies lasting several days, to which people flocked by the thousands. Men and women of all denominations, old and young, rich and poor, black and white, came from as far as a hundred miles away. They lived in their wagons or tents; the preaching and singing went on all day and often, whipped into a revivalist frenzy, all night. In spite of its emotional excesses, the camp meeting was the spawning ground for many beautiful, seemingly indestructible songs of faith, such as AMAZING GRACE, WONDROUS LOVE, and many others; the words "Mine eyes have seen the glory of the coming of the Lord" were set to a melody which was a rousing camp-meeting hymn long before it became the BATTLE HYMN OF THE REPUBLIC.

It was not only through oral tradition that these songs became widely known. Hymn books containing both words and music were published from the beginning of the century, often prefaced with an "introduction to the rudiments of music." Some of these books became immensely popular. William Walker's *The Southern Harmony and Musical Companion*, published in 1835, sold over a half million copies in the Midwest alone and could be purchased all over the country in general stores together with groceries, tobacco and other provisions. "Singing Billy" Walker, who compiled, arranged and partly composed the contents of this remarkable collection, was not an erudite musician but had —as did William Billings a half century before him—a deep, instinctive feeling for a truly indigenous vocal expression. His modal melodies and primitive harmonizations have an archaic, often medieval sound, but also have a distinctly native strength and character.

There are two other towering personalities of nineteenth-century American hymnody. Lowell Mason, who left the banking business to become the "father of American church music," was also a music educator of distinction through whose crusading efforts music instruction was introduced in our public schools in 1838. He was a very prolific and successful composer of hymns; MY FAITH LOOKS UP TO THEE is still one of the best-loved. In contrast to Billy Walker, whose inspiration was deeply rooted in the camp meeting and rural America, Mason followed somewhat more sophisticated, but at the same time musically more conventional, paths. The same can be said about his eminent contemporary Thomas Hastings, who composed over one thousand hymns, among them the imperishable ROCK OF AGES.

In addition to folk songs and hymns, the bulk of our popular-song repertory during the first half of the century consisted of the sentimental ballads and the lively tunes of minstrel shows. Singing, playing, and listening to these melodies was the main form of musical and social diversion all over urban and rural America, in the theaters, at concerts, clubs, picnics, quilting bees, and—most importantly—in the homes where the squeaky little "pump organ" had gradually been replaced by the piano. In an age when there were no radios, television sets or record players, the piano in the parlor was the focal point of family entertainment. "In many an humble home throughout our land," remarked Grover Cleveland, "the piano has

gathered about it the most sacred and tender association"; and often it did even more by giving the young daughter of the house an opportunity to "touch the heart of her future husband."

Early in the century, pianos still had to be imported from Europe at great cost and were relatively rare in private homes. But as soon as the manufacturing and distribution of the sturdily built American-made pianos began—the Chickerings in 1823, the Knabes in 1837, the Steinways in 1853, with many other brands following in rapid succession—the prices became more reasonable, or at least graduated enough to offer choices according to the means of the family. In 1851 there were 900 pianos made in the United States. In the 1860s the yearly sale amounted to 25,000 and—according to contemporary accounts—the piano "was only less important to the home than the kitchen sink." By the end of the century the number had grown to 1,000,000.

To supply printed music for the parlor upright a new industry, music publishing, began to prosper. At first publications were still in the form of the "songster," providing tunes for every conceivable occasion and taste: *Melodies for the Multitudes, The Parlor Companion or Polite Songster, The Rough and Ready Songster* and others *ad infinitum*. More and more, however, the outstanding popular songs of the day were published singly, in sheet-music form. The first of such copies were rather drab, black and white prints, but publishers soon discovered that an attractive multicolored design on the cover invariably helped sales. As a result of brisk competition among publishers to outdo each other in this field, the diligent researcher may discover among the song-fronts of the period works of the famous lithographer Nathaniel Currier, or may encounter the name of a then struggling young artist, Winslow Homer. By the middle of the century the amount of music published and the capacity of the consuming public to absorb it was truly phenomenal; in the year 1867 alone, there were 33,000 pieces of sheet music advertised in the country.

Who were the authors of this musical outpouring? Some, very few, were truly gifted, intuitive writers. Others, in the majority, were more or less capable craftsmen who, with their modest creative talents, were able to gauge the moods, the emotional needs, of the growing nation; they were in command of the formulae to exploit a generous sentimental vein in the American psyche and were attuned to the limited esthetic demands of their public. Any objective criticism of these writers must, however, be regarded as academic in view of the fact that their songs entertained millions and had that indefinable virtue of being impervious to obsolescence; they delighted several generations and, in many cases, have survived to our time.

Among the favored topics of our early sentimental ballads were the simple virtues of attachment to home, family, the old familiar places and things. The most enduring example of the genre, and one of the most popular songs of all time, HOME SWEET HOME, was published in 1823. It was loved and sung not only by the masses, but also became a favorite encore piece of Jenny Lind, Adelina Patti and other vocal celebrities. Another great favorite of the time, WOODMAN SPARE THAT TREE, was performed on nationwide tours by its composer, Henry Russell, who, as a singer, pianist and consummate showman, often left his audiences "perfectly overcome by emotion." These audiences, it seems, loved pathos and craved tear-drenched sentimentality. They were deeply moved by LILLY DALE, ROSALIE, THE PRAIRIE FLOWER, and an entire sorority of young maidens who shared a curiously similar fate; they died young, and were resting in a "flowery vale," in a "Fadeless Bow'r" under the mournful branches of the weeping willow, or amidst other heartbreakingly picturesque scenery. All this does not mean of course that these were inferior songs and did not deserve their popularity. Far from it. One of the great piano virtuosos of the nineteenth century, Sigismund Thalberg, composed a set of variations on the theme of LILLY DALE; and, with the right approach and the proper empathy for its naïveté, the cultivation of ROSALIE, THE PRAIRIE FLOWER can still prove very rewarding.

In contrast to the emotion-laden heart-throbs of the "genteel tradition," there were, of course, many other sturdier voices also heard in the land. "I hear America singing," said Walt Whitman in 1860; and, indeed, the line could have been written in any other decade of the century as well. While the piano tinkled away in the parlor, the nation kept growing, expanding, forging ahead in many areas of human endeavor, always accompanied by song. Ships plowed the oceans and churned the rivers, newly built canals teemed with barges, railroads were built, all echoing the chants and tunes of their particular lore. And when from California the cry of "Gold!" came across the continent and the leisurely pace of westward movement became a stampede, the countless hardships encountered on the trek were eased by song. "Sweet Betsy from Pike" with her lover Ike were just one couple of many thousands who ". . . swam the wide rivers and crossed the tall peaks, and camped on the prairie for weeks upon weeks; starvation and cholera and hard work and slaughter, they reached California spite of hell and high water."

The forty-niners' experiences and adventures in their rush for gold not only enriched our popular-song repertory, but also dispersed it and made it known from ocean to ocean. From the 1840s the mobility of American song was also greatly enhanced by numerous traveling singing groups, of which one of the first and best-known was the Hutchinson Family. These four members of a large New England clan had a well-rehearsed, neatly harmonized repertory of sentimental, religious and comic songs, which they performed with their own effective instrumental accompaniment. Their long, successful career spanned several decades, and although through their songs they often espoused numerous and, for their time, quite controversial causes (temperance, woman suffrage, abolition), their style and entire approach to musical entertainment belonged safely in the genteel tradition. The infusion of zest, flamboyance and rhythmic effervescence into the song repertory of the times came from another source—minstrelsy.

On February 6, 1843, the Bowery Theater in New York was the scene of an important event, advertised in the *Tribune* as "First night of the novel, grotesque, original and surprisingly melodious Ethiopian band, entitled the *Virginia Minstrels,* being an exclusively musical entertainment combining the banjo, violin, bone castanets and tambourine. . . ." The cast of four men were dressed in colorful costumes of white pants, calico shirts, long, swallow-tailed blue coats, and had their faces blackened with burnt cork. One of them, playing the violin, was Daniel Decatur Emmett, who later became a successful writer of such famous songs as OLD DAN TUCKER and DIXIE. Their show, a mélange of songs, dances and comic patter in Negro dialect was an instant success. It quickly prompted the formation of other similar groups and became, with the cast gradually augmented and the format extended into a three-act unit, the mainstay of American theater entertainment for almost a half a century.

While the minstrel show, as an organized, evening-long entertainment, sprang into full bloom in the 1840s, its essential ingredients existed and were popular long before that time. The roots go back to the plantation, where the slave population often performed for its own amusement and for the diversion of the family and guests in the "big house." White entertainers adapted these songs, dances and comic impersonations for their own use; they blackened their faces and played the black man's instruments. All this was labeled "Ethiopian" entertainment and became a great fad.

One of the first successful blackface performers was George Washington Dixon, identified with the songs LONG TAIL BLUE and OLD ZIP COON (TURKEY IN THE STRAW). But the most famous and, in his influence, most important early minstrel was an itinerant singer-actor, Thomas Dartmouth Rice. In 1828, "Daddy" Rice was a member of a Louisville theatrical group, where he had the role of providing some light entertainment between the acts of a play, an accepted audience-catching device of those days. In search for proper materials to perform, Rice had the opportunity and good fortune to witness the antics of a Negro stable hand who, while at work sang a funny ditty and, when ending each refrain with the line "Eb'ry time

I wheel about I jump Jim Crow," performed an odd hop, shuffle and skip. Rice memorized and assimilated the entire routine—words, music, dance steps, tattered clothes and all—and it became an instant hit in all the big cities of the United States and, by 1836, even in London, making JUMP JIM CROW the first American song success of international proportions. The character it created was a coarse caricature of the good-natured, underprivileged Negro, but it also was the popular comic "hero," and not the "villain" of the minstrel show. It happened only later that the term "Jim Crow" became a colloquial stigma attached to our language symbolizing the segregation of black people. Minstrelsy, it should be remembered, was essentially the white man's show, utilizing and exploiting the rich vein of Negro lore. It was guilty of offensive distortions, but was also, in a sense, a tribute to the black man's deep human values and inborn musical genius.

During the height of its vogue, around 1860, there were as many as 150 minstrel troupes touring the country, performing a vast repertory of popular tunes. These songs, running the gamut from tuneful sentimentality to rhythmic exuberance, from comedy to pathos, substantially influenced subsequent development of our idiom. The shows were extremely popular and there were very few dissenting voices. A few churches here and there and some pedantic esthetes raised eyebrows or looked down their noses at minstrelsy; but the people, the masses, loved it. Mark Twain remarked that Hannibal, Missouri, greeted the first minstrel shows "as a glad and stunning surprise . . . they flocked to them and were enchanted." About a performance in London, Thackeray wrote: ". . . a vagabond with a corked face and a banjo sings a little song, strikes a wild note, which sets the heart thrilling with happy pity."

One of the writers who provided the materials for these thrills was America's first truly great songwriter, Stephen Collins Foster. He had a natural gift for expressing with words and melody simple thoughts in an easy, appealing manner. He wrote his first song at the age of sixteen and was only twenty-two when his reputation was established with OH! SUSANNA.

According to some reports, he received only ten dollars for the song, but the popular assumption that he was exploited and unrewarded throughout his life is not borne out by facts. Most of his publishers treated him fairly, and although his earnings were by no means commensurate with his gifts and importance, his misfortunes in life were due more to a weak and improvident personality and, in some measure, to the circumstances which plagued writers in general in those days.

Foster songs fall into two main categories. The first includes his comic minstrel songs and nostalgic plantation melodies such as OH! SUSANNA and OLD FOLKS AT HOME; the second group consists of genteel, sentimental ballads, including JEANIE WITH THE LIGHT BROWN HAIR and BEAUTIFUL DREAMER. At the beginning of his career he intended to cultivate only the latter style and tried to avoid identification with minstrelsy and the "Ethiopian" trend. He even permitted OLD FOLKS AT HOME to be published with the name of C. P. Christy, the minstrel, appearing as writer of the song. He soon changed his mind, however, and in 1852 he wrote to Christy: "I have concluded to reinstate my name on my songs and pursue the Ethiopian business without fear or shame . . ." A wise decision, without which the Foster *oeuvre* could not have attained its prominent place in the songwriters' Hall of Fame.

The quality and undiminished popularity of these melodies still provide a subject for constant and voluminous analysis. What is the mysterious chemistry of these simple vocal creations that made them so well-liked in their time and enabled them to survive and to outlive so many transient trends of popular music styles? The answer is elusive. May it suffice to say here that Foster had the unique ability to absorb a variety of diverse influences—the music of the Negro, the Anglo-Celtic folk song, the mood and tempo of the American frontier—and to transmute them into a melodic mold of his own, which somehow had, and still has, the secret of universal appeal.

Home, Sweet Home

Words by
John Howard Payne

Music by
Henry R. Bishop

Gently moving

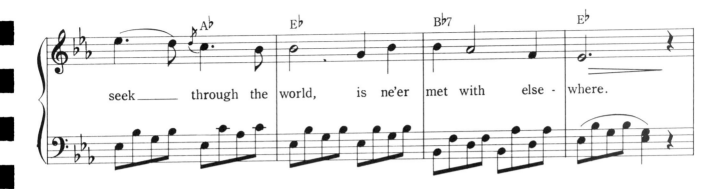

seek _____ through the world, is ne'er met with else - where.

Home! home! sweet, sweet home! There's

no _____ place like home! _____ There's no _____ place like home.

2. I gaze on the moon as I tread the drear wild,
   And feel that my mother now thinks of her child;
   As she looks on that moon from our own cottage door,
   Through the woodbine whose fragrance shall cheer me no more.
   Chorus

3. An exile from home, splendor dazzles in vain;
   Oh, give me my lowly thatched cottage again;
   The birds singing gaily, that came at my call;
   Give me them, and that peace of mind, dearer than all.
   Chorus

Woodman, Spare That Tree

Words by
George P. Morris

Music by
Henry Russel

2. That old familiar tree!
   Its glory and renown
   Are spread o'er land and sea,
   And would'st thou hew it down?

Woodman, forbear thy stroke!
Cut not its earth-bound ties;
Oh! spare that aged oak,
Now tow'ring to the skies.

Springfield Mountain

(The Pesky Sarpent)

Folk Song

Slowly moving

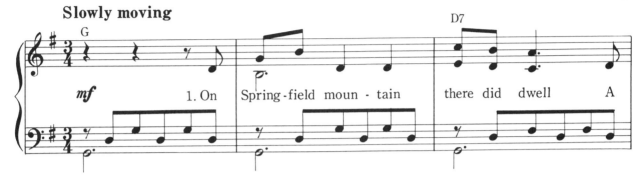

2.   One Monday morning he did go
     Down to the meadow for to mow.
     Chorus

3.   He scarce had mowed half round the field
     When a pesky sarpent bit his heel.
     Chorus

4.   They took him home to Molly dear
     Which made her feel so very queer.
     Chorus

5.   Now Molly had two ruby lips
     With which the pizen she did sip.
     Chorus

6.   Now Molly had a rotten tooth
     And so the pizen killed them both.
     Chorus

[57]

Poor Wayfaring Stranger

Religious Folk Ballad

2. I know dark clouds will gather 'round me,
   I know my way is rough and steep;
   Yet beauteous fields lie just before me,
   Where God's redeemed their vigils keep.
   I'm going there to see my mother,
   She said she'd meet me when I come;
   I'm only going over Jordan,
   I'm only going over home.

3. I'll soon be freed from every trial,
   My body asleep in the church-yard;
   I'll drop the cross of self-denial,
   And enter on my great reward.
   I'm going there to see my brothers
   Who've gone before me one by one;
   I'm only going over Jordan,
   I'm only going over home.

4. I want to wear a crown of glory,
   When I get home to that good land;
   I want to shout salvation's story,
   In concert with the blood-washed band.
   I'm going there to see my Savior,
   To sing His praise forever more;
   I'm only going over Jordan,
   I'm only going over home.

Amazing Grace

Words by
Rev. John Newton

Folk Hymn

Slowly (*in a freely ornamented style*)

1. A - maz - ing grace, how sweet the sound, That saved a wretch like me; once was lost but now I'm found, Was blind, but now I see.

2. "Twas grace that taught my heart to fear,
   And grace my fears relieved;
   How precious did that grace appear,
   The hour I first believed.

3. Through many dangers, toils and snares,
   I have already come.
   'Tis grace hath brought me safe thus far,
   And grace will lead me home.

4. How sweet the name of Jesus sounds
   In a believer's ear.
   It soothes his sorrows, heals his wounds,
   And drives away his fear.

5. Must Jesus bear the cross alone
   And all the world go free?
   No, there's a cross for everyone
   And there's a cross for me.

Wondrous Love

Words by
Rev. Alex Means

Folk Hymn

Moderately slow

2. When I was sinking down, sinking down, sinking down,
   When I was sinking down, sinking down;
   When I was sinking down,
   Beneath God's righteous frown,
   Christ laid aside his crown for my soul, for my soul;
   Christ laid aside his crown for my soul.

3. And when from death I'm free, I'll sing on, I'll sing on;
   And when from death I'm free, I'll sing on.
   And when from death I'm free,
   I'll sing and joyful be,
   And through eternity I'll sing on, I'll sing on,
   And through eternity I'll sing on.

Blow The Man Down

Heartily, with a swing

Sea Chantey

1. Come all ye young fel-lows that fol-low the sea, To me

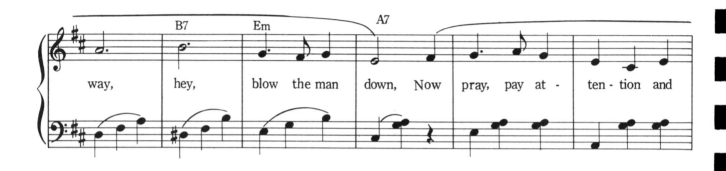

way, hey, blow the man down, Now pray, pay at-ten-tion and

lis-ten to me, Give me some time to blow the man down.

2. As I was a-walking down Paradise Street,
To me way, hey, blow the man down!
A pretty young damsel I chanced for to meet,
Give me some time to blow the man down!

3. She hailed me with her flipper, I took her in tow,
To me way, hey, blow the man down!
Yard-arm to yard-arm away we did go,
Give me some time to blow the man down!

4. But as we were going she said unto me,
To me way, hey, blow the man down!
"There's a spanking full-rigger just ready for sea."
Give me some time to blow the man down!

5. But soon as that packet was clear of the bar,
To me way, hey, blow the man down,
The mate knocked me down with the end of a spar,
Give me some time to blow the man down!

6. And as soon as that packet was out on the sea,
To me way, hey, blow the man down!
'Twas devilish hard treatment of every degree,
Give me some time to blow the man down!

7. So I give you fair warning before we belay,
To me way, hey, blow the man down!
Don't ever take heed of what pretty girls say,
Give me some time to blow the man down!

Shenandoah

Riverboat Chantey

Slowly and freely

1. Oh, Shen-an-doah,____ I long to hear you,____ A-

way,____ you rol-ling riv-er!____ Oh, Shen-an-doah,__ I long to hear you,____ A-

way,____ I'm bound a- way, 'Cross the wide Mis- sour-i.____

2. The white man loved an Indian maiden,
    Away, you rolling river!
    With notions his canoe was laden,
    Away, I'm bound away,
    'Cross the wide Missouri.

3. Oh, Shenandoah, I love your daughter,
    Away, you rolling river!
    For her I've crossed the stormy water,
    Away, I'm bound away,
    'Cross the wide Missouri.

4. Farewell, my dear, I'm bound to leave you,
    Away, you rolling river!
    Oh, Shenandoah, I'll not deceive you,
    Away, I'm bound away!
    'Cross the wide Missouri.

Jump Jim Crow

Words and music by
Thomas D. Rice

2. I'm a rorer on de fiddle,
    An' down in ol' Virginny,
    Dey say I play de skientific,
    Like massa Pagganninny. *Chorus*

3. I went down to de river,
    I didn't mean to stay,
    But there I see so many gals,
    I couldn't get away. *Chorus*

4. I met Miss Dina Scrub one day,
    I gib her sich a buss;
    An' den she turn an' slap my face,
    An' make a mighty fuss. *Chorus*

5. De udder gals dey 'gin to fight,
    I tel'd dem wait a bit;
    I'd hab dem all, jis one by one,
    As I tourt fit. *Chorus*

Long Tail Blue

Minstrel Tune

2. Some people they have but one coat,
   But you see I've got two;
   I wears a jacket all the week,
   And Sunday my long tail blue. *Chorus*

3. As I was going up Fulton Street,
   I holler'd after Sue,
   The watchman came and took me up,
   And spoilt my long tail blue. *Chorus*

4. I took it to a Tailor's shop,
   To see what he could do;
   He took a needle and some thread,
   And mended my long tail blue. *Chorus*

5. If you want to win the Ladies' hearts,
   I'll tell you what to do:
   Go to a tiptop Tailor's shop,
   And buy a long tail blue. *Chorus*

[65]

Turkey In The Straw

（Old Zip Coon）

With a lively beat

Traditional Square Dance Tune

1. As I was go - in'___ down the road, with a tired___ team___ and a heav - y load, I cracked my whip___ and the lead - er sprung, I___ says day - hay___ to the wag - on tongue.

Chorus

Tur - key in the straw, tur - key in the hay, Tur - key in the straw, tur - key in the hay, Roll 'em up and twist 'em up a

high tuck-a-haw, And ___ hit 'em up a tune ___ called ___ Tur-key in the Straw.

D.C.

2. Oh, I went out to milk, and I didn't know how;
   I milked a goat instead of a cow.
   A monkey sittin' on a pile of straw,
   A-winkin' his eye at his mother-in-law.
   Chorus

3. Well, I met Mister Catfish comin' down the stream;
   Says Mister Catfish, "What do you mean?"
   I caught Mister Catfish by the snout
   And I turned that Catfish wrong side out.
   Chorus

4. Then I come to the river and I couldn't get across,
   So I paid five dollars for a blind horse.
   Well he wouldn't go ahead, and he wouldn't stand still,
   So he went up and down like an old saw mill.
   Chorus

5. As I came down a new cut road,
   I met Mister Bull frog a-courtin' Miss Toad,
   And every time Miss Toad would sing,
   The old Bull frog cut a pigeon wing.
   Chorus

6. Oh, I jumped in the seat, and I gave a little yell,
   The horses ran away, broke the wagon all to hell,
   Sugar in the gourd and honey in the horn,
   I never been so happy since the day I was born.
   Chorus

[67]

Old Dan Tucker

Words and music by
Daniel Decatur Emmett

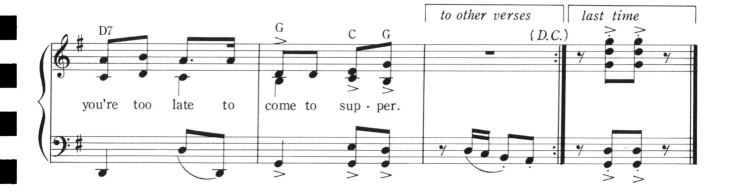

2. Now Old Dan Tucker was a mighty man,
   He washed his face in a frying pan,
   Combed his head with a wagon wheel,
   An' died with a toothache in his heel.
   Chorus

3. Old Dan Tucker he got drunk,
   He fell in the fire an' he kicked up a chunk,
   The red hot coals got in his shoe
   An' whee-ee! how the ashes flew!
   Chorus

4. Old Dan Tucker is a nice old man,
   He used to ride our darby ram;
   He sent him whizzin' down the hill,
   If he hadn't got up, he'd lay there still.
   Chorus

5. Now Old Dan Tucker begun in early life
   To play the banjo an' the fife,
   He'd play the boys and gals to sleep,
   An' then into his bunk he'd creep.
   Chorus

6. Now Old Dan Tucker is come to town,
   Riding a billy goat, leading a hound,
   Hound dog bark and the billy goat jump,
   Landed Dan Tucker on top of a stump.
   Chorus

7. Old Dan Tucker he clumb a tree,
   His Lord and Master for to see,
   The limb it broke an' Dan got a fall,
   Never got to see his Lord at all.
   Chorus

8. Old Dan Tucker is back in town,
   Swingin' the ladies all aroun',
   First to the right and then to the left,
   An' then to the gal that he loves best.
   Chorus

9. Ol' Dan an' me we did fall out,
   An' what do you reckon it was about?
   He stepped on my corn, I kicked him on the shin,
   An' that's the way this row begin.
   Chorus

10. An' now Old Dan is a gone sucker,
    And never can go home to supper;
    Ol' Dan he has had his last ride,
    An' the banjo's buried by his side.
    Chorus

The Blue Tail Fly

Minstrel Song

2. And when he'd ride in the afternoon
   I'd follow after with a hickory broom;
   The pony being rather shy
   When bitten by a blue-tail fly. *Chorus*

3. One day he ride around the farm,
   The flies so numerous they did swarm;
   One chanced to bite him on the thigh;
   The devil take the blue-tail fly. *Chorus*

4. The pony run, he jump, he pitch;
   He threw my master in the ditch.
   He died and the jury wondered why-
   The verdict was the blue-tail fly. *Chorus*

5. They lay him under a 'simmon tree;
   His epitaph is there to see:
   "Beneath this stone I'm forced to lie,
   Victim of the blue-tail fly." *Chorus*

For He's A Jolly Good Fellow

(We Won't Go Home Until Morning – The Bear Went Over The Mountain)

Traditional

For he's a jol-ly good fel - low, For he's a jol-ly good

fel - low, For he's a jol-ly good fel - low, Which no-bod-y can de - ny.

Fine

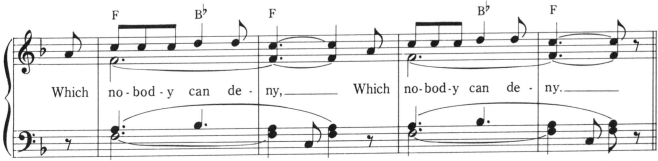

Which no-bod-y can de - ny,____ Which no-bod-y can de - ny.____

D.C. al Fine

We Won't Go Home Until Morning

We won't go home until morning,
We won't go home until morning,
We won't go home until morning,
'Til daylight doth appear!
'Til daylight doth appear,
'Til daylight doth appear.
We won't go home until morning,
We won't go home until morning,
We won't go home until morning,
'Til daylight doth appear!

The Bear Went Over The Mountain

The bear went over the mountain,
The bear went over the mountain,
The bear went over the mountain,
To see what he could see.
And all that he could see,
And all that he could see,
Was the other side of the mountain,
The other side of the mountain,
The other side of the mountain,
Was all that he could see!

My Faith Looks Up To Thee

Words by
Ray Palmer

Music by
Lowell Mason

Moderately; with devotion

1. My faith looks up to Thee, Thou Lamb of Cal - va - ry,

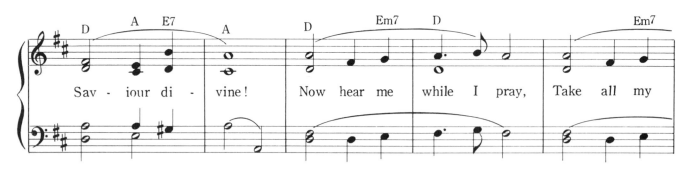

Sav - iour di - vine! Now hear me while I pray, Take all my

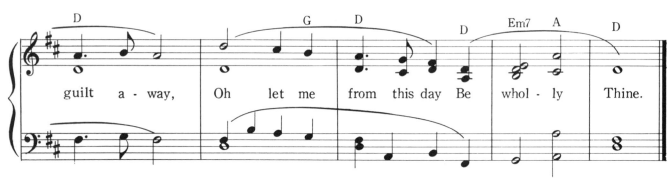

guilt a - way, Oh let me from this day Be whol - ly Thine.

2. May Thy rich grace impart
   Strength to my fainting heart,
   My zeal inspire;
   As Thou hast died for me,
   O may my love to Thee
   Pure, warm, and changeless be,
   A living fire!

3. While life's dark maze I tread,
   And griefs around me spread,
   Be Thou my guide;
   Bid darkness turn to day,
   Wipe sorrow's tears away,
   Nor let me ever stray
   From Thee aside.

4. When ends life's transient dream,
   When death's cold sullen stream
   Shall o'er me roll,
   Blest Saviour, then, in love,
   Fear and distrust remove;
   O bear me safe above,
   A ransomed soul!

Rock Of Ages

Words by
Augustus M. Toplady

Music by
Thomas Hastings

2. Could my zeal no respite know,
    Could my tears forever flow,
    All for sin could not atone,
    Thou must save, and Thou alone;
    Nothing in my hand I bring,
    Simply to Thy cross I cling.

3. While I draw this fleeting breath,
    When my eyelids close in death,
    When I soar to worlds unknown,
    And behold Thee on Thy throne,
    Rock of ages, cleft for me,
    Let me hide myself in Thee.

Old Rosin The Beau

(Acres of Clams)

Traditional
words and music

(*Continue, as above*):

2. I've traveled this country over
    And now to the next I will go,
    For I know that good quarters await me
    To welcome old Rosin, the Beau.
        To welcome old Rosin, the Beau, (etc.)

3. In the gay round of pleasures I've traveled.
    Nor will I behind leave a foe,
    And when my companions are jovial
    They will drink to old Rosin, the Beau.
        They will drink to old Rosin, the Beau, (etc.)

4. But my life is now drawn to a closing,
    As all will at last be so.
    So we'll take a full bumper at parting
    To the name of old Rosin, the Beau.
        To the name of old Rosin, the Beau, (etc.)

5. When I'm dead and laid out on the counter,
    The people all making a show,
    Just sprinkle plain whiskey and water
    On the corpse of old Rosin, the Beau.
        On the corps of old Rosin, the Beau, (etc.)

6. Then pick me out six trusty fellows
    And let them stand all in a row,
    And dig a big hole in the meadow
    And in it toss Rosin, the Beau.
        And in it toss Rosin, the Beau, (etc.)

7. Then bring out two little brown jugs:
    Place one at my head and my toe;
    And do not forget to scratch on them
    The name of old Rosin, the Beau.
        The name of old Rosin, the Beau, (etc.)

Acres of Clams

1. I've wandered all over this country,
    Prospecting and digging for gold;
    I've tunnel'd, hydraulicked and cradled,
    And I nearly froze in the cold.
        And I nearly froze in the cold, (etc.)

2. For one who got wealthy by mining
    I saw many hundreds get poor.
    I made up my mind to digging
    For something a little more sure.
        For something a little more sure, (etc.)

3. I rolled up my grub in my blanket,
    I left all my tools on the ground,
    I started one morning to shank it
    For the country they call Puget Sound.
        For the country they call Puget Sound, (etc.)

4. No longer the slave of ambition,
    I laugh at the world and its shams,
    And think of my happy condition
    Surrounded by acres of clams.
        Surrounded by acres of clams, (etc.)

Cape Ann

(from the repertory of The Hutchinson Family)

Old New-England Folk Song

Moderately lively

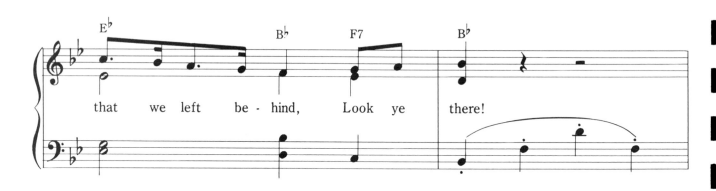

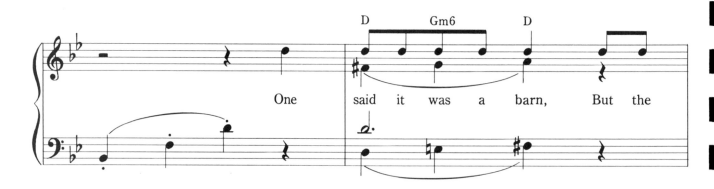

oth - er said nay; He said it was a Meet - ing - house, With the

stee - ple blown a - way, Look ye there!

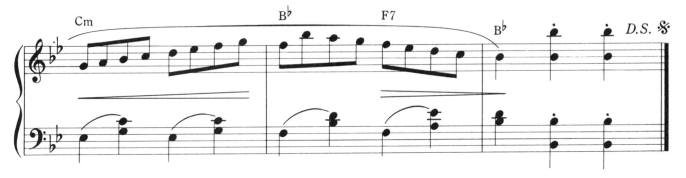

2. So we hunted and we halloed,
   And the next thing we did find
   Was the Moon in the element,
   And that we left behind,
   Look ye there!
   One said it was the Moon,
   But the other said nay;
   He said it was a Yankee cheese,
   With the one half cut away,
   Look ye there!

3. So we hunted and we halloed,
   And the next thing we did find
   Was a frog in the Mill pond,
   And that we left behind,
   Look ye there!
   One said it was a frog,
   But the other said nay;
   He said it was a canary bird,
   With its feathers washed away,
   Look ye there!

4. So we hunted and we halloed,
   And the next thing we did find
   Was the light-house in Cape Ann,
   And that we left behind,
   Look ye there!
   One said it was the light-house,
   But the other said nay;
   He said it was a sugar loaf,
   With the paper blown away,
   Look ye there!

5. So we hunted and we halloed,
   And the last thing we did find
   Was the owl in the olive bush,
   And that we left behind,
   Look ye there!
   One said it was an owl,
   But the other said nay;
   He said it was the Evil One,
   And we all three ran away,
   Look ye there!

Long, Long Ago

Words and music by
Thomas H. Bayly

[78]

Let me be - lieve that you love as you loved,

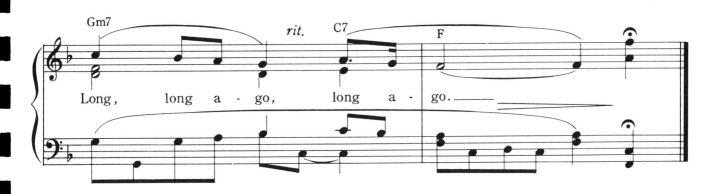

Long, long a - go, long a - go.

2. Do you remember the path where we met,
   Long, long ago, long, long ago,
   Ah, yes, you told me you ne'er would forget,
   Long, long ago, long ago.
   Then, to all others my smile you preferred,
   Love, when you spoke, gave a charm to each word,
   Still my heart treasures the praises I heard,
   Long, long ago, long ago.

3. Tho' by your kindness my fond hopes were raised,
   Long, long ago, long, long ago,
   You by more eloquent lips have been praised,
   Long, long ago, long ago.
   But, by long absence your truth has been tried,
   Still to your accents I listen with pride,
   Blessed as I was when I sat by your side,
   Long, long ago, long ago.

[79]

Peter Gray

Folk and Minstrel Tune

Moderately lively

1. Once on a time there lived a man, his name was Pe-ter Gray._ He
2. Now Pe-ter fell in love all with a nice_ young_ girl._ The

lived way down in that 'ere town called Penn-syl-van-i-a.
first three let-ters of her name were Lu-cy An-nie Pearl.

Chorus

Blow, ye winds of morn - ing, Blow, ye winds, high - o,

Blow, ye winds of morn - ing,_ blow, blow, blow.

3. Just as they were 'bout to wed
her father did say no,
And consequently she was sent
beyond the Ohio. *Chorus*

4. When Peter heard his love was lost,
he knew not what to say,
He'd half a mind to jump into
the Susquehan-ni-a. *Chorus*

5. Now Peter went away out west
for furs and other skins,
But he was caught and scalp-i-ed
by bloody Indians. *Chorus*

6. When Lucy Annie heard the news,
she straightway took to bed,
And never did get up again
until she di-i-ed. *Chorus*

Buffalo Gals

Minstrel Tune

Lively walking tempo

1. As I was walk-ing down the street, Down the street, down the street, A pret-ty gal I chanced to meet Un-der the sil-ver-y moon.

Chorus

Buf-fa-lo gals, won't you come out to-night, Come out to-night, come out to-night Buf-fa-lo gals won't you come out to-night, And dance by the light of the moon.

2. I asked her if she'd stop and talk,
    Stop and talk, stop and talk,
    Her feet covered up the whole sidewalk,
    She was fair to view.   *Chorus*

3. I asked her if she'd be my wife,
    Be my wife, be my wife,
    Then I'd be happy all my life,
    If she'd marry me.   *Chorus*

[81]

Gaily The Troubadour

Words and music by
Thomas H. Bayley

2. She for the Troubadour hopelessly wept;
Sadly she tho't of him when others slept;
Singing, "In search of thee would I might roam;
Troubadour, Troubadour, come to thy home."

3. Hark! 'twas the Troubadour breathing her name;
Under the battlement softly he came;
Singing, "From Palestine, hither I come;
Lady love, lady love, welcome me home."

Ho! Westward Ho!

Words and music by
Ossian E. Dodge

With robust, lively motion

1. "The Star of Em-pire" po-ets say, Ho! West-ward Ho! "For-
this be prov-en in our land,

It ev-er takes its on-ward way!" Ho! West-ward Ho! That
seems Je-ho-vah's great com-mand,

Ho!

Chorus

Ho! West-ward! Soon the world shall know That

all is grand in the west-ern land; Ho! west-ward Ho!

2. Our Pilgrim Fathers sang the song,   Still westward many thousands flock,
   Ho! Westward Ho!   Ho! Westward Ho!
   Hear Right should triumph over Wrong? And sing the shout from Plymouth Rock,
   Ho! Westward Ho!   Ho! Westward Ho!   *Chorus*

The Old Oaken Bucket

Words by
Samuel Woodworth

Music by
George Kiallmark

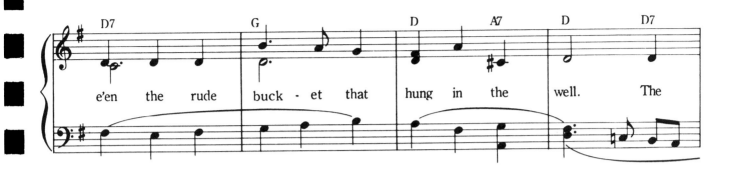

e'en the rude buck - et that hung in the well. The

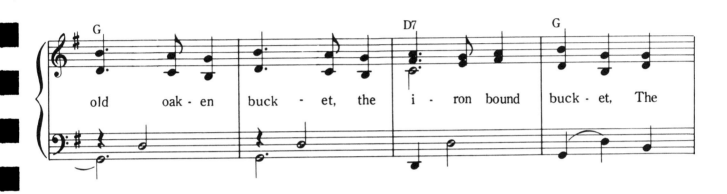

old oak - en buck - et, the i - ron bound buck - et, The

moss - cov - ered buck - et that hung in the well.

2. The moss-covered bucket I hailed as a treasure,
For often at noon when returned from the field,
I found it the source of an exquisite pleasure,
The purest and sweetest that nature can yield.
How ardent I seized it with hands that were glowing,
And quick to the white-pebbled bottom it fell;
The soon, with the emblem of truth overflowing
And dripping with coolness, it rose from the well.
The old oaken bucket, the iron-bound bucket,
The moss-covered bucket that hung in the well.

Sweet Betsy From Pike

Moderately lively

Folk Tune

2. Out on the prairie one bright starry night,
They broke out the whisky and Betsy got tight;
She sang and she shouted and danced o'er the plain,
And made a great show for the whole wagon train. *Chorus*

3. The Injuns came down in a wild yelling horde,
   And Betsy was skeered they would scalp her adored;
   Behind the front wagon wheel Betsy did crawl,
   And fought off the Injuns with musket and ball.   *Chorus*

4. They soon reached the desert, where Betsy gave out,
   And down in the sand she lay rolling about;
   While Ike in great terror looked on in surprise,
   Saying, "Get up now, Betsy, you'll get sand in your eyes."   *Chorus*

5. The wagon tipped over with a terrible crash,
   And out on the prairie rolled all sorts of trash;
   A few little baby clothes done up with care
   Looked rather suspicious — though 'twas all on the square.   *Chorus*

6. The Shanghai ran off and the cattle all died,
   The last piece of bacon that morning was fried;
   Poor Ike got discouraged, and Betsy got mad,
   The dog wagged his tail and looked wonderfully sad.   *Chorus*

7. They swam the wide rivers and crossed the tall peaks,
   And camped on the prairie for weeks upon weeks.
   Starvation and cholera and hard work and slaughter,
   They reached California spite of hell and high water.   *Chorus*

8. Long Ike and sweet Betsy attended a dance,
   Where Ike wore a pair of his Pike County pants;
   Sweet Betsy was covered with ribbons and rings.
   Said Ike, "You're an angel, but where are your wings?"   *Chorus*

9. A miner said, "Betsy. will you dance with me?"
   "I will that, old hoss, if you don't make too free;
   But don't dance me hard. Do you want to know why?
   Doggone you, I'm chock-full of strong alkali."   *Chorus*

10. Long Ike, and sweet Betsy got married of course,
    But Ike, getting jealous, obtained a divorce;
    And Betsy, well satisfied, said with a shout,
    "Good-by, you big lummux, I'm glad you backed out."   *Chorus*

[87]

Hush Little Baby

Folk Lullaby

Gently

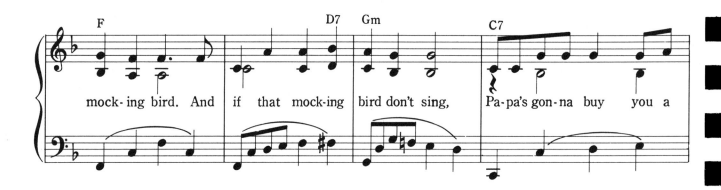

1. Hush, lit-tle ba-by, don't say a word; Pa-pa's gon-na buy you a mock-ing bird. And if that mock-ing bird don't sing, Pa-pa's gon-na buy you a

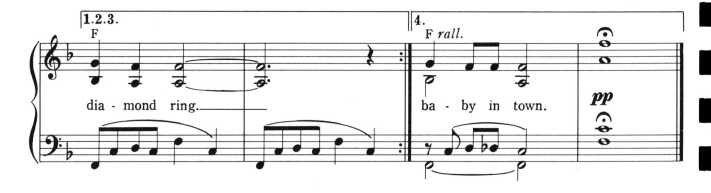

dia-mond ring.____ ba-by in town.

2. If that diamond ring is brass,
   Papa's gonna buy you a looking glass.
   And if that looking glass gets broke,
   Papa's gonna buy you a billy goat.

3. If that billy goat don't pull,
   Papa's gonna buy you a cart and bull.
   And if that cart and bull turn over,
   Papa's gonna buy you a dog named Rover.

4. If that dog named Rover don't bark,
   Papa's gonna buy you a horse and cart.
   And if that horse and cart fall down,
   You'll still be the sweetest little baby in town.

Cindy

Folk Tune

Lively

G

mf

1. You ought to see my Cin - dy, She lives a - way down

D7   G   G7   C   Cm   G   D7   G

South, And she's so sweet the hon - ey bees___ Swarm a - round her mouth.

Chorus

C   G

Get a - long home, Cin - dy, Cin - dy, Get a - long home, Cin - dy,

C   G   D7   G

Cin - dy, Get a - long home, Cin - dy, Cin - dy, I'll mar - ry you some day.

2. I wish I was an apple
A-hangin' on a tree,
And every time my Cindy passed
She'd take a bite of me. *Chorus*

3. I wish I had a needle,
As fine as I could sew,
I'd sew that gal to my coat-tail
And down the road I'd go. *Chorus*

4. Cindy got religion,
She had it once before,
But when she heard my old banjo
She 'uz the first one on the floor. *Chorus*

5. Cindy in the springtime,
Cindy in the fall,
If I can't have my Cindy,
I'll have no girl at all. *Chorus*

[89]

Wait For The Wagon

Words and music by
R. Bishop Buckley (?)

2. Where the river runs like silver
    And the birds they sing so sweet,
    I have a cabin, Phyllis,
    And something good to eat;
    Come listen to my story,
    It will relieve my heart;
    So jump into the wagon,
    And off we will start.   *Chorus*

3. Together, on life's journey,
    We'll travel till we stop,
    And if we have no trouble,
    We'll reach the happy top;
    Then come with me, sweet Phyllis,
    My dear, my lovely bride,
    We'll jump into the wagon,
    And all take a ride.   *Chorus*

There's Music In The Air

Words by
Fanny Crosby

Music by
George F. Root

1. There's music in the air, When the infant morn is nigh, And faint its blush is seen On the bright and laughing sky. Many a harp's ecstatic sound Thrills us with its joy profound, While we list, enchanted there, To the music in the air.

2.   There's music in the air,
    When the noontide's sultry beam
    Reflects a golden light
    On the distant mountain stream.
    When beneath some grateful shade
    Sorrow's aching head is laid,
    Sweetly to the spirit there
    Comes the music in the air.

3.   There's music in the air,
    When the twilight's gentle sigh
    Is lost on evening's breast,
    As its pensive beauties die;
    Then, oh, then, the loved ones gone
    Wake the pure, celestial song;
    Angelic voices great us there,
    In the music in the air.

Little Brown Jug

Words and music by
Joseph E. Winner(?)

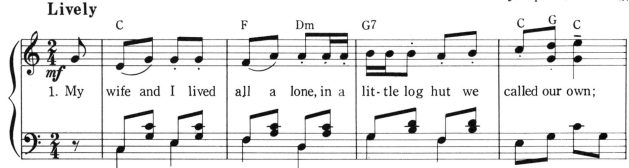

2. 'Tis you who makes my friends and foes,
'Tis you who makes me wear old clothes;
Here you are so near my nose,
So tip her up and down she goes.
Chorus

3. When I go toiling to my farm
I take little brown jug under my arm,
Place him under a shady tree,
Little Brown Jug, 'tis you and me.
Chorus

4. If all the folks in Adam's race
Were gathered together in one place
Then I'd prepare to shed a tear
Before I'd part with you, my dear.
Chorus

5. If I'd a cow that gave such milk,
I'd clothe her in the finest silk,
I'd feed her on the choicest hay,
And milk her forty times a day.
Chorus

6. The rose is red, my nose is, too,
The violet's blue and so are you;
And yet I guess, before I stop
I'd better take another drop.
Chorus

[92]

Pop! Goes The Weasel

Play Tune

2. A penny for a spool of thread,
   A penny for a needle,
   That's the way the money goes,
   Pop! goes the weasel.
   Johnny's got the whooping cough
   And Jenny's got the measles,
   That's the way the money goes,
   Pop! goes the weasel.

3. The butcher, when he charges for meat,
   Sticks in the bone and gristle,
   But that's the way the money goes,
   Pop! goes the weasel.
   The painter works with ladder and brush,
   The artist with the easel,
   The fiddler always snaps the strings,
   Pop! goes the weasel.

[93]

Lilly Dale

Words and music by
H. S. Thompson

Moderately slow

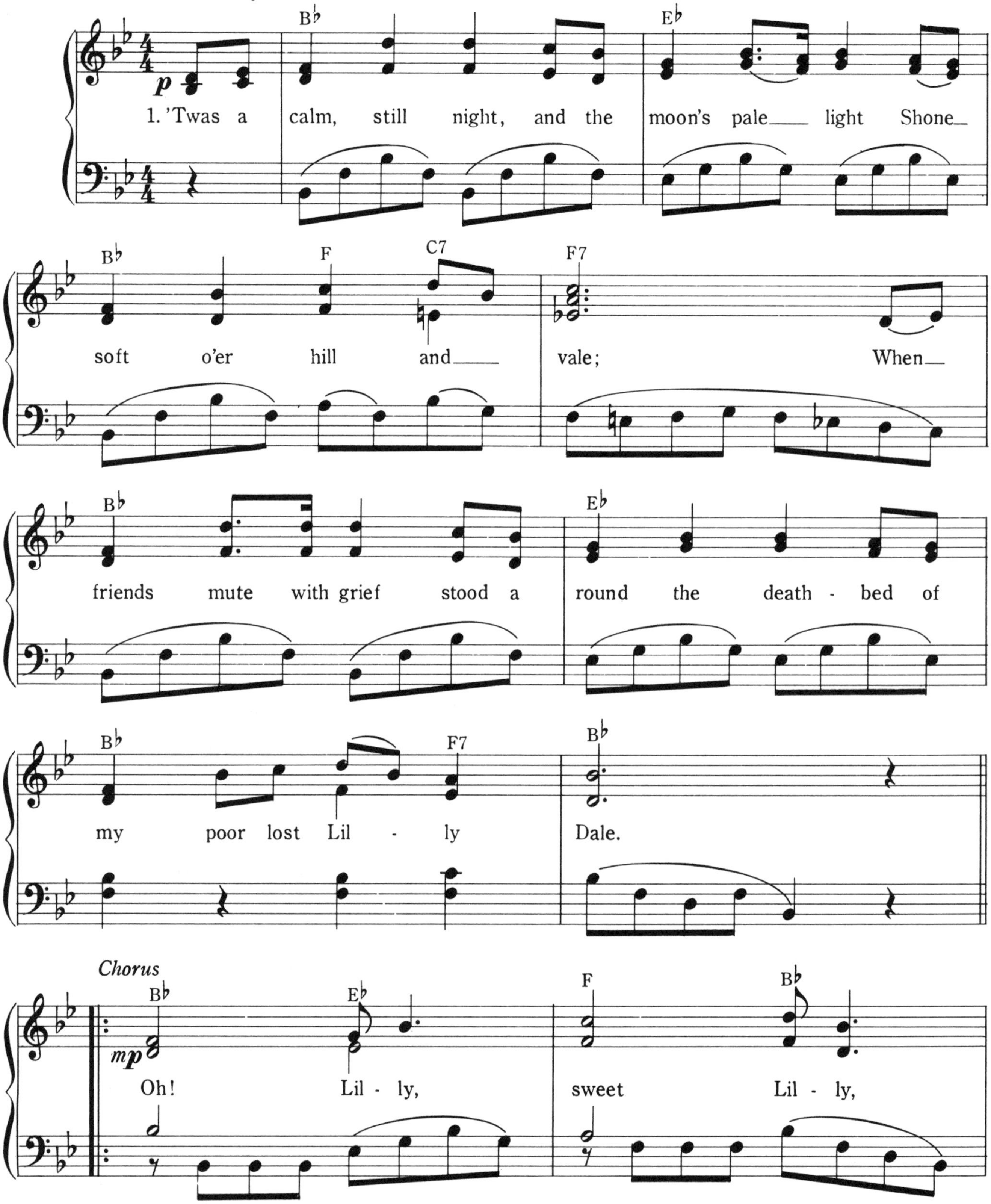

B♭ E♭
p
1. 'Twas a calm, still night, and the moon's pale light Shone
B♭ F C7 F7
soft o'er hill and vale; When
B♭ E♭
friends mute with grief stood a round the death - bed of
B♭ F7 B♭
my poor lost Lil - ly Dale.
Chorus
B♭ E♭ F B♭
mp
Oh! Lil - ly, sweet Lil - ly,

2. Her cheeks that once glowed with the rose tint of health,
   By the hand of disease had turned pale,
   And the death damp was on the pure white brow
   Of my poor lost Lilly Dale. *Chorus*

3. "I go," she said, "to the land of rest,
   And ere my strength shall fail,
   I must tell you where, near my own loved home,
   You must lay poor Lilly Dale." *Chorus*

4. 'Neath the chestnut tree, where the wild flow'rs grow,
   And the stream ripples forth thro' the vale,
   Where the birds shall warble their songs in spring,
   There lay poor Lilly Dale. *Chorus*

Kiss Me Quick And Go

Words by
Silas S. Steele

Music by
Fred Buckley

With a lively bounce

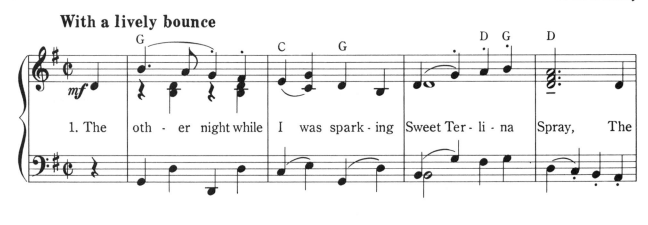

1. The oth - er night while I was spark - ing Sweet Ter - li - na Spray, The

more we whis - per'd our love talk - ing, The more we had to say. The

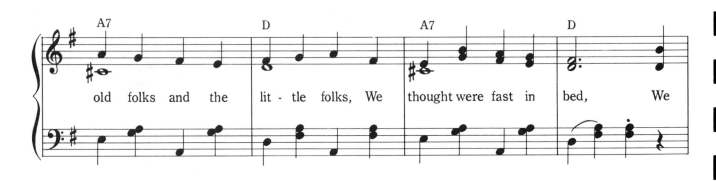

old folks and the lit - tle folks, We thought were fast in bed, We

heard a foot - step on the stairs, And what d'ye think she said? O!

2. Soon after that I gave my love
   A moonlight promenade,
   At last we fetch'd up to the door,
   Just where the old folks stay'd.
   The clock struck twelve, her heart struck too,
   And peeping overhead,
   We saw a nightcap raise the blind,
   And what d'ye think she said? *Chorus*

3. One Sunday night we sat together,
   Sighing, side by side,
   Just like two winter leaves of cabbage,
   In the sunshine fried.
   My heart with love was nigh to split,
   To ask her for to wed;
   Said I, "Shall I go for the priest?"
   And what d'ye think she said? *Chorus*

[97]

Jingle Bells

Words and music by
James Pierpont

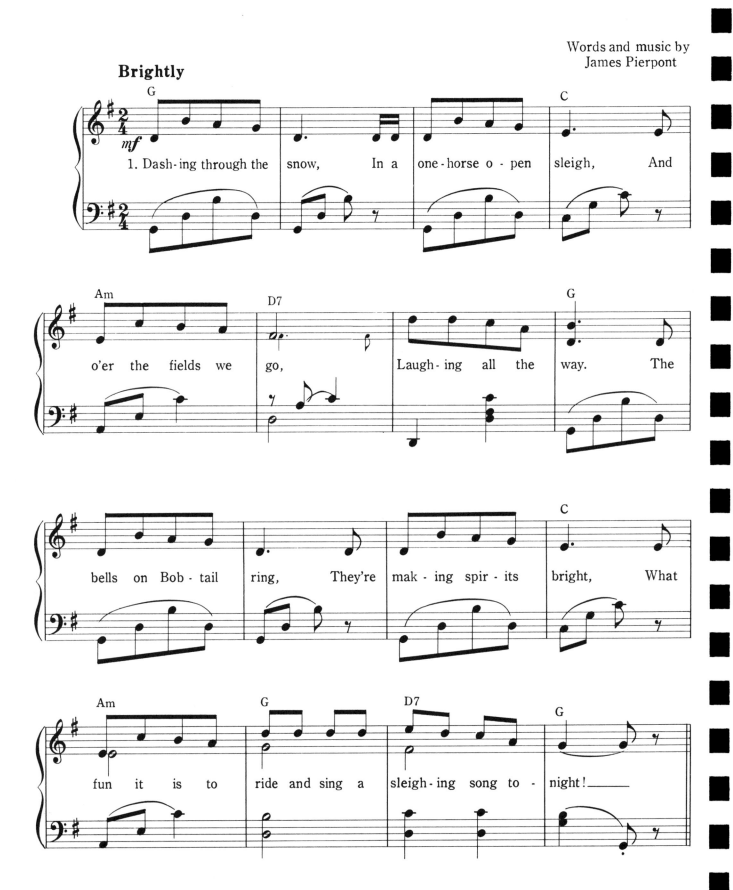

Chorus

Jin - gle bells! Jin - gle bells! Jin - gle all the way!

Oh, what fun it is to ride in a one - horse o - pen sleigh, ____

Jin - gle bells! Jin - gle bells! Jin - gle all the way!

Oh, what fun it is to ride in a one-horse o - pen sleigh! ____

2. A day or so ago,
   I thought I'd take a ride,
   And soon Miss Fannie Bright
   Was seated by my side.
   The horse was lean and lank,
   Misfortune seemed his lot,
   He got into a drifted bank,
   And we? We got upsot!
   Chorus

3. Now the ground is white,
   Go it while you're young,
   Take the girls tonight,
   And sing this sleighing song.
   Just get a bob-tailed nag,
   Two-forty for his speed,
   Then hitch him to an open sleigh,
   And crack! You'll take the lead.
   Chorus

[99]

Rosalie, The Prairie Flower

Words and music by
George Frederick Root

With a gentle, easy flow

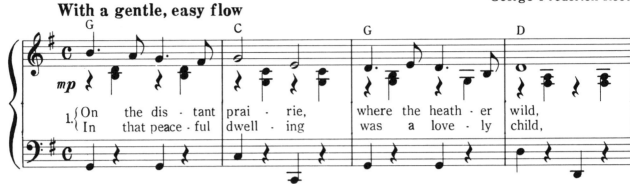

1. { On the dis - tant prai - rie, where the heath - er wild,
In that peace - ful dwell - ing was a love - ly child,

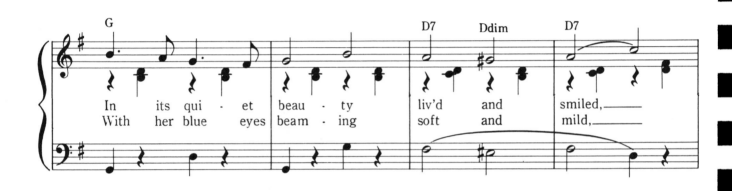

In its qui - et beau - ty liv'd and smiled,_____
With her blue eyes beam - ing soft and mild,_____

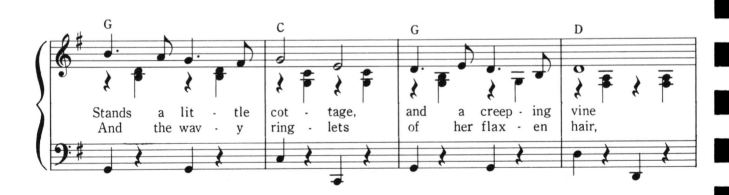

Stands a lit - tle cot - tage, and a creep - ing vine
And the wav - y ring - lets of her flax - en hair,

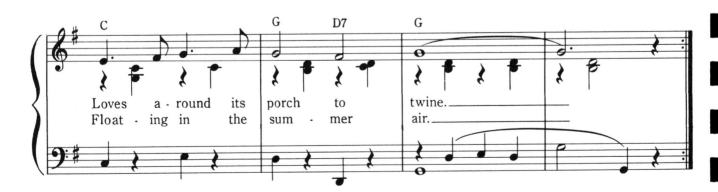

Loves a - round its porch to twine._____
Float - ing in the sum - mer air._____

2. On that distant prairie, when the days were long,
   Tripping like a fairy, sweet her song,
   With the sunny blossoms, and the birds at play,
   Beautiful and bright as they.
   When the twilight shadows gather'd in the west,
   And the voice of Nature sank to rest,
   Like a cherub kneeling, seem'd the lovely child,
   With her gentle eyes so mild.

   Fair as a lily, joyous and free,
   Light of that prairie home was she.
   Ev'ry one who knew her felt the gentle pow'r
   Of Rosalie, "The Prairie Flow'r".

3. But the summer faded, and a chilly blast,
   O'er that happy cottage swept at last:
   When the autumn song birds woke the dewy morn,
   Little "Prairie Flow'r" was gone.
   For the angels whisper'd softly in her ear,
   "Child, thy Father calls thee, stay not here"·
   And they gently bore her, rob'd in spotless white,
   To their blissful home of light.

   Though we shall never look on her more,
   Gone with the love and joy she bore,
   Far away she's blooming in a fadeless bow'r,
   Sweet Rosalie, "The Prairie Flow'r".

[101]

Listen To The Mocking Bird

Words by Alice Hawthorne
(Septimus Winner)

Melody by
Richard Milburn

Chorus

Listen to the mocking bird, lis-ten to the mock-ing bird, The

mock-ing bird is sing-ing o'er her grave; Lis-ten to the

mock-ing bird, Lis-ten to the mock-ing bird, Still

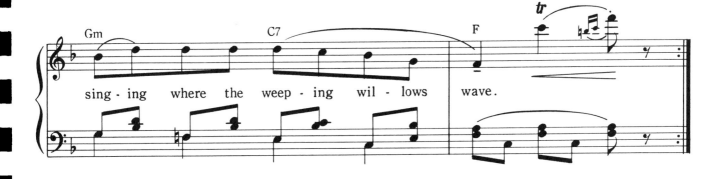

sing-ing where the weep-ing wil-lows wave.

2. Ah! well I yet remember,
   Remember, remember,
   Ah! well I yet remember
   When we gathered in the cotton side by side.

'Twas in the mild September,
September, September,
'Twas in the mild September
And the mocking bird was singing far and wide.

Chorus

[103]

The Erie Canal

Folk Song

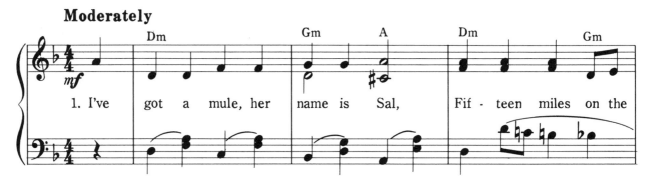

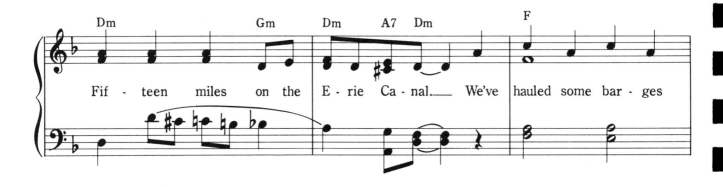

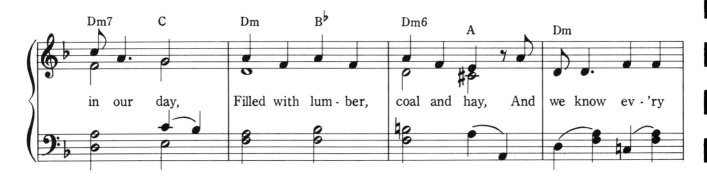

2. We better be on our way, old pal,
   Fifteen miles on the Erie Canal.
   'Cause you bet your life I'd never part with Sal,
   Fifteen miles on the Erie Canal.
   Get up there, mule, here comes a lock,
   We'll make Rome 'bout six o'clock,
   One more trip and back we'll go,
   Right back home to Buffalo.
   Chorus

Darling Nelly Gray

Words and music by
Benjamin Russel Hanby

2. One night I went to see her but "she's gone" the neighbors say,
   The white man bound her with his chain,
   They have taken her to Georgia for to wear her life away,
   As she toils in the cotton and the cane. *Chorus*

Oh! Susanna

Words and music by
Stephen Foster

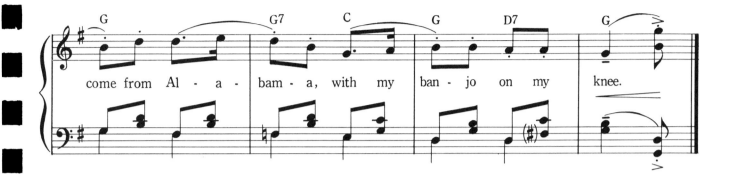

come from Al - a - bam - a, with my ban - jo on my knee.

2. I had a dream the other night,
    When everything was still;
    I thought I saw Susanna dear,
    A-coming down the hill.
    The buckwheat cake was in her mouth,
    The tear was in her eye,
    Said I, I'm coming from the south,
    Susanna don't you cry.   *Chorus*

3. I soon will be in New Orleans,
    And then I'll look all 'round,
    And when I find Susanna,
    I'll fall upon the ground.
    But if I do not find her,
    This darkey'll surely die,
    And when I'm dead and buried,
    Susanna don't you cry.   *Chorus*

Old Folks At Home

Words and music by
Stephen Foster

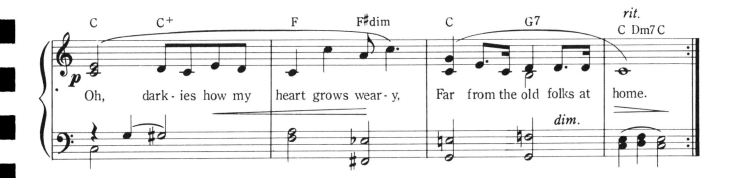

Oh, dark-ies how my heart grows wear-y, Far from the old folks at home.

2. All 'round the little farm I wandered
    When I was young,
    Then many happy days I squandered,
    Many the songs I sung.
    When I was playing with my brother
    Happy was I.
    Oh! take me to my kind old mother,
    There let me live and die.   *Chorus*

3. One little hut among the bushes,
    One that I love,
    Still sadly to my mem'ry rushes,
    No matter where I rove.
    When will I see the bees a-humming
    All 'round the comb?
    When will I hear the banjo strumming
    Down in my good old home?   *Chorus*

My Old Kentucky Home

Words and music by
Stephen Foster

2. They hunt no more for the 'possum and the 'coon
   On the meadow, the hill, and the shore;
   They sing no more by the glimmer of the moon,
   On the bench by the old cabin door.
   The day goes by like a shadow o'er the heart,
   With sorrow where all was delight,
   The time has come when the darkies have to part,
   Then, my old Kentucky home, good-night!   *Chorus*

3. The head must bow and the back will have to bend,
   Wherever the darky may go;
   A few more days and the trouble all will end,
   In the fields where the sugar-canes grow;
   A few more days for to tote the weary load,
   No matter, 'twill never be light,
   A few more days till we totter on the road,
   Then, my old Kentucky home, good-night!   *Chorus*

Jeanie With The Light Brown Hair

Words and music by
Stephen Foster

dream of Jea-nie with the light brown hair,

Float-ing like a va-por, on the soft sum-mer air.

2. I long for Jeanie with the day-dawn smile,
   Radiant in gladness, warm with winning guile;
   I hear her melodies, like joys gone by,
   Sighing 'round my heart o'er the fond hopes that die:
   Sighing like the night wind and sobbing like the rain,
   Wailing for the lost one that comes not again:
   Oh! I long for Jeanie and my heart bows low,
   Never more to find her where the bright waters flow.

3. I sigh for Jeanie, but her light form strayed
   Far from the fond hearts 'round her native glade;
   Her smiles have vanished and her sweet songs flown,
   Flitting like the dreams that have cheered us and gone
   Now the nodding wild flow'rs may wither on the shore
   While her gentle fingers will cull them no more:
   Oh! I sigh for Jeanie with the light brown hair,
   Floating, like a vapor, on the soft summer air.

[115]

Beautiful Dreamer

Words and music by
Stephen Foster

2. Beautiful dreamer, out on the sea,
   Mermaids are chanting the wild lorelie;
   Over the streamlet vapors are borne,
   Waiting to fade at the bright coming morn.
   Beautiful dreamer, beam in my heart,
   E'en as the morn on the streamlet and sea;
   Then will all clouds of sorrow depart,
   Beautiful dreamer, awake unto me!
   Beautiful dreamer, awake unto me!

III

BATTLE CRIES,
HEART-THROBS
AND HIGH-JINKS

VAUDEVILLE TUNES—SPIRITUALS—RAGS

THE entire history of the Civil War could be retold in detail through the hundreds of songs it produced. The patriotic muse was never more prolific than during this, the bloodiest and most bitter conflict in the nation's history. The tragic, one-people-divided nature of the struggle can best be illustrated by the fact that many of its songs were claimed by both sides and, with slight lyric alterations, were popular both north and south of the battle line.

The most popular and most stirring song of the Confederacy, DIXIE, was written by Daniel Decatur Emmett, a Northerner of strong Union sympathies. Born in Ohio, Emmett wrote his famous song in New York, before the outbreak of the hostilities, as a "walk-around" for the Bryant Minstrels. DIXIE was played at the inauguration of Jefferson Davis, President of the Confederacy, and was, at the same time, one of the favorite tunes of Abraham Lincoln. The North's BATTLE HYMN OF THE REPUBLIC by Julia Ward Howe, on the other hand, had its melodic origin in a southern camp-meeting hymn, which—after the Harper's Ferry incident—had the words "John Brown's body lies a-moldering in the grave" fitted to it. Hearing this version sung by Union soldiers moved Mrs. Howe to write her inspired stanzas for the soul-lifting marching song.

Many of the most popular songs of the war—TRAMP! TRAMP! TRAMP!, THE BONNIE BLUE FLAG and others which originally expressed the aspirations and fighting spirits of either the Blues or the Grays—usually seeped through the lines and appeared in a "reply" version or as a parody on the other side sooner or later. Some other songs, such as TENTING ON THE OLD CAMP GROUND, expressing the universal sentiments of longing for home and for peace, stayed safely neutral and could be enjoyed by both sides without alterations. WHEN JOHNNY COMES MARCHING HOME has the special distinction that it was sung not only by both North and South, but achieved even greater popularity more than three decades later during the Spanish-American War.

During the war years the genteel tradition of sentimental balladry was, understandably, somewhat subdued by the stronger topical emotions aroused by the bitter conflict. Immediately after the war, however, the cult of love songs, redolent with pathos, began to flourish again with renewed heart-throbs and a fresh supply of nostalgic tears. SWEET GENEVIEVE, SILVER THREADS AMONG THE GOLD, WHEN YOU AND I WERE YOUNG, MAGGIE, LOVE'S OLD SWEET SONG are all neatly constructed, inventive vocal variations on the same lyric idea; they all bemoan "the dear dead days beyond recall" and dream "the blissful dreams of long ago." In a more prosaic sense they also had in common spectacular commercial success, with combined sheet-music sales running into millions.

The mood, however, was by no means all sentimental and tearful along melody lane. The postwar decades could also boast a fine catalogue of merry, lively tunes, often spiced with a roguish, debonair zest. Some of these songs—CHAMPAGNE CHARLIE, MAN ON THE FLYING TRAPEZE, CAPTAIN JINKS—were written by English immigrants and are unmistakable echoes of the British music-hall tradition.

Minstrelsy was still popular during the postwar years, when Negroes also began to form their own companies. But by this time the genre, as a whole, was on the decline; the old format underwent fundamental changes in the direction of the variety show and eventually was replaced by vaudeville. Two songs stand out in the repertory of the late minstrel shows: THE BIG SUNFLOWER, a charming ditty which for years was the theme song of the period's most famous minstrel, Billy Emerson; and CARRY ME BACK TO OLD VIRGINNY, a perfect blend of simple words and music and a worthy successor to the Stephen Foster legacy. Its writer, James A. Bland, was the first successful black songwriter in America.

The emancipation of the Negro had deep and far-reaching effects on the music of America and especially on the development of a distinguishable American song idiom. It was only during the 1870s that the country at large began to become aware of that large body of beautiful songs of slavery days—the spirituals. Initially, this happened through the efforts of a group of black singers from Fisk University in Nashville, Tennessee, who called themselves The Fisk Jubilee Singers. This vocal ensemble of seven women and four men toured the country, and later Europe too, enthralling audiences everywhere with a program consisting largely of these hitherto unknown gems of Negro folklore. What are these songs, the spirituals, which had such an emotional impact that audiences were "carried away with a whirlwind of delight?" In general terms, they are deeply felt, spontaneous vocal expressions of an oppressed and, in spite of all the hardships, a remarkably creative people. Singing these chants gave the slaves faith, courage, a bond of unity and hope. The personalities and events of the Bible became symbols of their own experiences. The words "let my people go" applied not only to Israel in Egypt's land but was also their own cry for freedom; the "boats," the "chariots," the "gospel trains" all became vehicles for deliverance both in the spiritual and physical sense. Spirituals were not only religious songs; they also helped to ease the burden of work and were especially helpful with any kind of labor that could be performed at a cadence—rowing, hammering, digging, planting.

The musical substance of the spirituals has been the subject of intensive study and research for decades, and the main sources influencing its evolution have been well established: a West-African musical heritage with its feeling for a strong rhythmic pulse and a characteristic tonal inflection; white hymnody, and especially the high-pitched emotional fervor of the camp-meeting songs; Anglo-Saxon folk songs—all contributed. But the question as to how, by what steps of progression, these various elements fused, at that time in history, at that particular geographic location, under those social conditions, to produce this unique and vital catalogue of songs, is still unanswered and probably will ever remain so.

Minstrelsy, vaudeville, and burlesque were responsible for launching a good portion of our popular-song repertory during the second half of the nineteenth century. In those days burlesque had not yet acquired its later notoriety, being merely a show of song, dance and slapstick comedy. Sex, however, did raise its grinning countenance through another form of theatrical entertainment known as the *extravaganza*. It was in 1866 that the first and most successful representative of this genre, *The Black Crook*, opened in New York and created an immediate sensation. This was a five-hour-long, cleverly mounted stage spectacle, employing a large *corps de ballet* of buxom girls, dressed in low-cut, tight-waisted bodices, abbreviated skirts and pink tights. The essence of the entire show was neatly summarized by the *Tribune*: "The scenery is magnificent; the ballet is beautiful; the drama—rubbish." Other press comments were less kind: "The police should arrest all engaged in such a violation of public decency and morality," fulminated the *Herald*. There was also a constant barrage of denunciations from the pulpit. One minister accused *The Black Crook* of being responsible for the male members' slackening interest in the affairs of the congregation; instead of listening to the "pealing of the bells," they have their eyes fixed on "the peeling of the belles." It was, of course, due precisely to such comments that the populace lined up to view this revolutionary exposure of feminine charms and assured the show's unprecedented success. The hit song of the production, YOU NAUGHTY, NAUGHTY MEN might well deserve attention even today from warblers of the night-club circuit.

During the 1870s and '80s the theatrical partnership of Harrigan and Hart, in collaboration with their English-born musical director, David Braham, created a whole catalogue of rollicking tunes that swept the country. Most of these songs were developed by the famous comedy team into satirical song sketches, staged in vaudeville style, depicting amusing episodes in the everyday life of big-city ethnic groups: the Irish, the German, the Jewish, the Italian and—in the tradition of minstrelsy—the Negro. Among their most famous song skits were THE MULLIGAN GUARD, a caricature of uniform-loving social fraternities and WALKING FOR THAT CAKE, an early, mildly syncopated cakewalk-quadrille reviving an old plantation custom.

The establishment of vaudeville as family entertainment was due largely to the talent and ingenuity of Tony Pastor. As singer, performer, and entrepreneur, he realized very early in his career that, by making his variety shows acceptable to female audiences, he could tap a huge new reservoir of theater customers. Accordingly, he eliminated smoking and drinking in the audience, saw to it that nothing offensive took place on the stage, and even offered door prizes of groceries, kitchenware, dress patterns and such. His efforts were eminently successful; the women came with the men, Tony prospered and moved into larger and larger theaters. To appear in his shows became the hallmark of success for performers of the period; Lillian Russell, Eddie Foy, Gus Williams, Weber and Fields, George M. Cohan, all established their names at Tony Pastor's.

In the meantime back in the hinterlands, on the great plains, driving the herds of Texas longhorn through hundreds of miles of still untamed territory, a new folk hero was born, the cowboy; and with him emerged an entire new literature of songs describing the West and the hard life and pleasures of these roughhewn, colorful horsemen. All this evolved very swiftly, in a matter of two or three decades. The first railroad spanning the country was opened in 1869; stockyards were established at the railheads and towns sprang up overnight; cattle and drovers came in a steady stream, overcoming sandstorms, stampedes and Indian raids. By 1890, after about six million longhorns had walked north to the market, the burgeoning new railroad networks made the cattle drive obsolete and the saga of the trail ended. But the songs linger on, and the appeal of the range "where the buffalo roam . . . and the antelope play" is still as fresh as ever.

In writing about the musical and social history of America, the last three decades of the nineteenth century are usually tagged with certain alliterative epithets such as the "sentimental" seventies, the "elegant" eighties, the "naughty" or "gay" nineties. In fact, no such blanket characterizations of these decades is appropriate. Sentimentality, nostalgia, romantic love were, of course, not exclusive earmarks of the seventies; they had been ever present in our song literature throughout the century and well beyond. Also, for every tear-drenched refrain there always was another jolly tune to quicken the pulse and elicit a happy smile. So, if the sudden stopping of GRANDFATHER'S CLOCK left an audience hushed and subdued, reaching for the LITTLE BROWN JUG could well brighten things up. Also, while many adieus in our ballads were sad and final, some were just a promising and flirtatious KISS ME QUICK AND GO.

A similar juxtaposition of moods, with perhaps even sharper contrasts, is discernible in the songs of the 1880s and '90s. These were decades of an America bursting with activity—years marked by unprecedented industrial expansion, the birth of big business, the emergence of the United States as a world power. We had acquired the telephone, the electric light, the horseless carriage, the talking machine, but we also had periodic depressions, bank failures and workers' strikes. Some of the songs were boisterously gay, others were tightly packed with melodrama: children lost or dying, women wronged, lovers torn apart and reunited, vice decried and virtue triumphant. But, again, for every doleful ditty there was a lusty echo of TA-RA-RA BOOM-DER-É, and for every pathetic BIRD IN A GILDED CAGE there was a lucky DAISY BELL pedaling her way to happy matrimony on a bicycle built for two.

In addition to all this variety there was also something else: the emergence of an excitingly new musical phenomenon, which made the last decade of the century one of the most fascinating and important chapters in the history of American music. This new popular style was ragtime. It was at the Chicago World's Fair in 1893 that Americans in great numbers first had an opportunity to hear this exuberantly new music-making, through the playing of a young black musician named Scott Joplin and other pianists. For three or four years, "ragging" spread and gained momentum underground in midwestern honky-tonks and Mississippi riverfront saloons, until, in 1896, it erupted into a national craze. The man generally credited with starting this explosive trend was Benjamin R. Harney, who opened at Tony Pastor's in New York with his "piano playing in cyncopated [sic] or 'rag time,' singing his own 'Coon' melodies and doing his original dancing." The advertisement added that the act was "an absolute hit everywhere," which, if anything, was an understatement. Overnight, countless other entertainers were doing the same thing; ragtime "clicked" and spread like wildfire through piano players, piano rolls, brass bands and sheet-music promotions; within a few months people everywhere were playing it, singing it, dancing it, from big cities to the smallest hamlets.

It was the rhythmic effervescence and infectious gaiety of the twin phenomena, cakewalk and ragtime, that captivated the country. In essence, neither the dance nor the music was new. Cakewalk was originally a plantation dance of antebellum days; the slaves got dressed up on Sundays and—for their own and the master's amusement—did a high-kicking, prancing walkaround, with much bowing back and forward and frequent salutatory gestures toward the audience. The prize of a cake was given to the best-performing couple. Blackface minstrels incorporated the dance into their shows, and from there it was transferred to vaudeville. The earliest minstrel tunes—OLD DAN TUCKER, ZIP COON and others—years before had contained the basic rhythmic element, the heart of ragtime: syncopation.

There was, of course, an interaction of numerous other elements in the evolution of this idiom: West-African and Caribbean dance rhythms, the Negro folk song with its "blue" scale of flatted thirds and sevenths, the form patterns of various social dances such as the quadrille, the polka, the march. The fusion of these elements could take place only after emancipation, when the Negro attained a degree of mobility, made inroads in the entertainment field, and—most importantly—gained access to the piano. Ragtime is, essentially and *par excellence*, piano music, in which the solid oom-pah, oom-pah bass of the left hand supports the richly syncopated melodic flourishes of the right hand. It was the Negro player's affinity with the keyboard, his natural gift to exploit its technical and expressive possibilities in a unique way, that provided the needed catalyst to fuse the above ingredients into a new mold, a type of music and a style of piano playing which, together with the blues, became the principal tributaries of twentieth-century jazz. Among the many fine instrumental rags of the period the works of Scott Joplin stand out with their spark and originality. MAPLE LEAF RAG, the most successful of them all, became a classic of the genre and was, with unusually clever lyrics added, also popular as a song.

The syncopated revelry of ragtime found vocal expression in many popular tunes of the period. Called "coon songs"—an offensive term by our standards—they were cultivated by writers and performers of both races and represented a healthy contrast to the maudlin sentimentality of the many lachrymose ballads. They may have been crude at times, as were the many Irish, Jewish and Chinese spoofs, but did not carry connotations of an intentional ethnic slur. A feeling of tuneful vitality and unashamedly boisterous fun pervaded these songs and was the reason for their immense popularity. THE BULLY SONG, AT A GEORGIA CAMP MEETING, A HOT TIME IN THE OLD TOWN TONIGHT, BILL BAILEY, HELLO, MA BABY, and UNDER THE BAMBOO TREE were among the many favorite representatives of this category and of the era. It was to their lively cakewalk beat and to the lilting strains of many waltz tunes—among them THE BAND PLAYED ON, THE SIDEWALKS OF NEW YORK, AFTER THE BALL— that America sang and danced its way into the twentieth century.

Dixie

Words and music by
Daniel Decatur Emmet

1. I wish I was in the land of cotton, old times there are not for-got-ten, Look a - way! Look a - way! Look a - way! Dix - ie Land. In Dix - ie Land where I was born in, ear - ly on one frost - y morn-in', Look a - way! Look a - way! Look a - way! Dix - ie Land. Then I wish I was in Dix - ie, Hoo - ray! Hoo

ray! In Dix - ie Land, I'll take my stand to live and die in

Dix - ie. A - way, a - way, a - way down south in

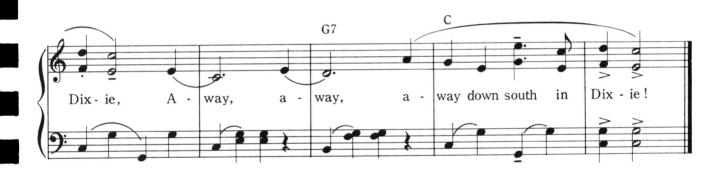

Dix - ie, A - way, a - way, a - way down south in Dix - ie!

2. Ole Missus marry "Will the weaver",
   Willium was a gay deceiver;
   Look away! Look away!
   Look away! Dixie Land!
   But when he put his arm around 'er,
   He smiled fierce as a forty pounder,
   Look away! Look away!
   Look away! Dixie Land!   *Chorus*

3. His face was sharp as a butcher's cleaver,
   But that did not seem to grieve 'er;
   Look away! Look away!
   Look away! Dixie Land!
   Ole Missus acted the foolish part,
   And died for a man that broke her heart,
   Look away! Look away!
   Look away! Dixie Land!   *Chorus*

4. Now here's a health to the next ole Missus,
   An' all the gals that want to kiss us;
   Look away! Look away!
   Look away! Dixie Land!
   But if you want to drive 'way sorrow,
   Come and hear this song tomorrow,
   Look away! Look away!
   Look away! Dixie Land!   *Chorus*

5. There's buckwheat cakes and Injun batter,
   Makes you fat or a little fatter;
   Look away! Look away!
   Look away! Dixie Land!
   Then hoe it down and scratch your gravel,
   To Dixie's Land I'm bound to travel,
   Look away! Look away!
   Look away! Dixie Land!   *Chorus*

[127]

The Battle Hymn Of The Republic

John Brown's Body

Words by
Julia Ward Howe

Music by
William Steffe(?)

Majestic march tempo

2. I have seen Him in the watchfires of a hundred circling camps;
They have builded Him an altar in the evening dews and damps,
I can read His righteous sentence by the dim and flaring lamps;
His day is marching on.
Chorus

3. I have read a fiery gospel writ in burnished rows of steel:
"As ye deal with My contemners, so with you My grace shall deal":
Let the Hero born of woman crush the serpent with His heel,
Since God is marching on.
Chorus

4. He has sounded forth the trumpet that shall never call retreat;
He is sifting out the hearts of men before His judgment seat.
Oh, be swift, my soul, to answer Him! be jubilant, my feet!
Our God is marching on.
Chorus

5. In the beauty of the lilies Christ was born across the sea,
With a glory in His bosom that transfigures you and me;
As He died to make men holy let us die to make men free,
While God is marching on.
Chorus

John Brown's Body

1. John Brown's body lies amould'ring in the grave,
John Brown's body lies amould'ring in the grave,
John Brown's body lies amould'ring in the grave,
His soul goes marching on!

Chorus
Glory, glory! Hallelujah! Glory, glory! Hallelujah!
Glory, glory! Hallelujah! His soul is marching on.

2. He captured Harper's Ferry with his nineteen men so true,
And he frightened old Virginia till she trembled through and through;
They hung him for a traitor, themselves the traitor crew,
But His soul is marching on!
Chorus

3. John Brown died that the slave might be free,
John Brown died that the slave might be free,
John Brown died that the slave might be free,
But his soul goes marching on!
Chorus

4. The stars of heaven are looking kindly down,
The stars of heaven are looking kindly down,
The stars of heaven are looking kindly down,
On the grave of old John Brown!
Chorus

The Bonnie Blue Flag

Words by
Harry McCarthy

Traditional Irish Melody

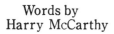

Spirited march tempo

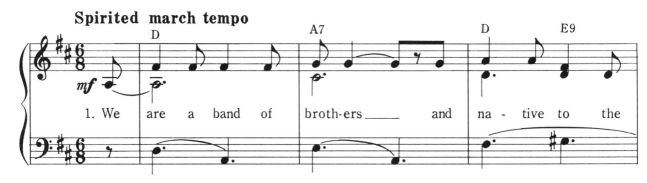

1. We are a band of broth-ers_____ and na - tive to the

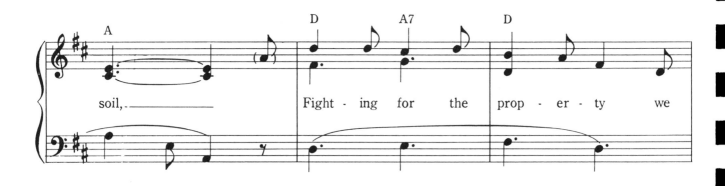

soil,._____ Fight - ing for the prop - er - ty we

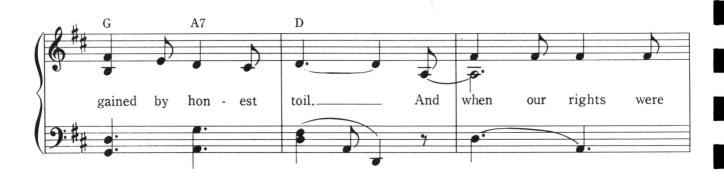

gained by hon - est toil._____ And when our rights were

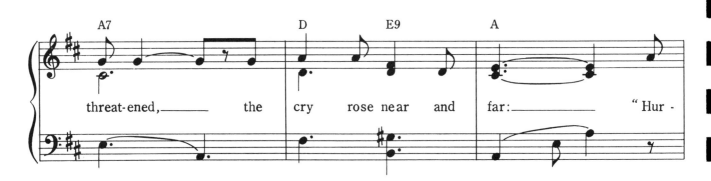

threat-ened,_____ the cry rose near and far:_____ "Hur -

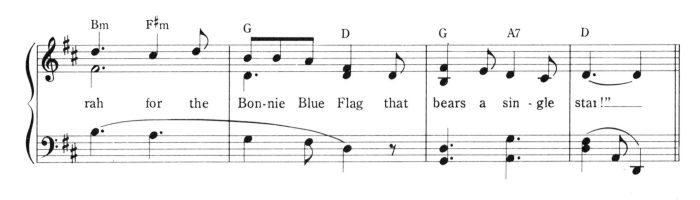

rah   for   the   Bon-nie Blue Flag that   bears a sin-gle   star!"

Chorus

Hur - rah!_____   Hur - rah!_____   for

South - ern   rights hur - rah!_____   Hur - rah   for   the

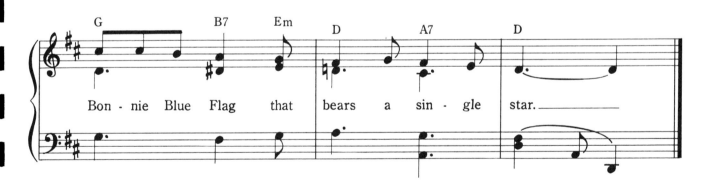

Bon - nie Blue Flag   that   bears a sin - gle   star._____

2.   As long as the Union was faithful to her trust,
      Like friends and brethren, kind were we, and just;
      But now, when Northern treachery attempts our rights to mar,
      We hoist on high the Bonnie Blue Flag that bears a single star.
      Chorus

3.   Then here's to our Confederacy, strong we are and brave,
      Like patriots of old we'll fight, our heritage to save;
      And rather than submit to shame, to die we would prefer,
      So cheer for the Bonnie Blue Flag that bears a single star.
      Chorus

[131]

Tramp! Tramp! Tramp!

Words and music by
George F. Root

Cheer up, com-rades, they will come. And be-
neath the star-ry flag, We shall breathe the air a-gain, Of the
free land in our own be-lov-ed home. home.

2. In the battle front we stood,
   When their fiercest charge they made,
   And they swept us off a hundred men or more,
   But before we reached their lines,
   They were beaten back dismayed,
   And we heard the cry of vict'ry o'er and o'er.
   Chorus

3. So within the prison cell
   We are waiting for the day
   That shall come to open wide the iron door,
   And the hollow eye grows bright,
   And the poor heart almost gay,
   As we think of seeing home and friends once more.
   Chorus

Southern Version:

1. In my prison cell I sit,
   Thinking, Mother, dear, of you,
   And my happy Southern home so far away;
   And my eyes they fill with tears
   'Spite of all that I can do,
   Though I try to cheer my comrades and be gay.

2. In the cruel stockade-pen
   Dying slowly day by day,
   For weary months we've waited all in vain;
   But if God will speed the way
   Of our gallant boys in gray,
   I shall see your face, dear Mother, yet again.

Chorus
Tramp! Tramp! Tramp!
The boys are marching;
Cheer up, comrades, they will come.
And beneath the stars and bars
We shall breathe the air again
Of freemen in our own beloved home.

[133]

Tenting Tonight

(Tenting On The Old Camp Ground)

Words and music by
Walter Kittredge

[134]

see   the   dawn   of   peace.   Tent - ing   to - night,

tent - ing   to - night,   Tent - ing   on   the   old   camp   ground.

2.   We've been tenting tonight on the old camp ground,
     Thinking of days gone by,
     Of the loved ones at home that gave us the hand,
     And the tear that said, "Good-bye."
     Chorus

3.   We are tired of war on the old camp ground,
     Many are dead and gone,
     Of the brave and true who've left their home,
     Others been wounded long.
     Chorus

4.   We've been fighting tonight on the old camp ground,
     Many are lying near;
     Some are dead and some are dying,
     Many are in tears.
     Chorus

[135]

When Johnny Comes Marching Home

Words and music by
Patrick S. Gilmore

2. The old church bell will peal with joy,
Hurrah! Hurrah!
To welcome home our darling boy,
Hurrah! Hurrah!
The village lads and lassies say
With roses they will strew the way,
And we'll all feel gay
When Johnny comes marching home.

3. Get ready for the Jubilee,
Hurrah! Hurrah!
We'll give the hero three times three,
Hurrah! Hurrah!
The laurel wreath is ready now
To place upon his loyal brow
And we'll all feel gay
When Johnny comes marching home.

Aura Lee

Words by
W. W. Fosdick

Music by
George R. Poulton

When You And I Were Young Maggie

Words by
George W. Johnson

Music by
James A. Butterfield

you and — I were — young. — And now we are a-ged and

gray, Mag-gie, And the tri-als of life — near-ly done; — Let us

sing of the days that are gone, Mag-gie, When you and — I were — young.

2. A city so silent and lone, Maggie,
   Where the young and the gay and the best,
   In polished white mansions of stone, Maggie,
   Have each found a place of rest,
   Is built where the birds used to play, Maggie,
   And join in the songs that were sung;
   For we sang as gay as they, Maggie,
   When you and I were young.   *Chorus*

3. They say I am feeble with age, Maggie,
   My steps are less sprightly than then;
   My face is a well-written page, Maggie,
   But time alone was the pen.
   They say we are aged and gray, Maggie,
   As spray by the white breakers flung;
   But to me you're as fair as you were, Maggie,
   When you and I were young.   *Chorus*

The Big Sunflower

Words and music by
Bobby Newcomb

2. As days passed on and we became
   Like friends of olden times,
   I thought the question I would pop,
   And ask her to be mine.
   But the answer I received next day,
   How could she treat me so?
   Instead of being mine for life,
   She simply answered "No."
   Chorus

3. I went next day dressed in my best,
   This young girl for to see,
   To ask her if she would explain
   Why she had shaken me.
   She said she really felt quite sad
   To cause me such distress,
   And when I said: "Won't you be mine?"
   Of course she answered: "Yes."
   Chorus

Sweet Genevieve

Words by
George Cooper

Music by
Henry Tucker

Slowly, with much expression

Chorus

G   D7   G   Gdim G

mp

1. O,   Gen - e - vieve, sweet Gen - e - vieve, The   days may come, the   days___ may go, But

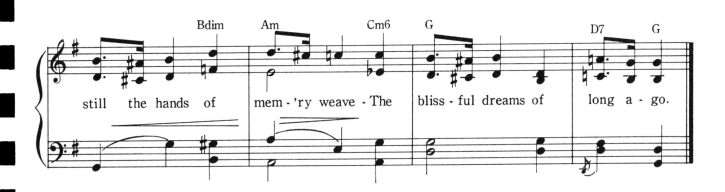

Bdim   Am   Cm6   G   D7   G

still   the hands of   mem - 'ry weave - The   bliss - ful dreams of   long a - go.

2.   Fair Genevieve, my early love,
The years but make thee dearer far!
My heart shall never, never rove,
Thou art my only guiding star.
For me the past has no regret
Whate'er the years may bring to me;
I bless the hour when first we met,
The hour that gave me love and thee!
Chorus

You Naughty, Naughty Men

Words by
T. Kennick

from "The Black Crook"

Music by
G. Bicknell

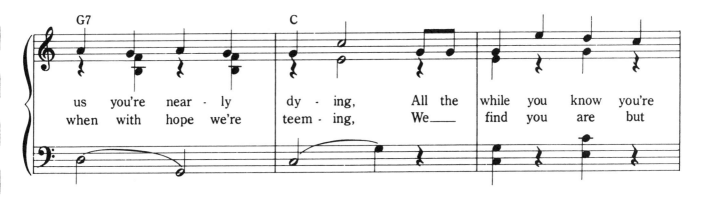

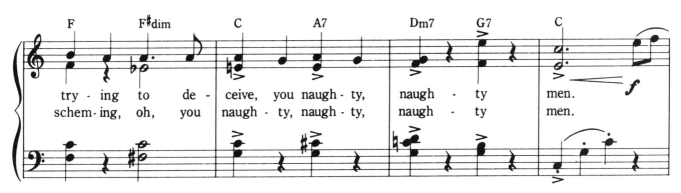

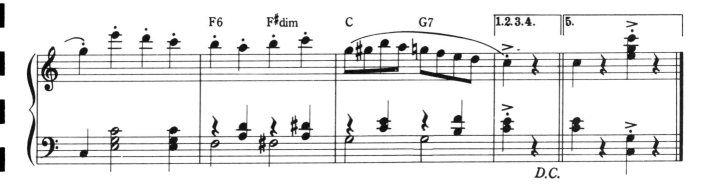

3. If a fortune we inherit, you see in us every merit,
   And declare we're girls of spirit, oh! you naughty, naughty men;
   But too often, matrimony is a mere matter of money,
   We get bitters 'stead of honey from you naughty, naughty men.
       Chorus: But too often, matrimony is a mere matter of money,
               We get bitters 'stead of honey from you naughty, naughty, naughty men.

4. And when married how you treat us, and of each fond hope defeat us,
   And there's some will even beat us, oh! you naughty, naughty men;
   You take us from our mothers, from our sisters and our brothers,
   When you get us, flirt with others, oh! you cruel, wicked men.
       Chorus: You take us from our mothers, from our sisters and our brothers,
               When you get us, flirt with others, oh! you naughty, cruel, wicked men.

5. But with all your faults, we clearly, love you wicked fellows dearly,
   Yes, we dote upon you dearly, oh! you naughty, naughty men;
   We've no wish to distress you, we would sooner far caress you,
   And when kind we'll say, oh, bless you, oh! you dear, delightful men.
       Chorus: We've no wish to distress you, we would sooner far caress you,
               And when kind we'll say, oh, bless you, oh! you naughty, dear, delightful men.

[145]

Grandfather's Clock

Words and music by
Henry C. Work

Moderately

1. My grand-fa-ther's clock was too large for the shelf, So it stood nine-ty years on the floor; It was tall-er by half than the old man him-self, Though it weighed not a pen-ny-weight more. It was bought on the morn of the day that he was born, And was al-ways his treas-ure and pride; But it stopp'd short, nev-er to go a-gain, when the old man

died. Nine-ty years with-out slum-ber-ing, tick, tock, tick, tock, His

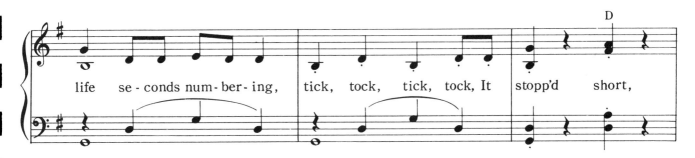

life se-conds num-ber-ing, tick, tock, tick, tock, It stopp'd short,

nev-er to so a-gain, when the old man died.

2. In watching its pendulum swing to and fro,
   Many hours had he spent while a boy;
   And in childhood and manhood the clock seemed to know,
   And to share both his grief and his joy.
   For it struck twenty-four when he entered the door,
   With a blooming and beautiful bride.
   But it stopp'd short, never to go again,
   When the old man died.   *Chorus*

3. My grandfather said, that of those he could hire,
   Not a servant so faithful he found;
   For it wasted no time, and had but one desire,
   At the close of each week to be wound.
   And it kept in its place, not a frown upon its face,
   And its hands never hung by its side;
   But it stopp'd short, never to go again,
   When the old man died.   *Chorus*

4. It rang an alarm in the dead of the night,
   An alarm that for years had been dumb;
   And we knew that his spirit was pluming its flight,
   That his hour of departure had come.
   Still the clock kept the time, with a soft and muffled chime,
   As we silently stood by his side;
   But it stopp'd short, never to go again,
   When the old man died.   *Chorus*

[147]

Kingdom Coming

（Year of Jubilo）

Words and music by
Henry C. Work

ho!   It mus' be now de king-dom com-in', an' de year of Ju-bi- lo!

2.   He' six foot one way, two foot t'udder
      An' he weigh t'ree hundred pound,
      His coat's so big he couldn't pay de tailor
      An' it won' go half way 'round.
      He drill so much dey calls him Cap'n,
      An' he gets so mighty tanned,
      I 'spec he'll try to fool dem Yankees
      For to tink he's contraband.
      Chorus

3.   De darkeys got so lonesome libin'
      In de log hut on de lawn,
      Dey move dere t'ings into massa's parlor,
      For to keep it while he's gone.
      Dar's wine an' cider in de kitchen
      An' de darkeys dey'll hab some;
      I 'spose dey'll all be confiscated,
      When de Linkun sojers come.
      Chorus

4.   De oberseer he make us trouble,
      An' he dribe us 'round a spell;
      We lock him up in de smoke-house cellar,
      Wid de key t'rown in de well.
      De whip is los', de han'-cuff broken,
      But de massa'll hab his pay;
      He's ole enough, big enough, ought to know better
      Dan to went an' run away.
      Chorus

Champagne Charlie

Words by
George Leybourne (?)

Music by
Alfred Lee

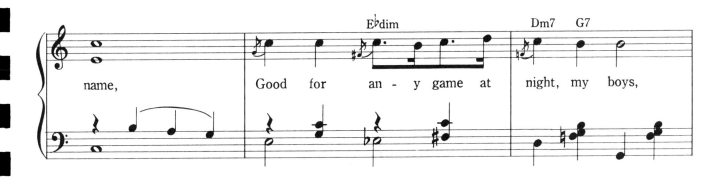

2. I've seen a deal of gaiety throughout my noisy life,
But with all my grand accomplishments I've ne'er obtained a wife.
The thing I mostly excel in is the "midnight supper game",
A noise all night, in bed all day, and swimming in champagne. *Chorus*

Silver Threads Among The Gold

Words by
Eben E. Rexford

Music by
Hart P. Danks

me.　Dar - ling, I am grow - ing,　grow - ing old,

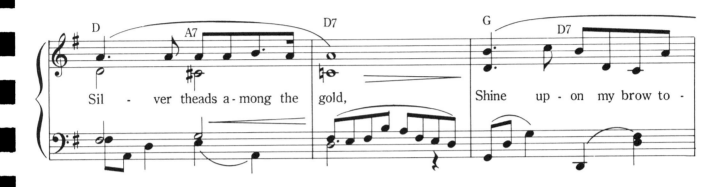

Sil - ver theads a - mong the　gold,　Shine up - on my brow to -

day＿＿＿＿　Life is fad - ing fast a - way.

2.　When your hair is silver white,
　　And your cheeks no longer bright,
　　With the roses of the May
　　I will kiss your lips and say:
　　Oh! my darling, mine alone, alone,
　　You have never older grown!
　　Yes, my darling, mine alone,
　　You have never older grown!　*Chorus*

3.　Love can never more grow old,
　　Locks may lose their brown and gold;
　　Cheeks may fade and hollow grow,
　　But the hearts that love will know,
　　Never, never winter's frost and chill;
　　Summer warmth is in them still;
　　Never winter's frost and chill,
　　Summer warmth is in them still.　*Chorus*

[153]

In The Gloaming

Words by
Mete Orred

Music by
Annie F. Harrison

Moderately, with tenderness

1. In the gloam - ing, O my dar - ling! When the lights are dim and low, And the qui - et shad - ows fall - ing, Soft - ly come and soft - ly go. When the winds are sob - bing faint - ly With a gen - tle, un - known woe, Will you think of me and

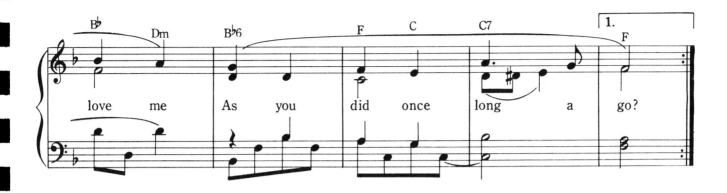

love me As you did once long a go?

me. It was best to leave you thus,

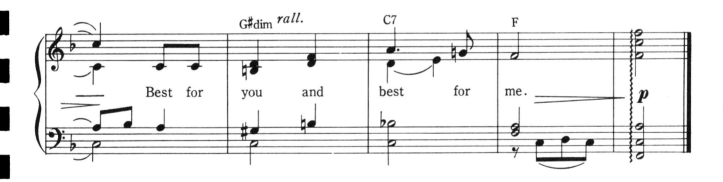

Best for you and best for me.

2. In the gloaming, O my darling!
    Think not bitterly of me!
    'Tho I passed away in silence,
    Left you lonely, set you free.
    For my heart was crushed with longing,
    What had been could never be.
    It was best to leave you thus, dear,
    Best for you and best for me.
    It was best to leave you thus,
    Best for you and best for me.

[155]

Captain Jinks

Words by
William Horace Lingard

Music by
T. Maclagan

ar - my. I'm___ Cap - tain Jinks of the Horse Ma - rines; I

feed my horse on corn and beans, And oft - en live be -

yond my means, Tho'a cap - tain in the ar - my.

2. I joined my corps when twenty-one,
    Of course I thought it capital fun;
    When the enemy came, of course I run,
    For I'm not cut out for the army.
    When I left home, Mama, she cried,
    Mama, she cried, Mama, she cried,
    When I left home, Mama, she cried,
    "He's not cut out for the army."
    Chorus

3. The first time I went out to drill,
    The bugle sounding made me ill;
    Of the battlefield I'd had my fill,
    For I'm not cut out for the army.
    The officers, they all did shout,
    They all did shout, they all did shout,
    The officers they all did shout,
    "Why! kick him out of the army."
    Chorus

[157]

The Mulligan Guard

Words by
Ned Harrigan

Music by
David Braham

2. When the band play'd Garry Owen,
   Or the Connamara Pet;
   With a rub a dub, dub, we'd march in the mud,
   To the military step.
   With the green above the red, boys,
   To show where we come from,
   Our guns we'd lift with the right shoulder shift,
   As we'd march to the bate of the drum.
   Chorus

3. When we got home at night, boys,
   The divil a bite we'd ate,
   We'd all set up and drink a sup
   Of whiskey strong and nate.
   Thin we'd all march home together,
   As slippery as lard,
   The solid min would all fall in,
   And march with the Mulligan Guard.
   Chorus

Carry Me Back To Old Virginny

Words and music by
James A. Bland

Moderately slow

1. Car-ry me back to old Vir-gin-ny, There's where the cot-ton and the corn and ta-ters grow; There's where the birds war-ble sweet in the spring-time, There's where this old dark-ey's heart am long'd to go. There's where I la-bored so hard for old Mas-sa, Day aft-er day in the field of yel-low corn; No place on earth do I love more sin-cere-ly

Than old Vir-gin- ny, the state where I was born.

Chorus

Car-ry me back to old Vir- gin- ny, There's where the cot-ton and the corn and ta- ters grow; There's where the birds war- ble sweet in the spring-time There's where this old dark - ey's heart am long'd to go.

2. Carry me back to old Virginny,
   There let me live till I wither and decay.
   Long by the old dismal swamp have I wandered,
   There's where this old darkey's life will pass away.
   Massa and missis have long gone before me,
   Soon we will meet on that bright and golden shore.
   There we'll be happy and free from all sorrow,
   There's where we'll meet and we'll never part no more. *Chorus*

The Man On The Flying Trapeze

Words by
George Leybourne

Music by
Alfred Lee

With a merry swing

1. Oh, once I was hap-py, but now I'm for-lorn, like an old coat that is tat-tered and torn. I'm left in this wide world to weep and to mourn, be-trayed by a maid in her teens. ___ Now this girl that I loved, she was hand-some, ___ and I tried all I knew her to please. ___ But I nev-er could please her one

2. Now the young man by name was Senor Boni Slang,
   Tall, big and handsome, as well made as Chang.
   Where'er he appeared, how the hall loudly rang,
   With ovations from all people there.
   He'd smile from the bar on the people below
   And one night he smiled on my love,
   She winked back at him, and she shouted "Bravo!"
   As he hung by his nose from above. Oh!   *Chorus*

3. Her father and mother were both on my side,
   And tried very hard to make her my bride.
   Her father, he sighed, and her mother, she cried
   To see her throw herself away.
   'Twas all no avail, she went there every night
   And threw her bouquets on the stage,
   Which caused him to meet her - how he ran me down,
   To tell it would take a whole page. Oh!   *Chorus*

4. One night I as usual went out to her home,
   And found there her mother and father alone.
   I asked for my love, and soon 'twas made known,
   To my horror, that she'd run away.
   She packed up her boxes and eloped in the night,
   With him with the greatest of ease.
   From two stories high he had lowered her down
   To the ground on his flying trapeze. Oh!   *Chorus*

5. Some months after that I went into a hall;
   To my surprise I found there on the wall
   A bill in red letters which did my heart gall,
   That she was appearing with him.
   He'd taught her gymnastics, and dressed her in tights
   To help him live at his ease.
   He'd made her assume a masculine name,
   And now she goes on the trapeze. Oh!

   Final Chorus
   She floats through the air with the greatest of ease;
   You'd think her a man on the flying trapeze.
   She does all the work while he takes his ease,
   And that's what's become of my love.

Walking For That Cake

Words by
Ed Harrigan

Music by
Dave Braham

Lively, strutting tempo

'Twas down at Aun - ty Jack - son's There was a big re -
cep - tion, Of high - toned so - cie - ty peo - ple So
full of sweet af - fec - tion. Such sing - ing and such
danc - ing, We made the ceil - ing shake, The
cream of all the ev - 'ning was A - walk - ing for that cake.

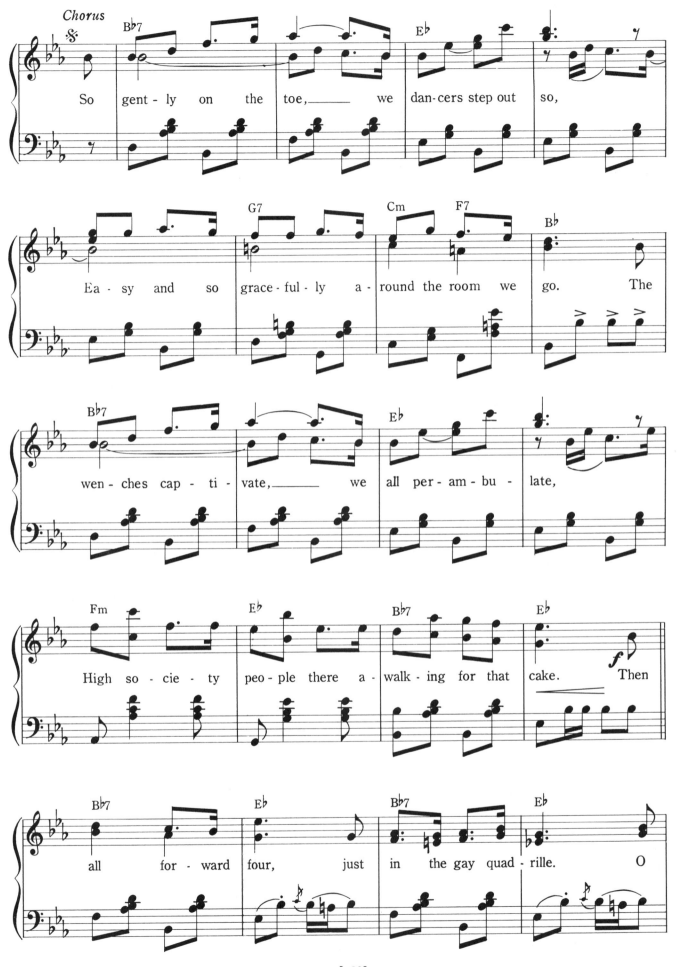

[166]

Baby Mine

Words by
Charles Mackey

Music by
Archibald Johnston

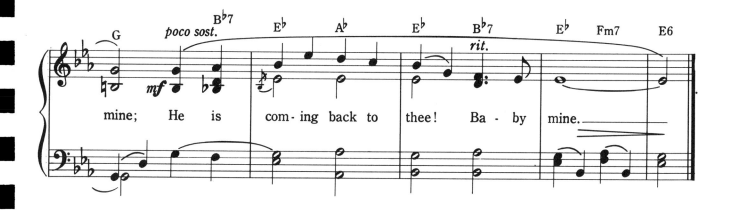

mine; He is com- ing back to thee! Ba - by mine. _____

2. Oh, I long to see his face, Baby mine, Baby mine;
   In his old accustom'd place, Baby mine, Baby mine;
   Like the rose of May in bloom, like a star amid the gloom,
   Like the sunshine in the room, Baby mine, Baby mine!
   Like the sunshine in the room, Baby mine!

3. I'm so glad, I cannot sleep, Baby mine, Baby mine;
   I'm so happy, I could weep, Baby mine, Baby mine;
   He is sailing o'er the sea, he is coming home to me,
   He is coming back to thee! Baby mine! Baby mine;
   He is coming back to thee! Baby mine!

Nobody Knows The Trouble I've Seen

Spiritual

Slowly moving; with deep feeling

No - bod - y knows the trouble I've seen, No - bod - y knows but

Je - sus. No - bod - y knows the trouble I've seen,

Glo - ry Hal - le - lu - jah! *Fine* Some - times I'm up, some-
I nev - er shall for -

times I'm down, Oh, yes, Lord; Some - times I'm al - most
get that day, Oh, yes, Lord; When Je - sus washed my

to the ground, Oh, yes, Lord.
sins a - way, Oh, yes, Lord.

D.C. al Fine

Swing Low Sweet Chariot

Spiritual

Sometimes I Feel Like A Motherless Child

Spiritual

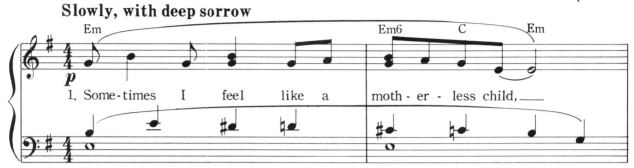

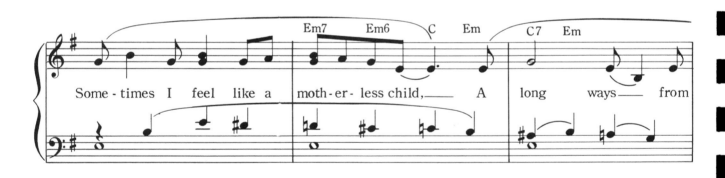

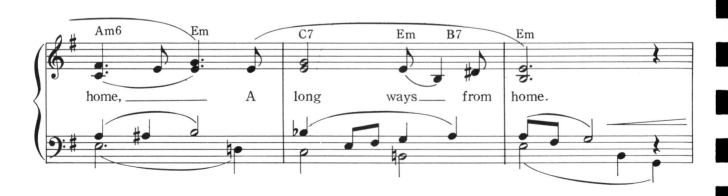

[172]

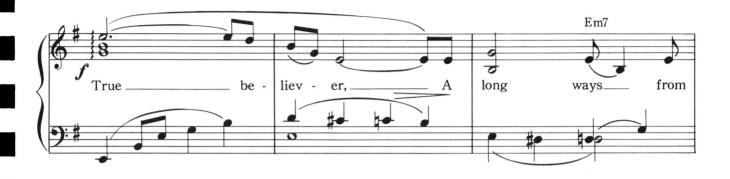

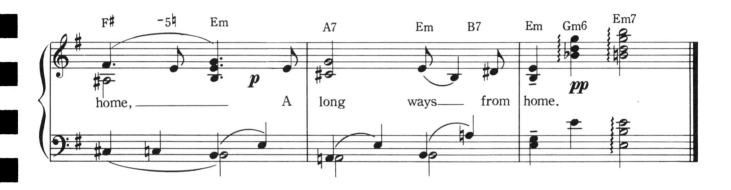

2. Sometimes I feel like I'm almost gone,
   Sometimes I feel like I'm almost gone,
   Sometimes I feel like I'm almost gone,
   Way up in the heavenly land,
   Way up in the heavenly land.
   True believer,
   Way up in the heavenly land,
   Way up in the heavenly land.

3. Sometimes I feel like a motherless child,
   Sometimes I feel like a motherless child,
   Sometimes I feel like a motherless child,
   A long ways from home,
   A long ways from home.
   True believer,
   A long ways from home,
   A long ways from home.

The Gospel Train

(Get On Board, Little Children)

Spiritual

2. The fare is cheap and all can go,
   The rich and poor are there;
   No second class aboard this train,
   No difference in the fare.   *Chorus*

3. I hear that train a-comin',
   She sure is speedin' fast,
   So get your tickets ready
   And ride to heaven at last.   *Chorus*

Look Down That Lonesome Road

Slow Blues Tempo

Folk Song

1. Look down, look down, that lone - some road, Hang down your head and sigh; The best of friends must part some day, And why not you and I?

2. True love, true love, what have I done,
    That you should treat me so?
    You caused me to walk and talk with you,
    Like I ne'er done before.

While Strolling Through The Park

Words and music by
Ed Haley

Love's Old Sweet Song

Words by
G. Clifton Bingham

Music by
James L. Molloy

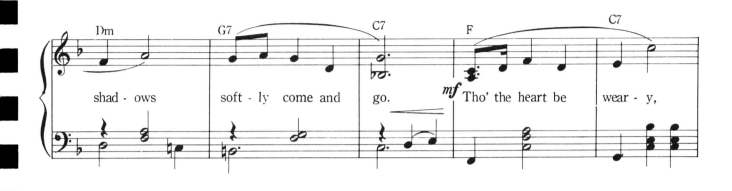

shad - ows   soft - ly come and   go.   *mf* Tho' the heart be   wear - y,

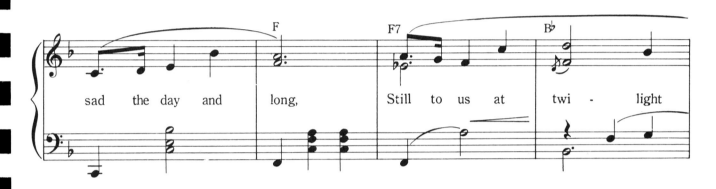

sad   the day   and   long,   Still   to   us   at   twi - light

comes   love's   old   song,   Comes   love's - old   sweet   song.

2.   Even today we hear love's song of yore,
Deep in our hearts it dwells for evermore.
Footsteps may falter, weary grow the way,
Still we can hear it at the close of day.
So till the end, when life's dim shadows fall,
Love will be found the sweetest song of all.   *Refrain*

There Is A Tavern In The Town

Traditional

Lively Polka

1. There is a tav-ern in the town, in the town, And there my dear love sits him down, sits him down,___ And___ drinks his wine 'mid laugh - ter___ free, And nev - er nev - er thinks of me. Fare thee well, for I must leave thee, Do not let the part-ing grieve thee, And re -

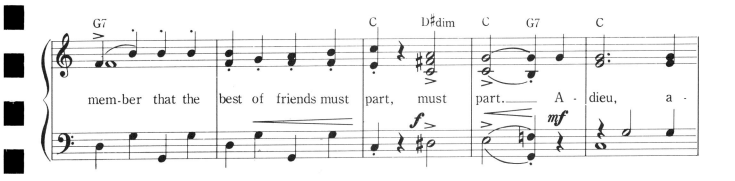

mem-ber that the best of friends must part, must part.___ A - dieu, a -

dieu, kind friends, a - dieu, a - dieu, a - dieu; I can no long - er stay with

you, stay with you;___ I'll___ hang my harp on a weep-ing wil - low

tree, And may the world go well with thee.

2. He left me for a damsel dark, damsel dark,
Each Friday night they used to spark, used to spark,
And now my love, once true to me,
Takes that dark damsel on his knee.   *Chorus*

3. Oh! dig my grave both wide and deep, wide and deep,
Put tombstones at my head and feet, head and feet,
And on my breast carve a turtle-dove,
To signify I died of love.   *Chorus*

Red River Valley

Cowboy Song

Chorus: (*sung to the melody above*)
Come and sit by my side if you love me,
Do not hasten to bid me adieu,
But remember the Red River Valley
And the girl that has loved you so true.

2. Won't you think of the valley you're leaving?
   Oh how lonely, how sad it will be,
   Oh think of the fond heart you're breaking,
   And the grief you are causing me.
   Chorus

3. I have promised you, darling, that never
   Will a word from my lips cause you pain;
   And my life, it will be yours forever
   If you only will love me again.
   Chorus

The Cowboy's Lament

(The Streets Of Laredo)

Folk Song

Moderately, with a lilt

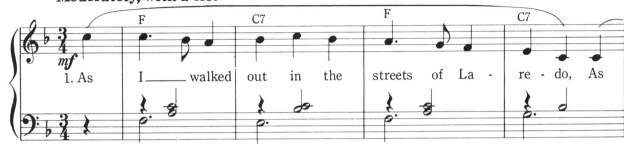

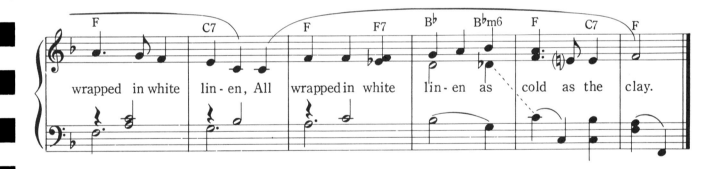

2. "I see by your outfit that you are a cowboy,"
   These words he did say as I calmly went by.
   "Come sit down beside me and hear my sad story,
   I'm shot in the breast and I know I must die."

3. "It was once in the saddle I used to go dashing,
   Once in the saddle I gallop'd away,
   First down to the barroom and then to the card house,
   Got shot in the breast, and I'm dying to-day."

4. "Get six of my buddies to carry my coffin,
   Six pretty maidens to sing a sad song,
   Take me to the valley and lay the sod o'er me,
   For I'm a young cowboy who knows he did wrong."

5. "Go fetch me a cup, a cup of cold water,
   To cool my parched lips," the cowboy then said,
   Before I returned, the spirit had left him,
   And gone to its Maker, the cowboy was dead.

6. — *(Repeat Verse No. 1.)*

Home On The Range

Traditional Cowboy Song

word,   And the skies are not cloud-y all day.

2. Oh, give me a land where the bright diamond sand
Flows leisurely down the stream;
Where the graceful white swan goes gliding along
Like a maid in a heavenly dream.   *Chorus*

3. How often at night when the heavens are bright
With the light of the glittering stars,
Have I stood here amazed and asked as I gazed
If their glory exceeds that of ours.   *Chorus*

4. Oh, I love these wild flowers in this dear land of ours;
The curlew I love to hear scream;
And I love the white rocks and the antelope flocks
That graze on the mountain-tops green.   *Chorus*

5. The red man was pressed from this part of the West,
He's likely no more to return
To the banks of Red River where seldom if ever
Their flickering campfires burn.   *Chorus*

6. Where the air is so pure, the zephyrs so free,
The breezes so balmy and light,
That I would not exchange my home on the range
For all the cities so bright.   *Chorus*

7. Oh, I would not exchange my home on the range,
Where the deer and the antelope play;
Where seldom is heard a discouraging word
And the skies are not cloudy all day.   *Chorus*

The Yellow Rose Of Texas

Southern Folk Tune

Lively march tempo

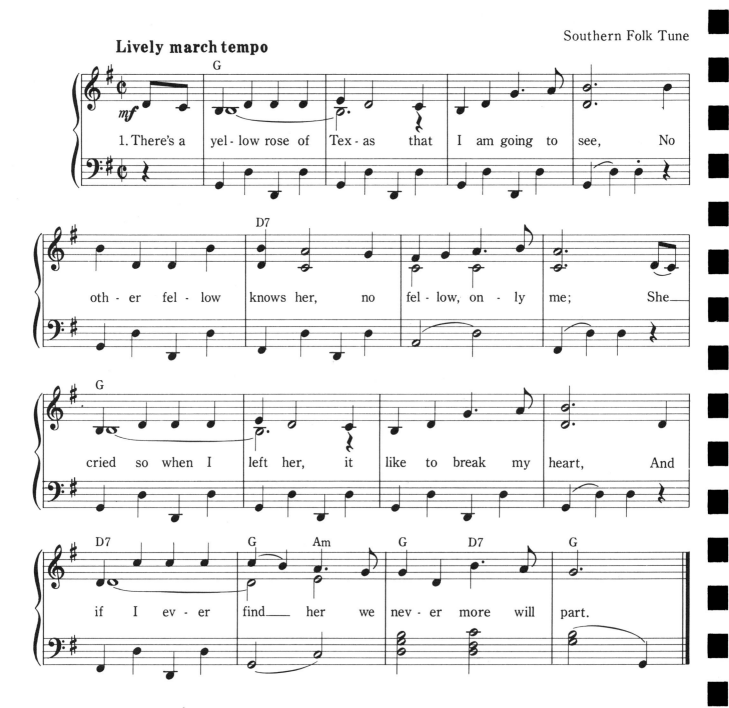

2. She's the sweetest rose of color
   a fellow ever knew,
   Her eyes are bright as di'monds
   they sparkle like the dew;
   You may talk about your dearest May
   and sing of Rosa Lee,
   But the Yellow Rose of Texas
   beats the belles of Tennessee.

3. Oh, now I'm going to find her,
   for my heart is full of woe,
   And we'll sing the song together,
   that we sung long ago;
   We'll play the banjo gaily,
   and we'll sing the songs of yore,
   And the Yellow Rose of Texas
   shall be mine forevermore.

4. *Repeat verse 2*

[186]

Li'l Liza Jane

Southern Folk Tune

2. Liza Jane looks good to me,
    Li'l Liza Jane.
    Sweetes' one I ever see,
    Li'l Liza Jane.   *Chorus*

3. I wouldn't care how far we roam,
    Li'l Liza Jane,,
    Where she's at is home, sweet home,
    Li'l Liza Jane.   *Chorus*

Frankie And Johnny

Traditional Barroom Ballad

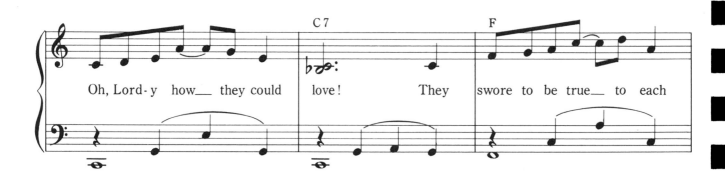

2. Frankie went down to the corner,
   Just for a bucket of beer,
   Says to the fat bartender,
   "Has my Johnny man been here?"
   He was her man, but he done her wrong.

3. "Well I ain't going to tell you no story,
   Ain't going to tell you no lie.
   Johnny went by, 'bout an hour ago,
   With a girl named Nellie Blye,
   He was your man, but he's doin' you wrong."

4. Frankie went home in a hurry,
   She didn't go there for fun,
   She hurried home to get a-hold
   Of Johnny's shootin' gun.
   He was her man, but he's doin' her wrong.

5. Frankie went down to South Clark Street,
   Looked in a window so high,
   Saw her Johnny man a-lovin' up
   That high brown Nellie Blye.
   He was her man, but he done her wrong.

6. Johnny saw Frankie a-comin',
   Out the back door he did scoot,
   But Frankie took aim with her pistol,
   And the gun went "Root a toot-toot!"
   He was her man, but he done her wrong.

7. "Oh roll me over so easy,
   Roll me over so slow,
   Roll me over easy boys,
   'Cause my wounds they hurt me so.
   I was her man, but I done her wrong."

8. "Oh, bring on your rubber-tired carriage,
   Bring on your rubber-tired hack;
   They're taking your man to the graveyard
   And they ain't goin' to bring him back.
   He was your man, but he done you wrong."

9. The sheriff arrested poor Frankie,
   Took her to jail that same day,
   He locked her up in a dungeon cell,
   And threw the key away.
   She shot her man, though he done her wrong.

10. This story has no moral,
    This story has no end,
    This story only goes to show
    That there ain't no good in men.
    He was her man, and he done her wrong.

Ta-ra-ra Boom-der-é

Words and music by
Henry J. Sayers

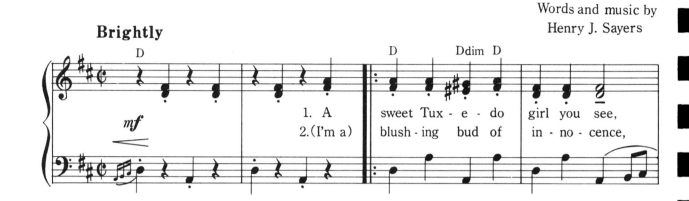

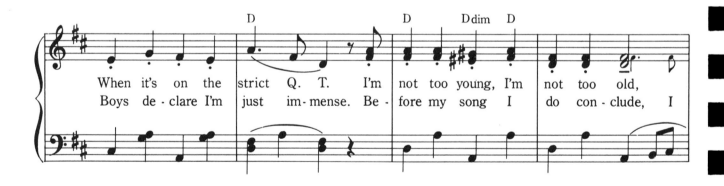

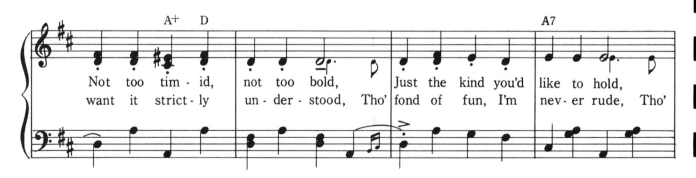

The Flowers That Bloom In The Spring

from "The Mikado"

Words by
William S. Gilbert

Music by
Arthur S. Sullivan

[193]

Prayer Of Thanksgiving

*English words by
Dr. Theodore Baker

Traditional Dutch Air

3. We all do extol Thee, Thou Leader in battle,
   And pray that Thou still our Defender wilt be.
   Let Thy congregation escape tribulation;
   Thy name be ever praised! O Lord, make us free!

After The Ball

Words and music by
Charles K. Harris

After the dancers' leaving, After the stars are gone; Many a heart is aching, If you could read them all; Many the hopes that have vanish'd After the ball.

2. "Bright lights were flashing
   in the grand ballroom,
   Softly the music, playing sweet tunes,
   There came my sweetheart,
   my love, my own,
   "I wish some water; leave me alone."
   When I returned, dear, there stood a man,
   Kissing my sweetheart, as lovers can.
   Down fell the glass, pet,
   broken, that's all,
   Just as my heart was, after the ball.

3. Long years have passed, child;
   I've never wed,
   True to my lost love, though she is dead.
   She tried to tell me,
   tried to explain;
   I would not listen, pleadings were vain.
   One day a letter came from that man;
   He was her brother, the letter ran.
   That's why I'm lonely,
   no home at all;
   I broke her heart, pet, after the ball.

The Bully Song

Words and music by
Charles E. Trevathan

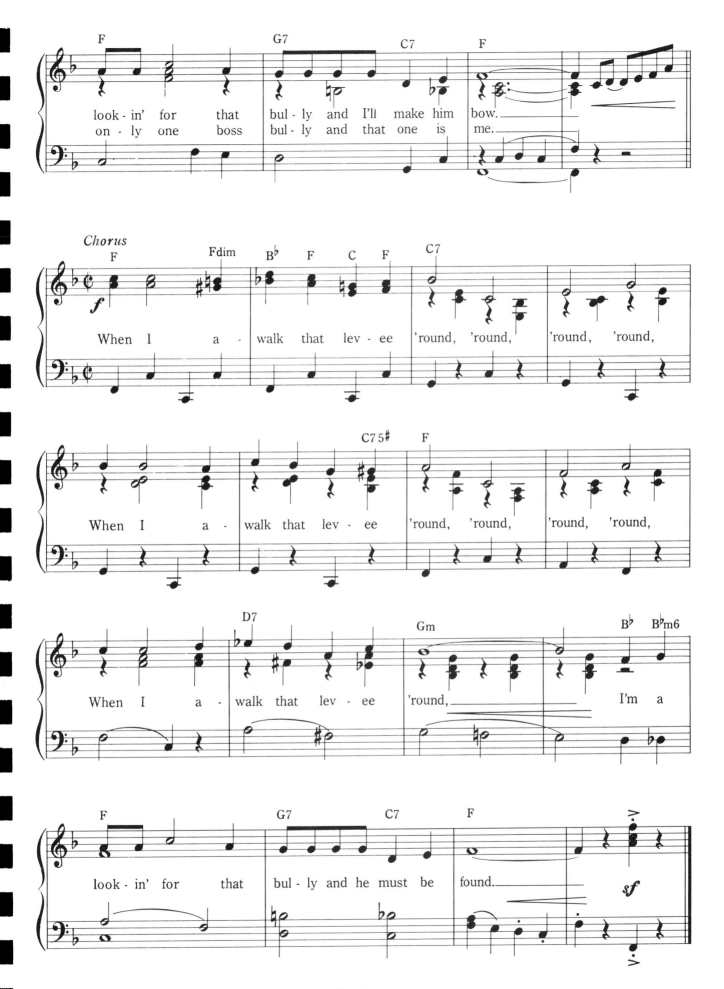

Clementine

Words and music by
Percy Montross

Moderately

1. In a cav-ern in a can-yon, Ex-ca-vat-ing for a mine, Dwelt a min-er for-ty nin-er, And his daugh-ter Clem-en-tine.

Chorus

Oh my dar-ling, oh my dar-ling, Oh my dar-ling Clem-en-tine! Thou art lost and gone for-ev-er, Dread-ful sor-ry, Clem-en-tine.

2. Light she was and like a fairy,
And her shoes were number nine,
Herring boxes without topses,
Sandals were for Clementine. *Chorus*

3. Drove she ducklings to the water,
Ev'ry morning just at nine,
Hit her foot against a splinter,
Fell into the foaming brine. *Chorus*

4. Ruby lips above the water,
Blowing bubbles soft and fine,
But, alas, I was no swimmer,
So I lost my Clementine. *Chorus*

5. How I missed her! How I missed her,
How I missed my Clementine,
But I kissed her little sister,
I forgot my Clementine. *Chorus*

Daisy Bell
（A Bicycle Built For Two）

Words and music by
Harry Dacre

Lively waltz tempo

1. There is a flow-er with-in my heart, Dai-sy, Dai-sy! Plant-ed one day by a glanc-ing dart, Plant-ed by Dai-sy Bell! Wheth-er she loves me or loves me not, Some-times it's hard to tell; Yet I am long-ing to

[201]

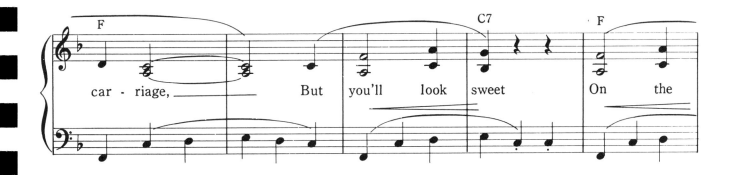

car - riage, _____ But you'll look sweet On the

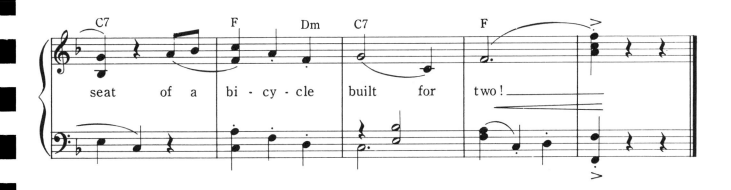

seat of a bi - cy - cle built for two! _____

2. We will go "tandem" as man and wife,
   Daisy, Daisy!
   "Peddling" away down the road of life,
   I and my Daisy Bell!
   When the road's dark we can both despise
   P'licemen and "lamps" as well;
   There are bright lights in the dazzling eyes
   Of beautiful Daisy Bell!   *Chorus*

3. I will stand by you in "wheel" or woe,
   Daisy, Daisy!
   You'll be the bell(e) which I'll ring, you know!
   Sweet little Daisy Bell!
   You'll take the "lead" in each "trip" we take,
   Then, if I don't do well,
   I will permit you to use the brake,
   My beautiful Daisy Bell!   *Chorus*

The Sidewalks Of New York

Words and music by
Charles B. Lawlor and
James W. Blake

Boys and girls to - geth - er,___ Me and Ma - mie Rorke,_____ We trip the light___ fan - tas - tic, On the side - walks

of New York. York.

2. That's where Johnny Casey,
    And little Jimmy Crowe,
    With Jakey Krause the baker,
    Who always had the dough;
    Pretty Nellie Shannon,
    With a dude as light as cork,
    First picked up the waltz-step
    On the sidewalks of New York. *Chorus*

3. Things have changed since those times,
    Some are up in "G,"
    Others, they are wand'rers,
    But they all feel just like me;
    They'd part with all they've got,
    Could they but once more walk,
    With their best girl and have a twirl
    On the sidewalks of New York. *Chorus*

The Band Played On

Music By
Charles B. Ward

Words by
John F. Palmer

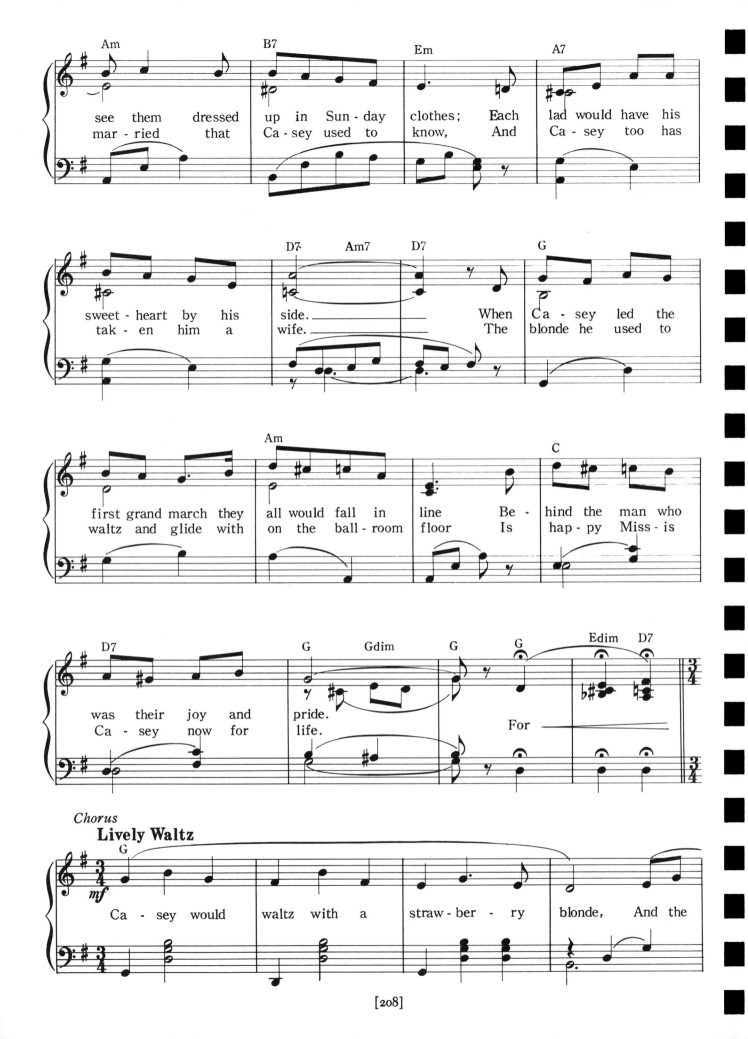

see them dressed up in Sun-day clothes; Each lad would have his
mar-ried that Ca-sey used to know, And Ca-sey too has

sweet-heart by his side._____ When Ca-sey led the
tak-en him a wife._____ The blonde he used to

first grand march they all would fall in line Be-hind the man who
waltz and glide with on the ball-room floor Is hap-py Miss-is

was their joy and pride. For
Ca-sey now for life.

Chorus
Lively Waltz

Ca - sey would waltz with a straw-ber-ry blonde, And the

There'll Be A Hot Time

Words by
Joe Hayden

Music by
Theodore A. Metz

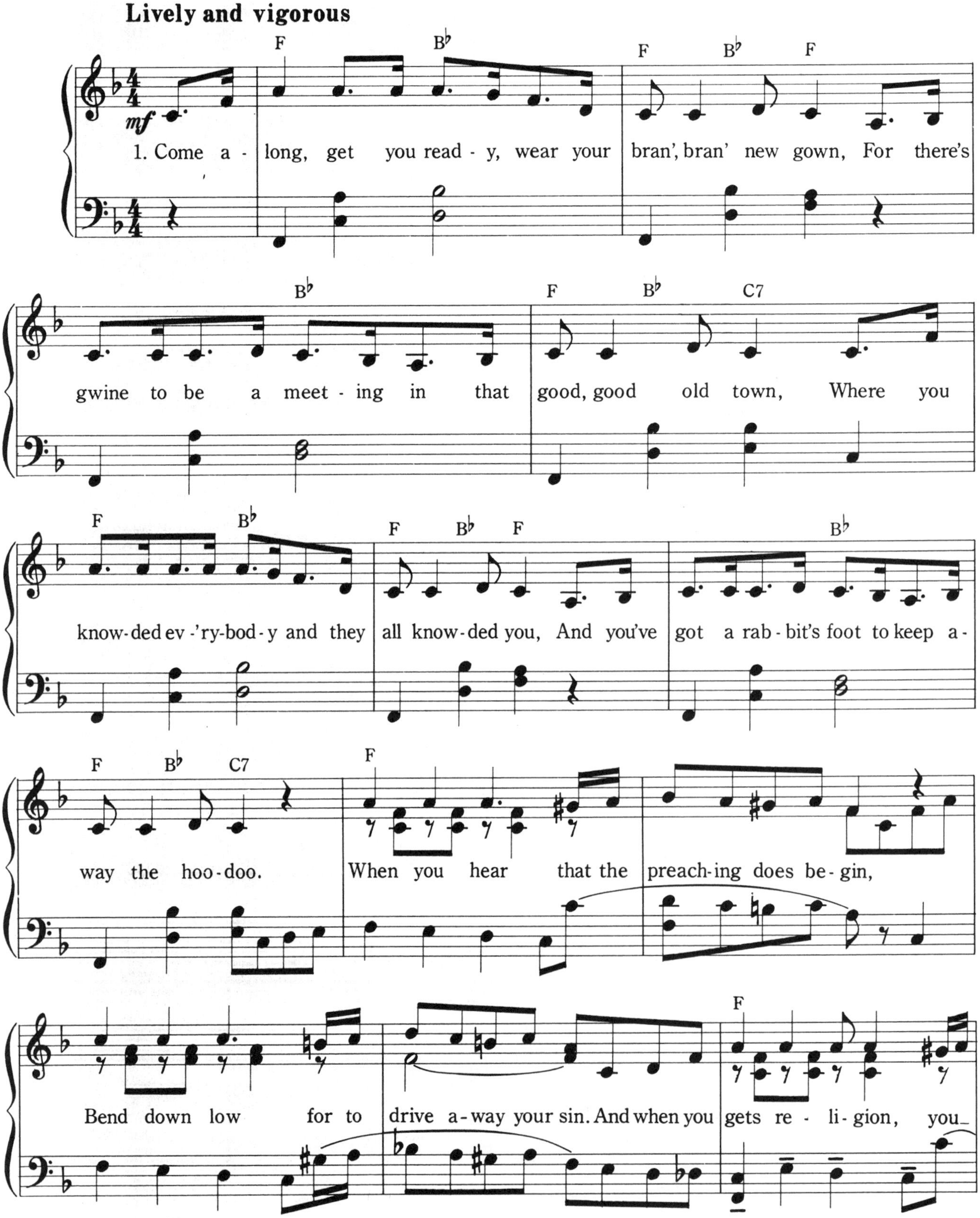
Lively and vigorous
F Bb F Bb F
mf
1. Come a - long, get you read - y, wear your bran', bran' new gown, For there's
Bb F Bb C7
gwine to be a meet - ing in that good, good old town, Where you
F Bb F Bb F Bb
know-ded ev-'ry-bod-y and they all know-ded you, And you've got a rab-bit's foot to keep a-
F Bb C7 F
way the hoo-doo. When you hear that the preach-ing does be-gin,
F
Bend down low for to drive a-way your sin. And when you gets re - li-gion, you

2. There'll be girls for ev'rybody in that good, good old town,
   For there's Miss Consola Davis an' there's Miss Gondolia Brown,
   And there's Miss Johanna Beasly, she am dressed all in red,
   I just hugged her and I kissed her and to me then she said:
   "Please, oh, please, oh, do not let me fall.
   You're all mine and I love you best of all;
   And you must be my man or I'll have no man at all.
   There'll be a hot time in the old town tonight, my baby." *Chorus*

The Sweetest Story Ever Told

Words and music by
R. M. Stults

Chorus
Tempo di Gavotte

Tell me, do you love me? Tell me soft-ly, sweet-ly as of old!

Tell me that you love me, For that's the sweet-est sto-ry ev-er

told. Tell me, do you love me?

Whis-per soft-ly, sweet-ly, as of old! Tell me that you

love me, For that's the sweet-est sto-ry ev-er told.

At A Georgia Camp Meeting

Words and music by
Kerry Mills

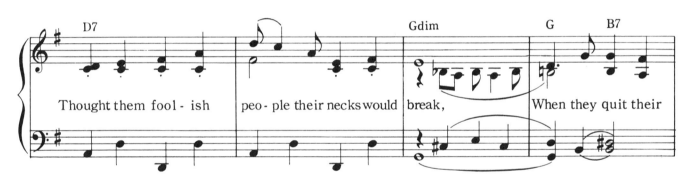

2. The old sisters raised sand, when they first heard the band;
    Way down in Georgia.
    The preacher did glare and the deacons did stare,
    At the young people prancing.
    The band played so sweet that nobody could eat,
    'Twas so entrancing.
    So the church folks agreed it was not a sinful deed,
    And they joined in with the rest.   *Chorus*

[215]

Maple Leaf Rag

(Song Version)

Words by
Sydney Brown

Music by
Scott Joplin

With a lively beat

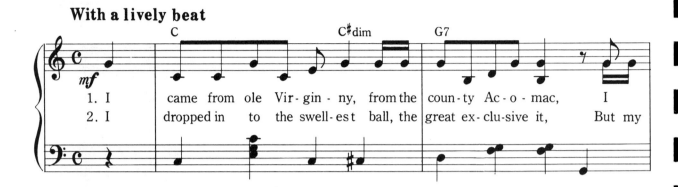

1. I came from ole Vir-gin-ny, from the coun-ty Ac-o-mac, I
2. I dropped in to the swell-est ball, the great ex-clu-sive it, But my

have no wealth to speak of 'cept the clothes up-on my back, I can
face was dead a-gainst me, and my trou-sers did-n't fit; But when

do the coun-try hoe-down, I can buck and wing to show-down, And
Ma-ple Leaf was start-ed, my ti-mi-di-ty de-part-ed, I

while I'm in the no-tion, just step back and watch my mo-tion.
lost my tre-pi-da-tion, you could taste the ad-mi-ra-tion.

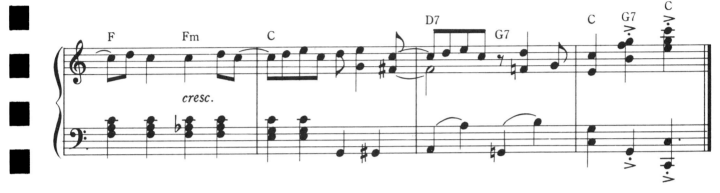

IV

FROM TIN PAN ALLEY
TO MAIN STREET

"EVEN POP CAN PLAY THE PIANOLA"

IT IS not certain how and by whom *Tin Pan Alley*—the collective term for writing, publishing and marketing popular songs in the first few decades of our century—was named. A few facts are known. The expression originated around 1900 to designate a block of brownstone buildings in Manhattan's Twenty-eighth Street where in those days nearly all offices of the burgeoning music publishing industry were located. These modest enterprises, which in most cases were started even without the proverbial shoestring, had to operate in rather tight quarters, with a minimum of equipment: a desk, a chair, and an upright piano. The close proximity of the offices, often not more than partitioned cubicles, necessitated the practice of muting the sound of the upright with sheets of newspaper placed between the hammers and strings. This was done not so much as a matter of polite consideration for the neighbor, but rather, one suspects, as a precautionary measure to camouflage an unpublished melody—always a potential hit—from eager ears of competition on the other side of the thin wall. The newsprint in the piano not only dampened the sound, but also gave it a metallic, clipped, tinny character. The simultaneous playing, singing, tap dancing and hubbub emanating from these buildings prompted the remark from someone that the whole block sounded like a "tin pan alley." The term stuck and was eventually applied not only to a geographic location but also to a certain commercial style of songwriting and methods of promotion.

During the nineteenth century, songs became popular in America through a natural sequence of circumstances, and almost no effort was made by the interested parties, writer and publisher, to interfere with the process. Songs were usually introduced on the stage, in minstrel shows or vaudeville, the audiences picked up the ones they liked, bought the sheet music for the parlor piano, and forgot the others. The only attempt to call attention to a song was by way of newspaper advertisements, a method which later was proven to be of negligible efficacy. The advent of Tin Pan Alley changed all this. From the 1890s on, the song and its audience did not meet and fall in love by chance; every step was planned and the romance promoted. As soon as the sheet music was off the press, the publisher began a campaign to have the song performed in as many places as possible, preferably where a large number of people could hear it. Daily visits were made to theaters, music halls, restaurants, saloons, sporting events. Singers, band leaders, singing waiters, theater and department store managers were contacted, buttonholed, cajoled. Whenever necessary, gifts, tips, and favors smoothed the way to get the tune a hearing. It soon became evident that the publisher alone could not perform this arduous task; needed were the services of a man who not only had the personality, ingenuity, stamina, and power of persuasion to have the song performed, but who, if necessary, could play or sing the tune himself. A new profession was born: the *song plugger*. Many great personalities of show business—Eddie Cantor, George Jessel, George M. Cohan, Irving Berlin, George Gershwin, to mention only a few—began their careers promoting songs in one way or another.

Versatility was the key word of show business in those days. Some of the most successful songwriters of the period had backgrounds of performing in the theater, in vaudeville, or minstrel shows. Also, they very often became publishers of their own songs. This trend was started by Charles K. Harris, who, discouraged by a royalty check of eighty-five cents he received for one of his tunes, decided to publish his next song himself. Its title was AFTER THE BALL and it sold over five million copies within a few years. This event did not pass unnoticed, and numerous other writers followed the example. One of these was Paul Dresser, older brother of the distinguished novelist Theodore Dreiser, who wrote and published ON THE BANKS OF THE WABASH, MY GAL SAL and many other hits. Another composer-publisher, one of the most prolific writers in the annals of our popular song was Harry Von Tilzer, who had to his credit more than two thousand songs. According to legend, it was in his office that the name "Tin Pan Alley" was coined. BIRD IN A GILDED CAGE and WAIT TILL THE SUN SHINES, NELLIE are fine examples of his prodigious output.

When it came to versatility, nobody could outdo that "Yankee Doodle Dandy born on the Fourth of July," George M. Cohan. He was not only a composer and lyricist, but also an actor, dancer, playwright and producer. He came from a stage family and got his training in vaudeville as a member of the Four Cohans, whose act he usually finished with his famous curtain speech: "My mother thanks you, my father thanks you, my sister thanks you and *I* thank you." His performing style, bubbling with an American brand of energy and optimism, had an irresistible appeal. So had his songs—GIVE MY REGARDS TO BROADWAY, MARY'S A GRAND OLD NAME and many others—which, after more than half a century of constant use could still elicit the remark from critic John S. Wilson: "They are part of our musical bloodstream. It is virtually impossible not to respond to the vigor and spirit of Cohan's melodies."

Not all the best-loved songs of the early twentieth century achieved their success by way of Tin Pan Alley. OH PROMISE ME by Reginald de Koven, THE ROSARY and MIGHTY LAK' A ROSE by Ethelbert Nevin, AT DAWNING by Charles Wakefield Cadman, BY THE WATERS OF MINNETONKA by Thurlow Lieurance were considered more in the art song tradition and were published by older, more conservative firms, which, however, did not in the least hinder their success or inhibit their huge sheet-music sales. Similarly, most publishers considered the songs of Carrie Jacobs Bond, including I LOVE YOU TRULY and A PERFECT DAY, too genteel and shyly sentimental for popular consumption. A widow at that time, Mrs. Bond converted the parlor of her house into a publishing office; with a little financial assistance from friends, she printed and promoted her songs; the rest—as they say—is history.

Andrew Carnegie is quoted as once having said: "My idea of heaven is to be able to sit and listen to all music by Victor Herbert that I want to." Most of the country agreed; the songs from *The Fortune Teller, The Red Mill, Mlle. Modiste,* and *Naughty Marietta* were immensely popular in their time and are still—in spite of the many changes in the popular idiom—entirely satisfying and ingratiating melodic statements today. Herbert was of Irish ancestry, had a thorough musical education in Germany and came to this country in the 1890s as a cello virtuoso and conductor of note. He began his career as a composer of symphonic works and operas. Although he has respectable credentials in that area, it was fortunate, for him and for American song, that he turned to the lighter muse and as a result became the foremost representative of European operetta traditions in America.

The sheet music of popular songs was still the principal merchandise of Tin Pan Alley in those days. Edison's phonograph made its appearance in 1900 and the voices of a few celebrated singers—Patti, Melba, Caruso—were recorded, but it was at least two decades before the phonograph record became an important commodity on the popular-music market. In the early 1900s the focus of music-making and listening was still the parlor piano, of which there were about one million in American homes. In 1905 the Sears, Roebuck Company listed a "Grand Concert Piano," really a massively built, ornate upright, for one hundred and sixty-five dollars and, so that the lack of ability to play should not deter a potential buyer, the same catalogue also offered instruction by mail! According to some accounts, there were at the time more pianos in American homes than there were bathtubs. By this time many of the instruments were equipped with a "player" mechanism; "Even Pop Can Play the Pianola" said the advertisement; it was necessary only to pump the pedals or to push a button; the perforated paper cylinder inserted in the instrument reproduced the sound of the latest hit tunes, and even the words of the song could be read as the roll unwound. The chronicles of American popular music, especially jazz, became richer and more authenticated by this method of recording. Many original ragtime pieces of the era, played by their composers, were preserved on piano rolls.

Ragtime enjoyed great popularity from the 1890s until the years of World War I, when another strain of the Negro's musical heritage emerged in the form of the blues. In contrast to ragtime's instrumental character and joyful spirit, the blues are vocal expressions of deep personal feelings: loneliness, poverty, lost love and other sorrows. In these wailing, haunting, richly improvised chants the intonation of certain notes often wavers between major and minor modes of the Western scale. The characteristic format of a three-line stanza, in which the second line repeats the first, corresponds to a twelve-bar form and chord sequence.

The introduction of this idiom into the mainstream of American music is inextricably linked to William Christopher Handy, composer of MEMPHIS BLUES, ST. LOUIS BLUES and other fine blues songs. The "Father of the Blues," Handy, who was born in Alabama, the son of a minister, heard and absorbed the music of his people from early childhood. His intuitive gifts as a writer, together with his many and varied musical experiences as cornetist, teacher and band leader enabled him to create a popular blues form of unique appeal and durability. His ST. LOUIS BLUES is one of the best-known and best-loved songs written in our land, one which has contributed greatly to the evolution of a distinctly native idiom in American popular song.

ST. LOUIS BLUES was published in 1914, and by 1917 a song on Tin Pan Alley claimed that "Everybody's Crazy 'Bout the Blues." In the same year, when our doughboys in Europe were singing the praises of MLLE. FROM ARMENTIÈRES, the magazine *Literary Digest* commented that "a strange word has gained widespread use in the ranks of our producers of popular music. It is 'jazz,' used mainly as an adjective descriptive of a band." The word was new perhaps, but not the music it stood for, which had been around for at least two decades before the country at large became aware of its existence. Jazz, the most truly American form of musical expression, had many contributing sources: Afro-American, Caribbean, Creole folk songs; minstrel tunes, spirituals, blues, ragtime. The confluence of these musical traditions and styles occurred in New Orleans, which, for geographic, ethnic and social reasons, proved to be an ideal location. This colorful, fun-loving city, more tolerant in its ways than the rest of the South, gave shelter and opportunity to many black musicians in the years following the Civil War. Street bands were formed and the city's special fondness for band music provided many occasions for performing: Mardi Gras, parades, rallies, funerals. We do not know exactly how these bands sounded, but it is certain that the renditions of whatever tunes they played were joyously improvised, richly syncopated and plenty "hot." At first their indoor employment was largely restricted to the notorious Storyville district, but gradually the bands were engaged to play for dancing elsewhere too. Around 1913, for various, mostly economic, reasons, an exodus of these pioneer musicians began to other big cities: Memphis, St. Louis, Chicago and New York. Jazz was on its way, and Tin Pan Alley was waiting with open arms.

A Bird In A Gilded Cage

Words by
Arthur J. Lamb

Music by
Harry Von Tilzer

Moderately lively waltz tempo

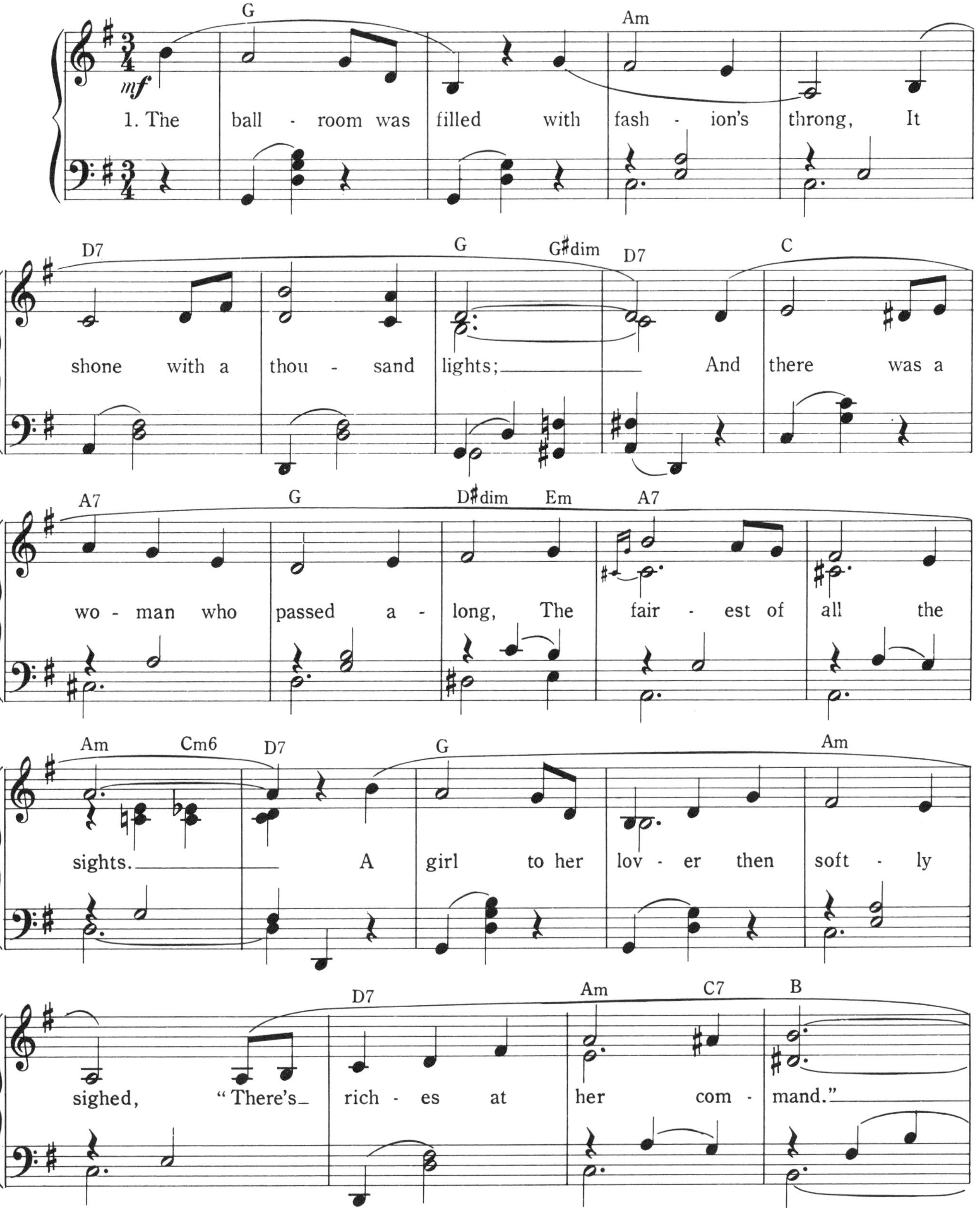

G
Am
mf
1. The ball - room was filled with fash - ion's throng, It
D7
G
G♯dim
D7
C
shone with a thou - sand lights; And there was a
A7
G
D♯dim
Em
A7
wo - man who passed a - long, The fair - est of all the
Am
Cm6
D7
G
Am
sights. A girl to her lov - er then soft - ly
D7
Am
C7
B
sighed, "There's rich - es at her com - mand."

2. I stood in a church-yard just at eve,
    When sunset adorned the West,
    And looked at the people who'd come to grieve
    For loved ones now laid at rest.
    A tall marble monument marked the grave
    Of one who'd been fashion's queen;
    And I thought, "She is happier here at rest,
    Than to have people say when seen:" *Chorus*

On The Banks Of The Wabash, Far Away

Words and music by
Paul Dresser

[230]

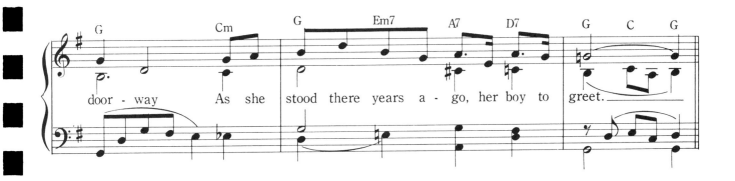

door-way   As she   stood there years a-go, her boy to   greet. ____

Chorus **Slowly, tenderly**

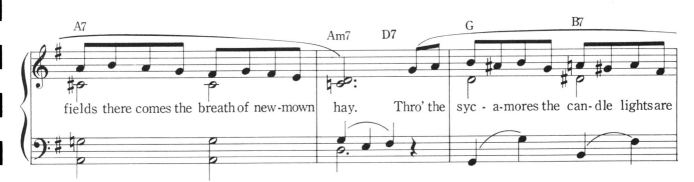

Oh, the   moon-light's fair   to - night a - long the   Wa - bash,   From the

fields there comes the breath of new-mown   hay.   Thro' the   syc - a-mores the can-dle lights are

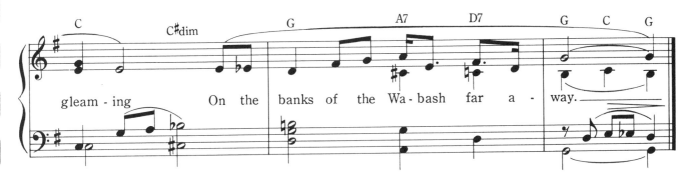

gleam - ing   On the   banks of the Wa - bash   far   a - way. ____

2. Many years have passed since I strolled by the river,
    Arm in arm with sweetheart Mary by my side.
    It was there I tried to tell her that I loved her,
    It was there I begged of her to be my bride.
    Long years have passed since I strolled thro' the churchyard,
    She's sleeping there, my angel Mary dear.
    I loved her but she thought I didn't mean it,
    Still I'd give my future were she only here.   *Chorus*

[231]

The Rosary

Words by
Robert Cameron Rogers

Music by
Ethelbert Nevin

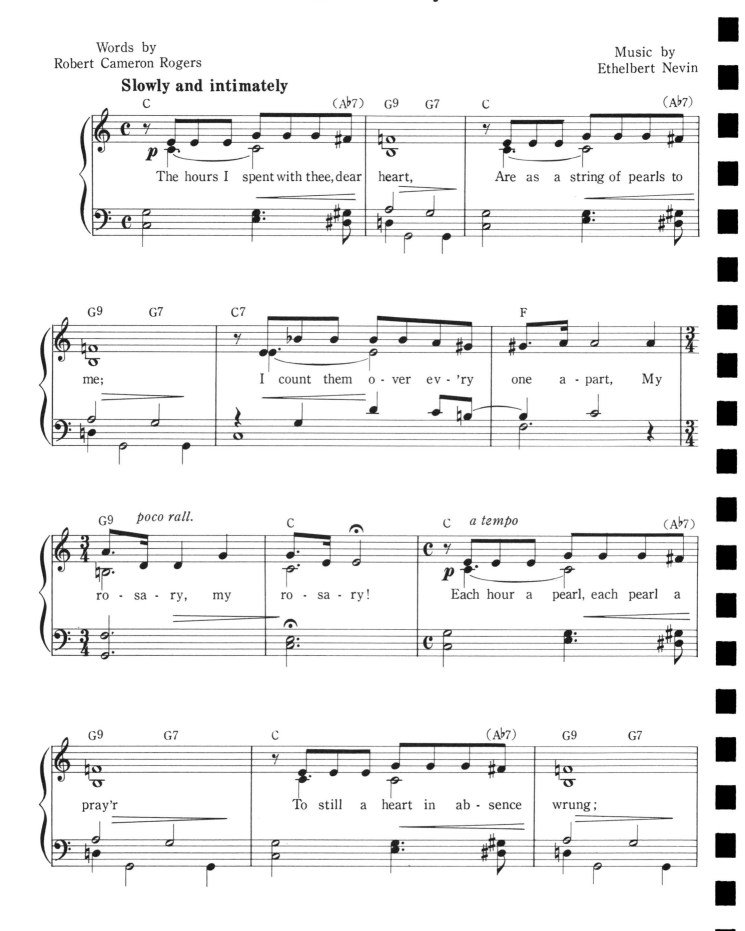

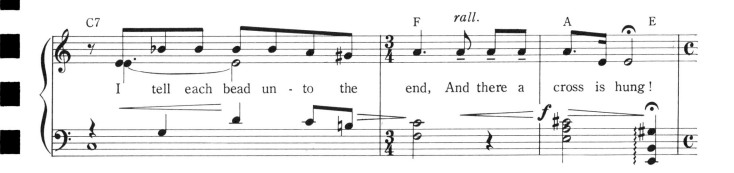

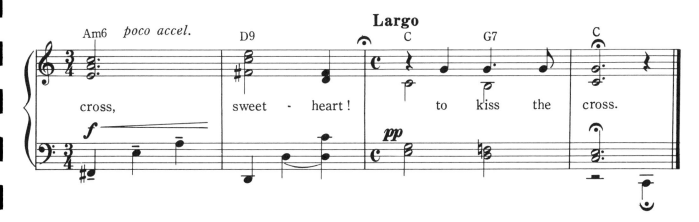

I Love You Truly

Words and music by
Carrie Jacobs Bond

1. I love you tru - ly, tru - ly, dear, Life with its sor - row, life with its tear, Fades in - to dreams when I feel you are near, For I love you tru - ly, tru - ly, dear.

2. Ah! love, 'tis something to feel your kind hand,
   Ah! yes, 'tis something by your side to stand;
   Gone is the sorrow, gone doubt and fear,
   For you love me truly, truly, dear.

My Wild Irish Rose

Words and music by
Chauncey Olcott

Freely moving

1. If you lis-ten, I'll sing you a sweet lit-tle song Of a flow-er that's now drooped and dead;____ Yet____ dear-er to me, yes, than all of its mates, Tho'__ each holds a - loft its proud head.____ 'Twas giv-en to me by a girl that I know, Since we've met, faith, I've known no re - pose.____

She is dear - er by far than the world's bright - est

star, And I call her my wild I - rish rose.

With much expression

Chorus

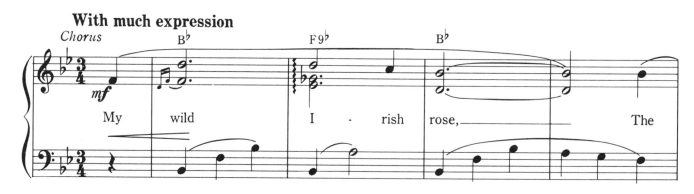

My wild I - rish rose, The

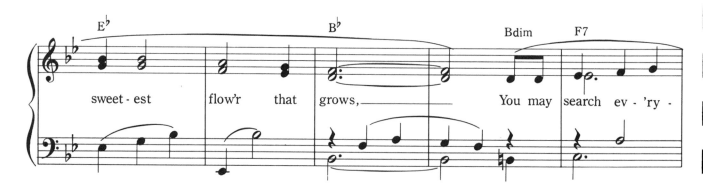

sweet - est flow'r that grows, You may search ev - 'ry -

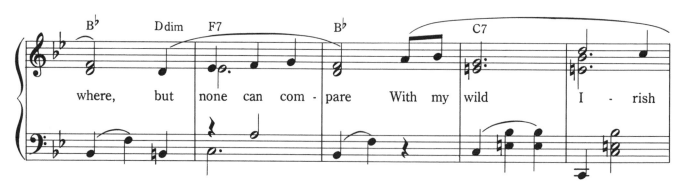

where, but none can com - pare With my wild I - rish

2. They may sing of their roses which by other names,
   Would smell just as sweetly, they say,
   But I know that my rose would never consent
   To have that sweet name taken away.
   Her glances are shy whene'er I pass by
   The bower where my true love grows;
   And my one wish has been that some day I may win
   The heart of my wild Irish rose. *Chorus*

Mighty Lak' A Rose

Words by
Frank L. Stanton

Music by
Ethelbert Nevin

Moderately slow; gently

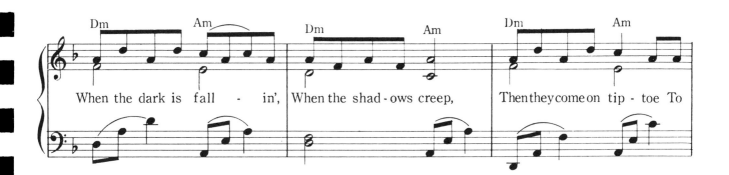

When the dark is fall - in', When the shad - ows creep, Then they come on tip - toe To

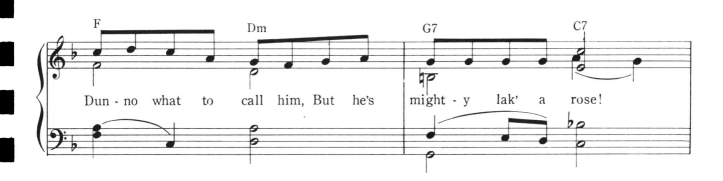

kiss 'im in his sleep. Sweet-est lit-tle fel - ler, Ev -'ry-bod- y knows;

Dun - no what to call him, But he's might - y lak' a rose!

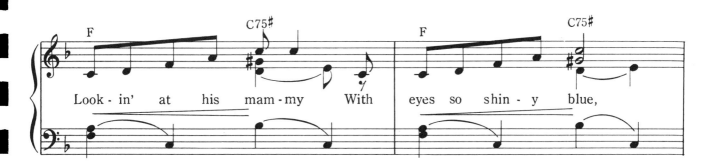

Look - in' at his mam - my With eyes so shin - y blue,

Make you think that heav'n _____ is com - in' close to you.

My Gal Sal

Words and music by
Paul Dresser

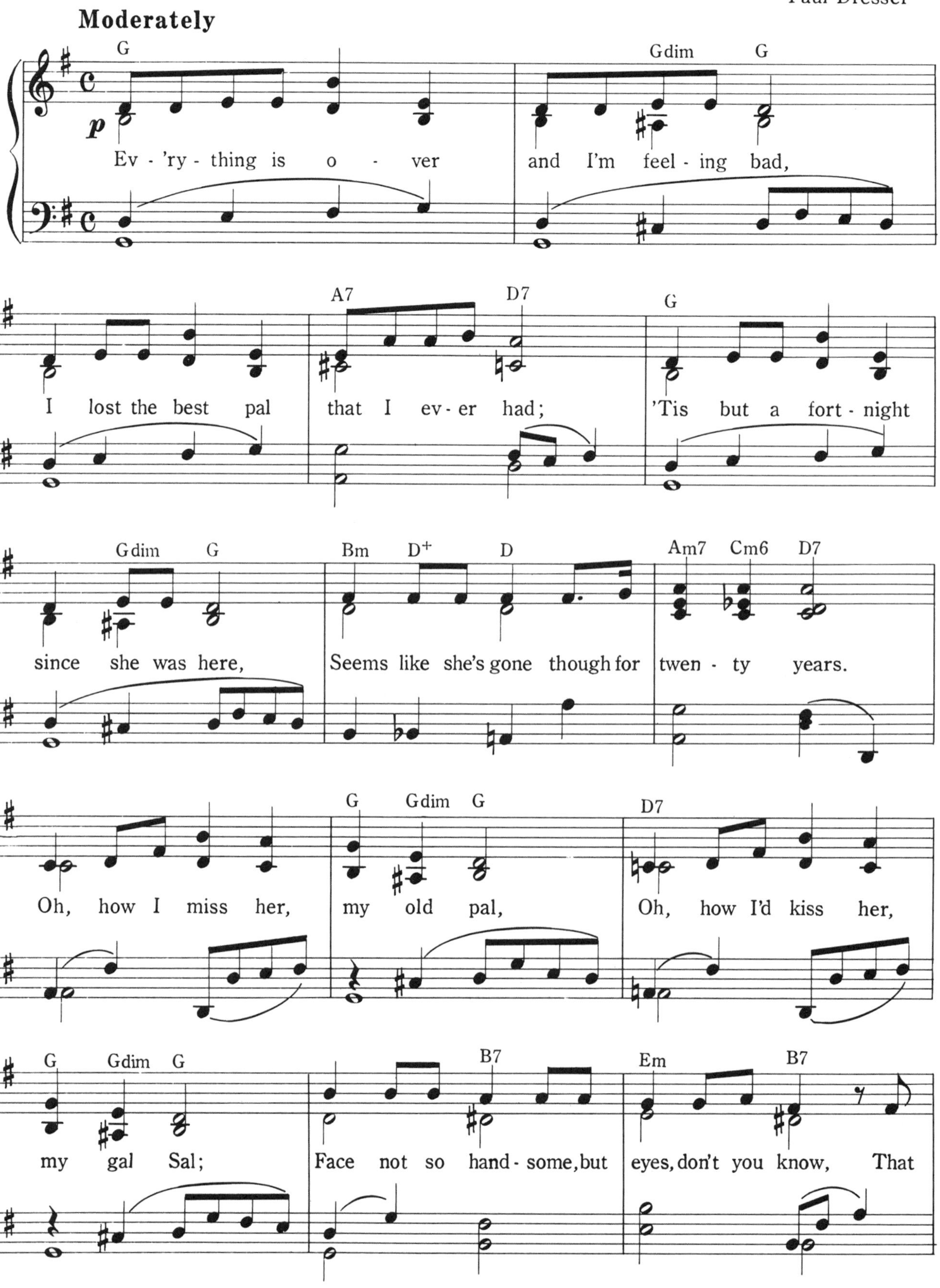

Moderately
G Gdim G
p
Ev - 'ry - thing is o - ver and I'm feel - ing bad,
A7 D7 G
I lost the best pal that I ev - er had; 'Tis but a fort - night
Gdim G Bm D+ D Am7 Cm6 D7
since she was here, Seems like she's gone though for twen - ty years.
G Gdim G D7
Oh, how I miss her, my old pal, Oh, how I'd kiss her,
G Gdim G B7 Em B7
my gal Sal; Face not so hand - some, but eyes, don't you know, That

2. Brought her little dainties just afore she died,
   Promised she would meet me on the other side.
   Told her how I loved her, she said "I know, Jim,
   Just do your best, leave the rest to Him."
   Gently I pressed her to my breast,
   Soon she would take her last long rest.
   She looked at me and murmured "Pal",
   And softly I whispered "Good-bye Sal."   *Chorus*

Under The Bamboo Tree

Words by
Bob Cole

Music by
J. Rosamond Johnson

If you lak-a-me, lak I lak-a-you, And we lak-a-both the same,

I lak-a say, this ver-y day, I lak-a change your name; 'Cause

I love-a-you, and love-a-you true, and if you-a-love-a- me,

One live as two, two live as one, Un-der the bam-boo tree.

2. This little story, strange but true,
Is often told in Mataboo,
Of how this Zulu tried to woo
His jungle lady in tropics shady.

Although the scene was miles away,
Right here at home, I dare to say,
You'll hear some Zulu ev'ry day
Gush out this soft refrain:

Chorus

Bill Bailey, Won't You Please Come Home

Words and music by
Hughie Cannon

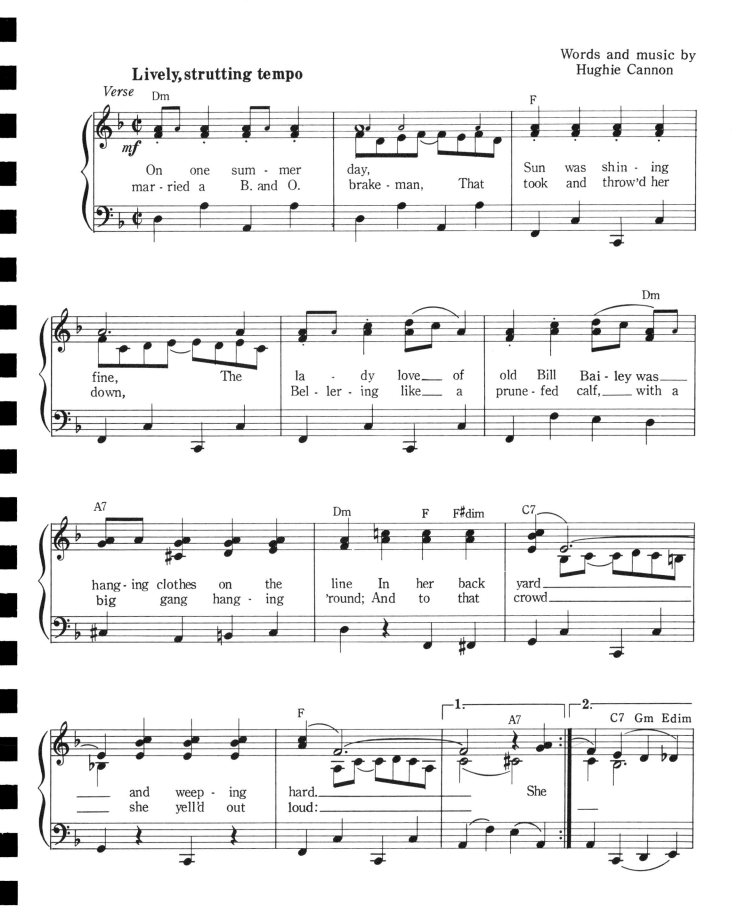

Lively, strutting tempo

On one sum-mer day, brake-man, That Sun was shin-ing
mar-ried a B. and O. took and throw'd her

fine, The la-dy love__ of old Bill Bai-ley was__
down, Bel-ler-ing like__ a prune-fed calf,__ with a

hang-ing clothes on the line In her back yard__
big gang hang-ing 'round; And to that crowd__

__ and weep-ing hard. She
__ she yell'd out loud:

[246]

Hello, Ma Baby

Words and music by
Joseph E. Howard and Ida Emerson

1. I've got a lit-tle ba-by, but she's out of sight, I talk to her a-cross the tel-e-phone; I'nev-er seen ma hon-ey but she's mine all right, So take my tip and leave this gal a-lone. Ev-'ry sin-gle morn-ing you will hear me yell "Hey,

2. This morning through the 'phone she said her name was Bess,
   And now I kind of know where I am at;
   I'm satisfied because I've got my babe's address,
   Here pasted in the lining of my hat.
   I am mighty scared 'cause if the wires get crossed
   'Twill separate me from ma baby mine,
   Then some other man will win her and my game is lost,
   And so each day I shout along the line.

   Chorus

In The Good Old Summertime

Words by
Ren Shields

Music by
George Evans

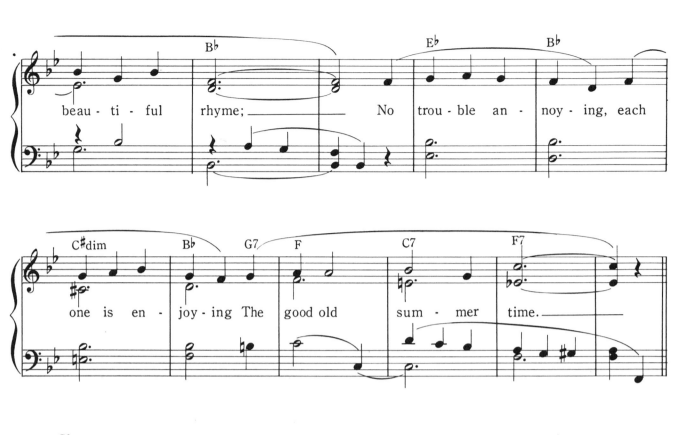

beau - ti - ful rhyme; ___ No trou - ble an - noy - ing, each

one is en - joy - ing The good old sum - mer time. ___

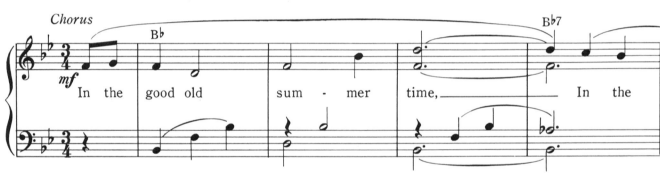

Chorus

In the good old sum - mer time, ___ In the

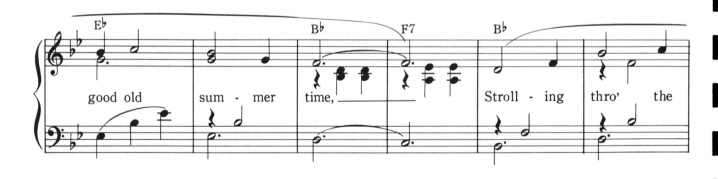

good old sum - mer time, ___ Stroll - ing thro' the

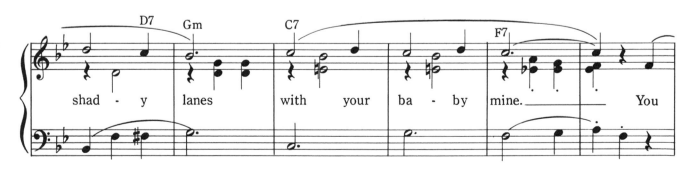

shad - y lanes with your ba - by mine. ___ You

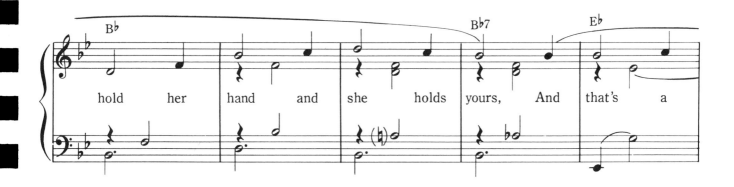

hold her hand and she holds yours, And that's a

ver - y good sign_____ That she's your toot - sey

woot - sey in the good old sum - mer time.

2. To swim in the pool you'd play "hooky" from school,
   Good old summer time.
   You'd play "ring arosie" with Jim, Kate and Josie,
   Good old summer time.
   Those days full of pleasure we now fondly treasure,
   when we never thought it a crime
   To go stealing cherries, with face brown as berries,
   Good old summer time.
   Chorus

[253]

Oh Promise Me

Words by
Clement Scott

Music by
Reginald De Koven

2. Oh promise me that you will take my hand,
   The most unworthy in this lonely land,
   And let me sit beside you, in your eyes
   Seeing the vision of our paradise;
   Hearing God's message while the organ rolls
   Its mighty music to our very souls;
   No love less perfect than a life with thee,
   Oh promise me! oh promise me!

Because

Words by
Edward Teschemacher

Music by
Guy d' Hardelot

Moderately slow

freely moving

Be - cause___ you come to me___ with naught save love,___ And hold my hand and lift mine eyes a - bove, A wid - er world of hope and joy I see, Be - cause___ you come to me.___ Be - cause you speak to me in ac - cents sweet,___ I find the ros - es wak-ing 'round my feet, And

Wait Till The Sun Shines, Nellie

Words by
Andrew B. Sterling

Music by
Harry Von Tilzer

On a Sun - day morn,___ sat a maid for - lorn,___ With her
sweet - heart by___ her side; Thro' the win - dow pane,___ she looked
at the rain,___ "We must stay home, Joe," she cried; "There's a
pic - nic too,___ at the Old Point View,___ I'ts a shame it rained___ to -
day." Then the boy drew near,___ Kissed a - way each tear,___ And she

Ida, Sweet As Apple Cider

Words by
Eddie Leonard

Music by
Eddie Munson

Kiss Me Again

from "Mlle. Modiste"

Words by
Henry Blossom

Music by
Victor Herbert

Toyland

from "Babes in Toyland"

Words by
Glen MacDonough

Music by
Victor Herbert

Slow and dreamy

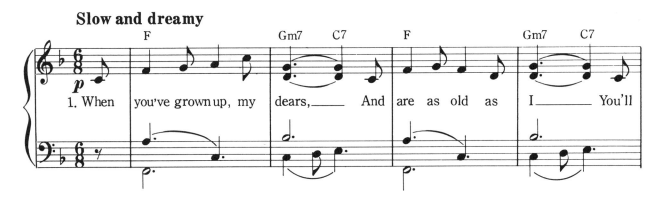

1. When you've grown up, my dears, And are as old as I You'll

oft - en pon - der on the years That roll so swift - ly by, my dears, That

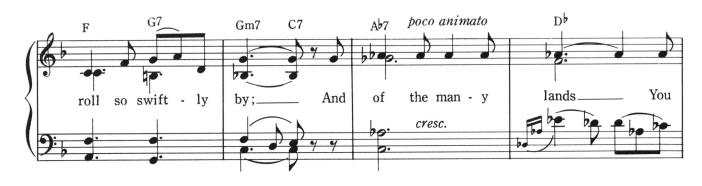

roll so swift - ly by; And of the man - y lands You

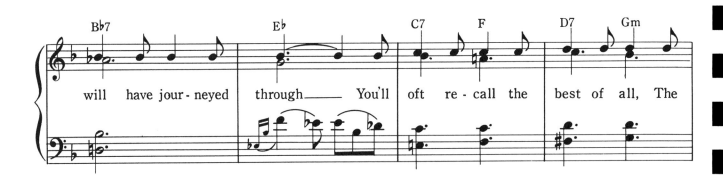

will have jour - neyed through You'll oft re - call the best of all, The

Because You're You

from "The Red Mill"

Words by
Henry Blossom

Music by
Victor Herbert

Moderate, graceful tempo

1. Love is a queer lit-tle el-fin sprite, Blest with the dead-li-est aim! Shoot-ing his ar-rows to left and right, Bag-ging the rar-est game, Fill-ing our hearts with a glad sur-prise, Al-most too good to be true! And still can you tell me why do you love me? On-ly be-cause you are you, dear!

optional duet part

Not that you are fair, dear, Not that you are true,

Not that I am fair, dear, Not that I am true,

Not your gol - den hair, dear, Not your eyes of

Not my gol - den hair, dear, Not my eyes of blue,

blue, When we ask the rea - son, Words are all too

When we ask the rea - son, Words are all too few!

few! I love you, dear, Be - cause you're you.

So I know I love you, dear, Be - cause you're you!

Glow Worm

Words by
Lila Cayley Robinson

Music by
Paul Lincke

Graceful walking tempo (Gavotte)

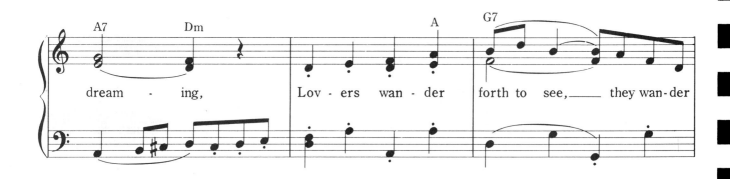

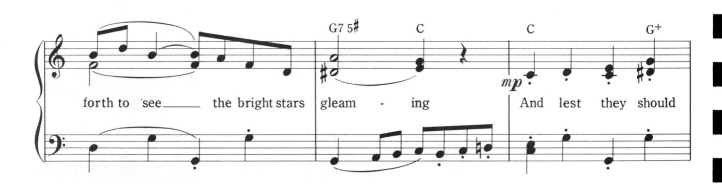

Lead us, lest too far we wan-der, Love's sweet voice is call-ing yon-der.

Shine lit-tle glow-worm, glim-mer, Shine lit-tle glow-worm glim-mer!

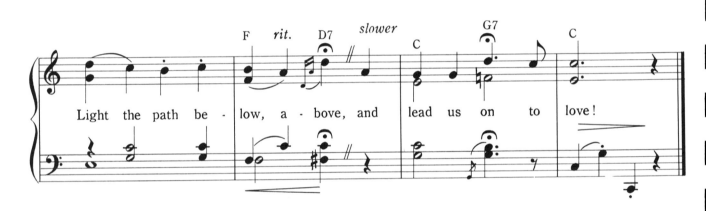

Light the path be-low, a-bove, and lead us on to love!

2. "Little glow-worm, tell me pray,
   Oh, glow-worm, tell me pray,
   How did you kindle
   Lamps that by the break of day,
   That by the break of day,
   Must fade and dwindle?"
   "Ah, this secret, by your leave,
   This secret, by your leave,
   Is worth the learning!
   When true lovers come at eve,
   True lovers come at eve,
   Their hearts are burning!
   Glowing cheeks and lips betray,
   How sweet the kisses tasted!
   'Till we steal the fire away,
   For fear lest it be wasted!"
   Refrain

The Yankee Doodle Boy

from "Little Johnny Jones"

Words and Music by
George M. Cohan

[273]

Mary's A Grand Old Name

from "Forty-five Minutes from Broadway"

Words and music by
George M. Cohan

be;_____ But with pro - pri - e - ty, so - ci - e - ty will

say Ma - rie._____ But it was Ma - ry,

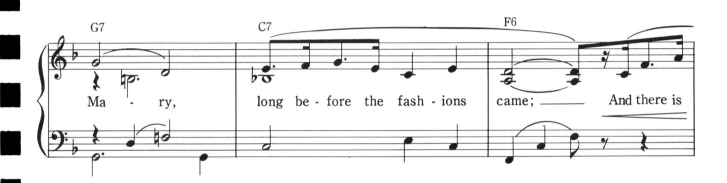

Ma - ry, long be - fore the fash - ions came;_____ And there is

some - thing there that sounds so fair, it's a grand old name!

2. Now, when her name is Mary, there is no falseness there;
When to Marie she'll vary, she'll surely bleach her hair.
Though Mary's ordinary,
Marie is fair to see;
Don't ever fear sweet Mary,
Beware of sweet Marie!   *Chorus*

At Dawning

Words by
Nelle Richmond Eberhart

Music by
Charles Wakefield Cadman

Moderately, with feeling

2. Dawn and dew proclaim my dream, I love you;
Chant the birds one thrilling theme, I love you;
All the sounds of morning meet,
Break in yearning at your feet,
Come and answer, come, my sweet;
I love you, I love you.

Give My Regards To Broadway

from "Little Johnny Jones"

Words and music by
George M. Cohan

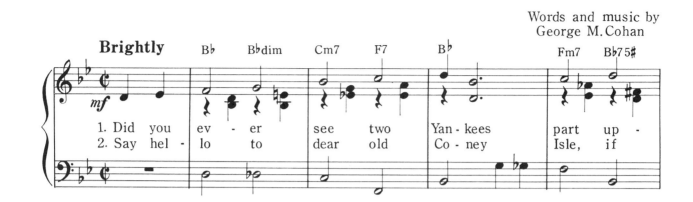

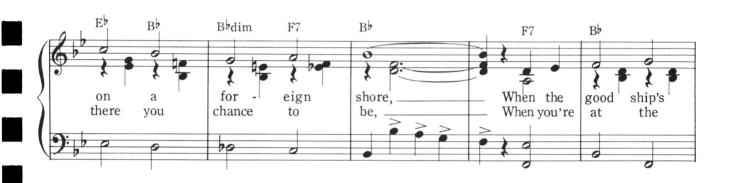

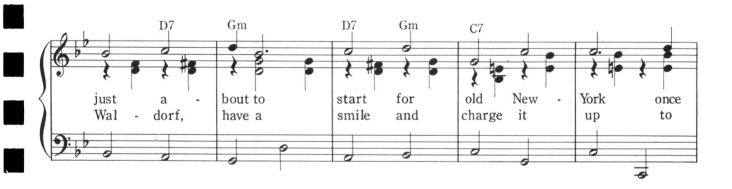

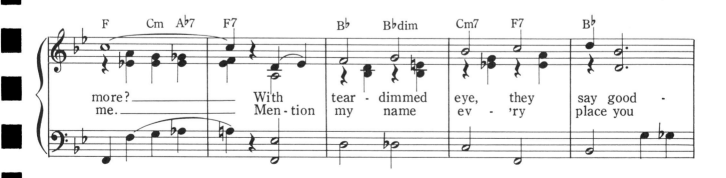

1. Did you ev - er see two Yan - kees part up - on a for - eign shore, When the good ship's just a - bout to start for old New - York once more? With tear - dimmed eye, they say good -

2. Say hel - lo to dear old Co - ney Isle, if there you chance to be, When you're at the Wal - dorf, have a smile and charge it up to me. Men - tion my name ev - 'ry place you

[279]

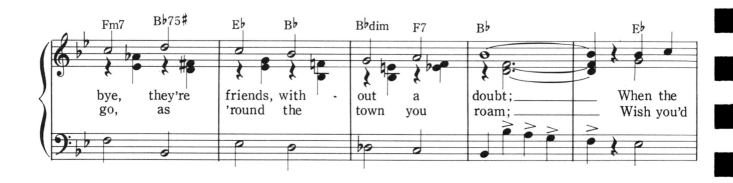

bye, they're friends, with - out a doubt;_____ When the
go, as 'round the town you roam;_____ Wish you'd

man on the pier_____ shouts "Let them clear", as the
call on my gal, now re - mem - ber, old pal, When you

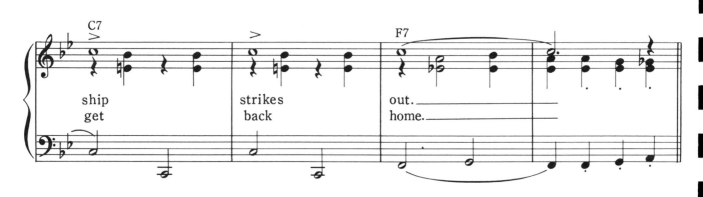

ship strikes out._____
get back home._____

Chorus

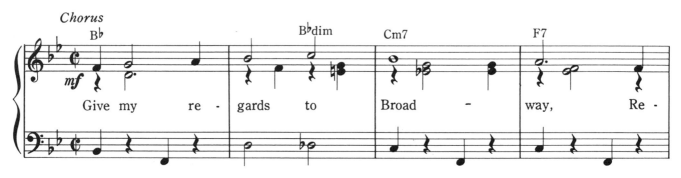

Give my re - gards to Broad - way, Re -

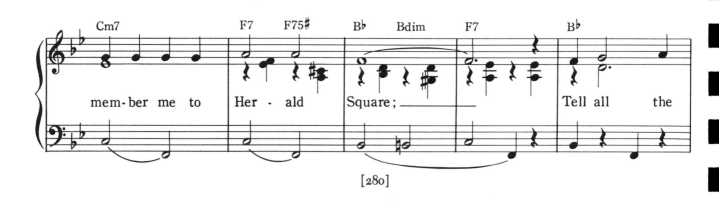

mem - ber me to Her - ald Square;_____ Tell all the

[280]

A Perfect Day

Words and music by
Carrie Jacobs-Bond

[282]

By The Waters Of Minnetonka

Words by
J. M. Cavanass

Music by
Thurlow Lieurance

For Me And My Gal

Words by
Edgar Leslie and
E. Ray Goetz

Music by
George W. Meyer

"The bells are ring-ing ____ for me and my gal, ____

____ The birds are sing-ing ____ for me and my gal. ____

____ Ev-'ry-bod-y's been know-ing ____ To a wed-ding they're

go-ing, ____ And for weeks they've been sew-ing, ____

____ Ev-'ry Su-sie and Sal. ____ They're con-gre-gat-ing ____

2. See the relatives there   It's a wonderful sight
   Looking over the pair!   As the fam'lies unite.
   They can tell at a glance   Gee! it makes the boy proud
   It's a loving romance.   As he says to the crowd:

Chorus

Saint Louis Blues

Arrangement by W.C. Handy

Words and music by
W.C. Handy

[290]

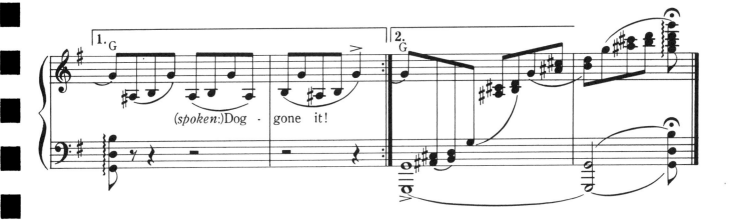

(spoken:) Dog - gone it!

2.   Been to de Gypsy to get ma fortune tole,
       To de Gypsy done got ma fortune tole,
       'Cause I'm most wile 'bout ma Jelly Roll.
       Gypsy done tole me, "Don't you wear no black."
       Yes she done tole me, "Don't you wear no black,
       Go to St. Louis, you can win him back."
       Help me to Cairo, make St. Louis by maself,
       Git to Cairo, find ma ole friend Jeff.
       Gwine to pin maself close to his side,
       If ah flag his train, I sho' can ride.

         Chorus

3.   You ought to see dat stove-pipe brown of mine,
       Lak he owns de Dimon' Joseph line,
       He'd make a cross-eyed o'man go stone blin'.
       Blacker than midnight, teeth lak flags of truce,
       Blackest man in de whole St. Louis,
       Blacker de berry, sweeter am de juice.
       About a crap game, he knows a pow'ful lot,
       But when worktime comes, he's on de dot.
       Gwine to ask him for a cold ten-spot,
       What it takes to git it, he's cert'nly got.

         Chorus

Extra Choruses

2.   A black-headed gal makes a freight train jump the track,
       Said a black-headed gal makes a freight train jump the track,
       But a long tall gal makes a preacher ball the jack.
3.   Lawd, a blonde-headed woman makes a good man leave the town,
       I said blonde-headed woman makes a good man leave the town,
       But a red-head woman makes a boy slap his papa down.
4.   Oh ashes to ashes and dust to dust,
       I said ashes to ashes and dust to dust,
       If my blues don't get you, my jazzing must.

Short'nin' Bread

Traditional Southern Tune

With a happy beat

1. Put on the skil - let, put on the led,

Mam - my's goin' to make a lit - tle short - 'nin' bread;

That ain't all she's go - in' to do,

Mam - my's goin' to make a lit - tle cof - fee too.

Chorus

Mam - my's lit - tle ba - by loves short - 'nin', short - 'nin',

[294]

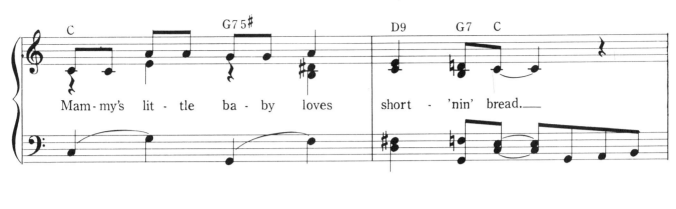

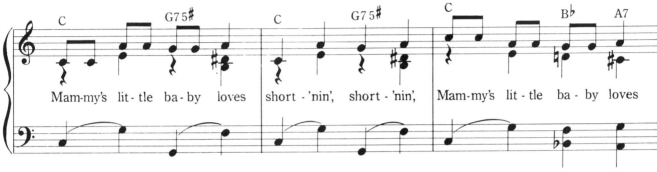

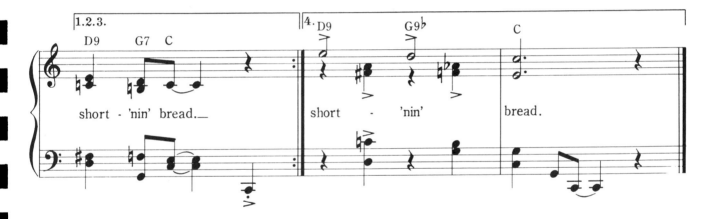

2. Three little fellers, lying in bed,
   Two was sick an' the other 'most dead;
   Sent for the doctor, the doctor said,
   "Feed those chillun on short'nin' bread." *Chorus*

3. Slip to the kitchen, slip up the led,
   Filled my pockets full of short'nin' bread;
   Stole the skillet, stole the led,
   Stole the gal makin' short'nin' bread. *Chorus*

4. Caught me with the skillet, caught me with the led,
   Caught me with the gal makin' short'nin' bread;
   Paid six dollars for the skillet, six dollars for the led,
   Spent six months in jail eatin' short'nin' bread. *Chorus*

[295]

The Boll Weevil Song

Traditional Southern Tune

Just a - look - in' for a home._____

2. Now, the first time I seen the boll weevil,
   He was sitting on the square.
   The next time I seen the boll weevil,
   He had all his family there -
   Just a-lookin' for a home, just a-lookin' for a home.
   Just a-lookin' for a home, just a-lookin' for a home.

3. The farmer took the boll weevil,
   And he put him in hot sand.
   The weevil said, "This is mighty hot,
   But I'll stand it like a man -
   This'll be my home, this'll be my home.
   This'll be my home, this'll be my home."

4. The farmer took the boll weevil,
   And he put him in a lump of ice.
   The boll weevil said to the farmer,
   "This is mighty cool and nice,
   It'll be my home, it'll be my home.
   It'll be my home, it'll be my home."

5. The boll weevil said to the farmer,
   "You better leave me alone;
   I ate up all your cotton,
   And I'm starting on your corn -
   I'll have a home, I'll have a home.
   I'll have a home, I'll have a home."

6. The merchant got half the cotton,
   The boll weevil got the rest.
   Didn't leave the farmer's wife
   But one old cotton dress -
   And it's full of holes, and it's full of holes.
   And it's full of holes, and it's full of holes.

7. The farmer said to the merchant,
   "We're in an awful fix;
   The boll weevil ate all the cotton up
   And left us only sticks -
   We got no home, we got no home.
   We got no home, we got no home."

8. The farmer said to the merchant,
   "We ain't made but one bale,
   And before we'll give you that one,
   We'll fight and go to jail -
   We'll have a home, we'll have a home.
   We'll have a home, we'll have a home."

9. And if anybody should ask you
   Who was it made this song;
   It was the farmer man
   With all but his blue jeans gone -
   A-lookin' for a home, a-lookin' for a home.
   A-lookin' for a home, a-lookin' for a home."

You're In The Army Now

Traditional Army Song

Mademoiselle From Armentières

(Hinky Dinky, Parlay-Voo)

Traditional Army Song

2. Our top kick in Armentières, parlay-voo,
   Our top kick in Armentières, parlay-voo,
   Our top kick in Armentières
   Soon broke the spell of forty years,
   Hinky dinky, parlay-voo.

3. The officers get all the steaks, parlay-voo,
   The officers get all the steaks, parlay-voo,
   The officers get all the steak
   And all we get is a belly ache,
   Hinky dinky, parlay-voo.

4. From gay Paree we heard guns roar, parlay-voo,
   From gay Paree we heard guns roar, parlay-voo,
   From gay Paree we heard guns roar,
   But all we heard was "Je t'adore",
   Hinky dinky, parlay-voo.

5. You might forget the gas and shell, parlay-voo,
   You might forget the gas and shell, parlay-voo,
   You might forget the gas and shell,
   You'll never forget the mademoiselle,
   Hinky dinky, parlay-voo.

I've Been Working On The Railroad

Traditional Song

She'll Be Comin' Round The Mountain

Traditional

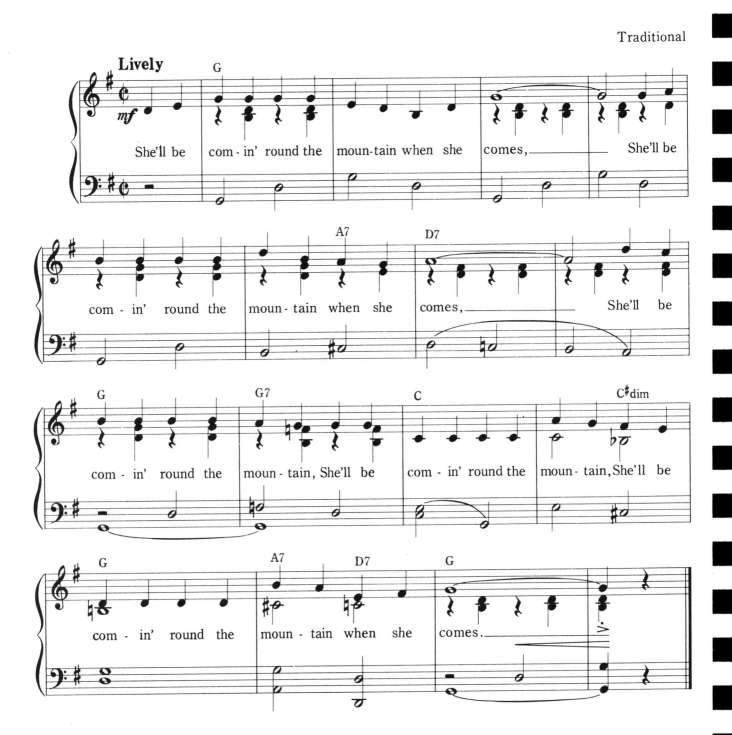

2. She'll be drivin' six white horses when she comes,   (etc.)

3. Oh, we'll all go out to meet her when she comes,   (etc.)

4. Oh, we'll kill the old red rooster when she comes,   (etc.)

V
THE HEYDAY OF
AMERICAN MELODY

THE GREAT WHITE WAY–THE AIRWAVES
–FOLKWAYS

THE 1920s were truly a golden age of American popular song. The new rhythmic and melodic patterns of jazz and blues offered irresistible stimuli for our writers. The flourishing musical theater, for which an increasingly large portion of our songs were written, allowed, indeed encouraged, the attainment of higher musical standards than were the cut-and-dried norms of Tin Pan Alley. Melodies became a bit more daring and sophisticated, the harmonic vocabulary was expanded, and song forms became more flexible. By this time phonograph records and radio broadcasting provided new, hitherto unavailable, avenues of dissemination and promotion. Through these media American jazz and popular songs became known with endemic swiftness the world over and attained a dominant position as yet unchallenged.

This roaring and restless decade of the speakeasies, the flappers and the Charleston was also a time which saw an unparalleled concentration of creative activity on the part of numerous, uncommonly gifted writers: Irving Berlin, Jerome Kern, George Gershwin, Vincent Youmans, Cole Porter, Richard Rodgers, and others, through whose works our popular music achieved its zenith of distinction. OL' MAN RIVER from *Show Boat*, TEA FOR TWO from *No, No, Nanette*, MY HEART STOOD STILL from *A Connecticut Yankee*, and I CAN'T GIVE YOU ANYTHING BUT LOVE from the review *Blackbirds of 1928*, should give a fair illustration of the variety and inventiveness inherent in the song repertory of the period.

The decade of the twenties, so rich in melody, ended on a sour economic note. "WALL ST. LAYS AN EGG" was the comment of the show business weekly, *Variety*, on the stock market fiasco of 1929. During the ensuing years of the Great Depression the country had to tighten its belt; the dancing and singing, however, still went on and it was business as usual on Tin Pan Alley. The tempo became somewhat subdued, to be sure; the frenzy of the Charleston, Black Bottom and Varsity Drag was largely replaced by the smoother Fox Trot and the beat of "sweet jazz." Hoagy Carmichael's enchanting tune STAR DUST, the first great hit of the decade, swept the country and the world; it sold records in the millions, and the words, by Mitchell Parish, were translated into more than forty languages.

By this time movies were talking and singing, and the tuneful dream world of film musicals offered an easy escape from the drab and harsh realities of the lean years. It also provided an entirely new mass medium for writers, publishers and performers of popular songs. Musical theater, too, was healthy as ever. Productions were trimmed from their former Ziegfeld proportions, but whatever was lost in lavishness was more than made up in maturity and literacy. Politics, social problems, and biting satire were no longer taboo, and, as Brooks Atkinson remarked when attending one of these musicals, "you need not check your brains with your hat." In 1932 the Pulitzer Prize for drama was given to *Of Thee I Sing*, which had a score by George and Ira Gershwin. It was the first time that such an honor had been awarded to a musical comedy.

During these "Gershwin years" George was at the height of his creative powers and popularity not only as a songwriter of incomparable flair and originality, but also as a composer of larger works. In RHAPSODY IN BLUE, CONCERTO IN F, and later in *Porgy and Bess* he successfully fused jazz and other American folk elements with the symphonic and operatic traditions of Europe. The artistic validity of this blend has been firmly proven by half a century of constant exposure while the appeal of his entire *oeuvre* remained undiminished. EMBRACEABLE YOU, with words by his brother Ira, is from the show *Girl Crazy*, which was described by one critic as "a never-ending bubbling of pure joyousness."

Fred Astaire opened on Broadway a year later in *Gay Divorcee* and launched the song NIGHT AND DAY. This great hit of the decade was written by Cole Porter, the most urbane, witty, and sophisticated of American songwriters. An erudite musician and fastidious craftsman, Porter wrote both words and music of his songs and richly deserves his pre-eminence on both counts. Beautiful melodic sweep, masterful construction and ingenious versification are the earmarks of his style. His greatest theatrical triumph, *Kiss Me, Kate*, came much later, in 1948, and the ballad SO IN LOVE from this score is one of his finest.

A representative sampling from the abundant song repertory of this era could not be complete without an entry from the pen of Harold Arlen, one of the top-rank creators of American popular song. The charming and ever-appealing I'VE GOT THE WORLD ON A STRING is a good illustration of his distinctive style: fresh melodic and harmonic inventiveness, buoyed by skillfully distilled jazz influences.

The tempo of the 1930s was enlivened and its rhythm spiced with the introduction of numerous Latin-American dances—the Rumba, Beguine, Conga. What turned out to be the characteristic beat of the decade, however, was a more indigenous development, an offshoot of jazz called "swing." In this idiom the heart of early jazz performance, free improvisation, was replaced by carefully notated arrangements which each player followed. The resulting loss of spontaneity was made up for by marvelously co-ordinated sound, and improvised solo passages were still retained within a planned framework. The apostles of the fad were the leaders of big bands—Benny Goodman, Artie Shaw, Tommy Dorsey and others; the faithful and exuberant mass of followers consisted mainly of teen-agers, the "hepsters" and "jitterbugs."

The end of the decade saw the gathering of war clouds over Europe. This did not dampen the high spirits of the "jive" set, but did cause some foreboding in many thoughtful people who felt an urgent need for strengthening the common bond of patriotism in the American people as they confronted the ominous danger signals from abroad. It was Irving Berlin, that foremost natural melodist of American song, who expressed the sentiment of the country most successfully with the words and music of GOD BLESS AMERICA. Introduced in late 1938, the song was enthusiastically received and nearly attained the status of a second national anthem. During his long and distinguished career of nearly six decades, Berlin has produced a uniquely rich catalogue of ageless songs in all styles. On his eightieth birthday President Lyndon B. Johnson said: "America is richer for his presence. God bless Berlin."

ALL THE THINGS YOU ARE was written in 1939 by Jerome Kern and Oscar Hammerstein II for a show that was a failure and was quickly forgotten. The song, however, has survived; it is one of Kern's most beautiful melodies and seems to be timeless. It is said that when Victor Herbert in 1914 first heard a musical score by the young Kern, he remarked: "This man will inherit my mantle." Indeed, Kern did even more. He not only became a master writer of theater songs, but, with *Show Boat*, he also established native American musical theater. Behind his flawless melodies lies meticulously controlled inventiveness. "Genius is surely not too extravagant a word for him . . ." said one of his eulogists.

World War II inspired a large number of tunes, as such great national efforts and trials usually do. THE MARINES' HYMN and THE CAISSONS GO ROLLING ALONG were among the many favorites, although written earlier. The most distinguished and best-loved songs of the 1940s, however, were not directly connected with the war; they originated in the theater and most often from the pen of Richard Rodgers. These were the songs written in collaboration with Oscar Hammerstein II for *Oklahoma!, Carousel* and *South Pacific,* the shows which elevated the

American musical theater to its highest degree of maturity and distinction. During the first twenty-five years of his career, Rodgers wrote his songs in partnership with Lorenz Hart, whose virtuosity as lyricist earned the accolades of at least two generations. Their first great ballad hit was MY HEART STOOD STILL in 1927, followed in quick succession by many other memorable tunes. The label "words and music by Rodgers and Hart" will always stand for a song of freshness, ingenuity and exquisite workmanship; nothing less could be said about the works of Rodgers and Hammerstein. The sunny, tuneful exuberance of JUNE IS BUSTIN' OUT ALL OVER from *Carousel* is a perennial reminder of this felicitous collaboration.

For afficionados of song and theater the year 1948 was notable for two events—the production of *Kiss Me Kate,* in which Cole Porter reached the summit of his artistry, and the Broadway debut of Frank Loesser as composer-lyricist of the show *Where's Charley?* in which Ray Bolger charmed his audiences with a memorable song-and-dance routine, the ever-popular ONCE IN LOVE WITH AMY. Loesser had a rare, instinctive mastery of words, music and stagecraft, and his shows—*Guys and Dolls, The Most Happy Fella,* and others—are important milestones in the annals of modern stage musicals.

A quickly passing fad of the late forties was "be-bop," a fast, discordant, offbeat jazz style, which—to no one's surprise—did not leave a legacy of hit tunes. Obviously, it was too difficult to develop a strong affinity for a vocal line which had to be sung to lyrics such as "oo-bop-sha-bam," or "bobba-doodle-dee, be-bop." Similarly, the dance craze, "twist," had no effect on our popular-song repertory, but did cause a high incidence of sacroiliac dislocations in the more elderly practitioners.

Of much greater significance and of substantial influence on the popular-music scene was the advent of "rock and roll," a teen-age-oriented, strongly accented blend of the Afro-American "rhythm and blues" idiom with the "country and western" music of rural string bands and vocalists. The high priest of the trend and idol of a multitude of screaming fans was a handsome young Tennesseean, ex-truck driver turned singer, Elvis Presley; but even his phenomenal success was overshadowed by the mass hysteria accompanying the appearance of that oddly groomed but extremely gifted quartet of young Englishmen, the Beatles. The long-range effect of this group was due not so much to their style of delivery as to the novel harmonic and constructional qualities of their songs, which enlarged their following by attracting the attention of adults and serious musicians as well. Parallel with the emergence of rock and roll there appeared a strong revival of interest in folk music. Whether it happened through "folk rock," or through the smoother, more mild-mannered renditions of various popular groups, the 1950s and '60s produced best-seller recordings of folk tunes year after year. TOM DOOLEY, ON TOP OF OLD SMOKY, THE YELLOW ROSE OF TEXAS and MICHAEL, ROW THE BOAT ASHORE are just a few examples of this parade of folk hits.

Songs written during the past two decades, including those in the various "rock" styles, are in most cases of too recent vintage for inclusion in the "best-loved" category. This term, as construed by the editor of this volume, implies not only a status of wide appeal and popularity, but also a certain indefinable quality of staying power which makes it impervious to the passage of time. Aging will not make a best-loved song obsolete; it will only encrust it with the patina of affection. Two songs selected from the repertory of the very recent past, both written for the theater, show every sign of proving this adage and qualifying for the honor of inclusion: Meredith Willson's SEVENTY SIX TROMBONES from *The Music Man,* the saga of a fast-talking instrument salesman from the bygone innocent years of the American Midwest; and THE IMPOSSIBLE DREAM by Joe Darion and Mitch Leigh, from *Man of La Mancha,* a 1965 musical version of the Cervantes classic. This grand ballad is much more than a popular song; it has become a slogan for the attainment of all the things we do not have and need most today: a better world.

Tea For Two

from "No No Nanette"

Words by
Irving Caesar

Music by
Vincent Youmans

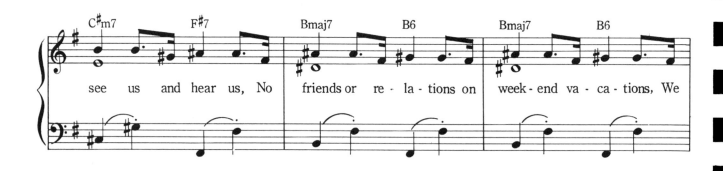

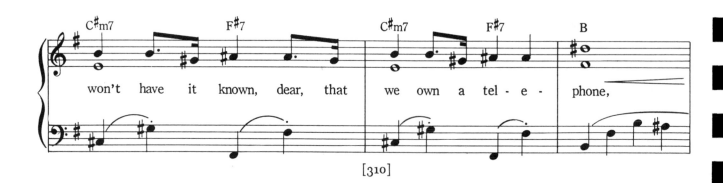

Ol' Man River

from "Show Boat"

Words by
Oscar Hammerstein II

Music by
Jerome Kern

Moderately

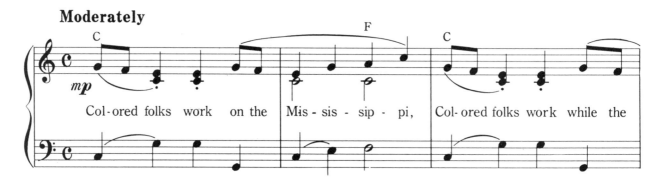

Col-ored folks work on the Mis-sis-sip-pi, Col-ored folks work while the

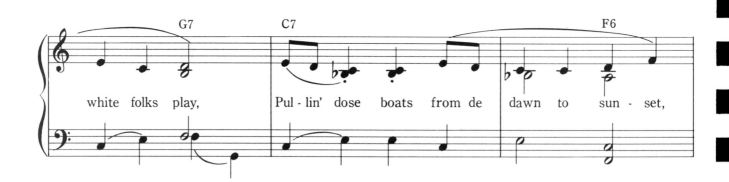

white folks play, Pul-lin' dose boats from de dawn to sun-set,

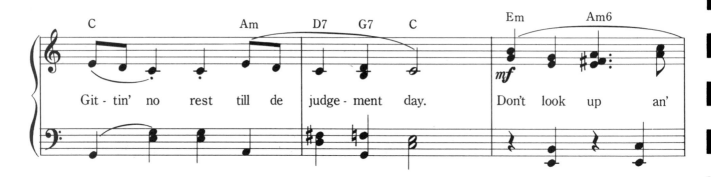

Git-tin' no rest till de judge-ment day. Don't look up an'

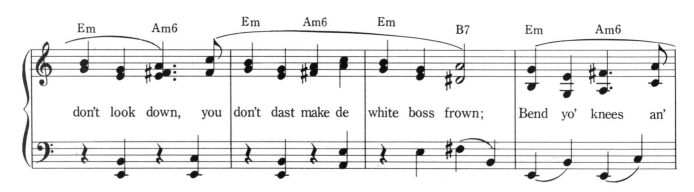

don't look down, you don't dast make de white boss frown; Bend yo' knees an'

[313]

I Love Life

Words by
Irwin M. Cassel

Music by
Mana-Zucca

Tempo I

I Can't Give You Anything But Love

Words by
Dorothy Fields

Music by
Jimmy McHugh

[319]

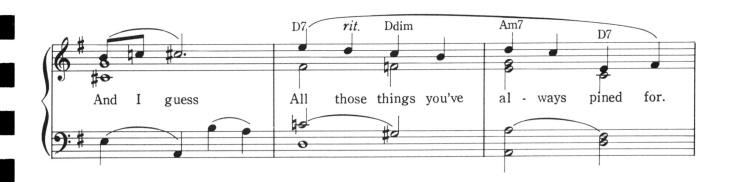

And I guess / All those things you've al - ways pined for.

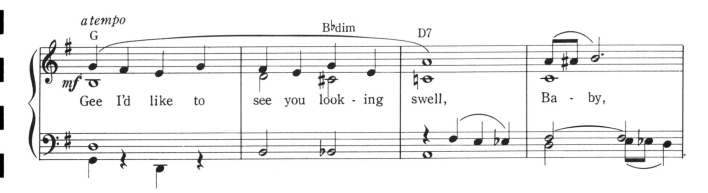

Gee I'd like to / see you look - ing swell, / Ba - by,

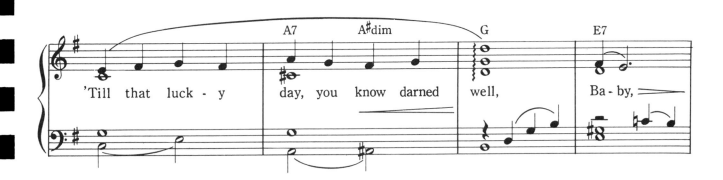

Dia - mond brace - lets / Wool - worth does - n't sell, / Ba - by,

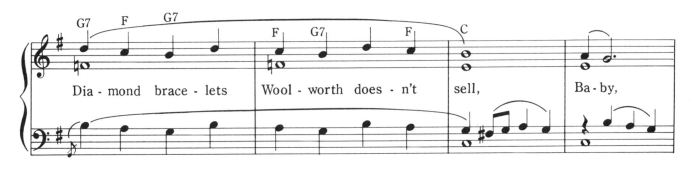

'Till that luck - y / day, you know darned well, / Ba - by, —

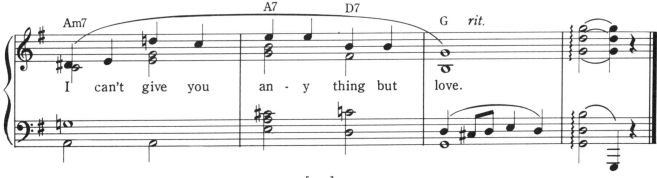

I can't give you / an - y thing but / love.

My Heart Stood Still

from "A Connecticut Yankee"

Words by
Lorenz Hart

Music by
Richard Rodgers

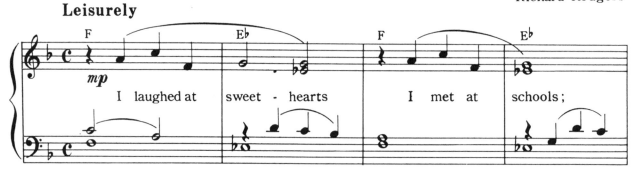

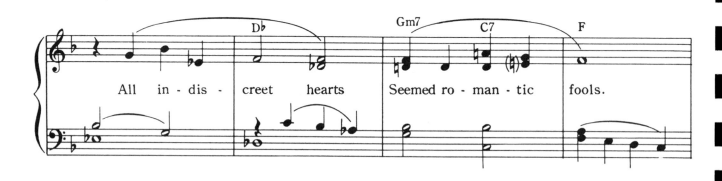

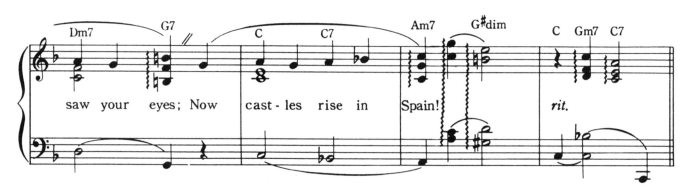

Leisurely

I laughed at sweet - hearts I met at schools;

All in - dis - creet hearts Seemed ro - man - tic fools.

A house in Ice - land Was my hearts do - main. I

saw your eyes; Now cast - les rise in Spain! *rit.*

Moderately, with a lilt

sin - gle word was spo - ken, I could tell you knew,____ That un - felt

clasp of hands____ Told me so well you knew.____

I nev - er lived at all un - til the thrill of that

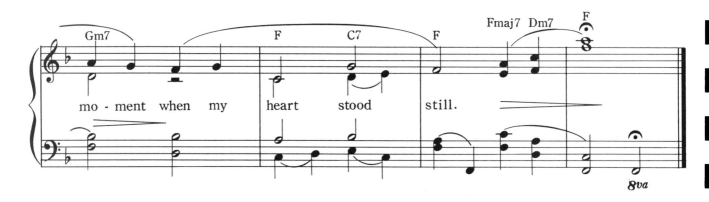

mo - ment when my heart stood still.

8va

Embraceable You

Words by
Ira Gershwin

from "Girl Crazy"

Music by
George Gershwin

Star Dust

Words by
Mitchell Parish

Music by
Hoagy Carmichael

side a gar - den wall, when stars are bright, you are in my arms, The

night - in' - gale tells his fair - y tale of par - a - dise, where ros - es

grew._____ Tho' I dream in vain,_____ In my

heart it will re - main: My star dust mel - o - dy,_____

___ The mem - o - ry of love's re - frain.

I've Got The World On A String

Words by
Ted Koehler

Music by
Harold Arlen

Moderately

Night And Day

from "Gay Divorcee"

Words and music by
Cole Porter

All The Things You Are

from "Very Warm For May"

Words by
Oscar Hammerstein 2nd

Music by
Jerome Kern

God Bless America

by Irving Berlin

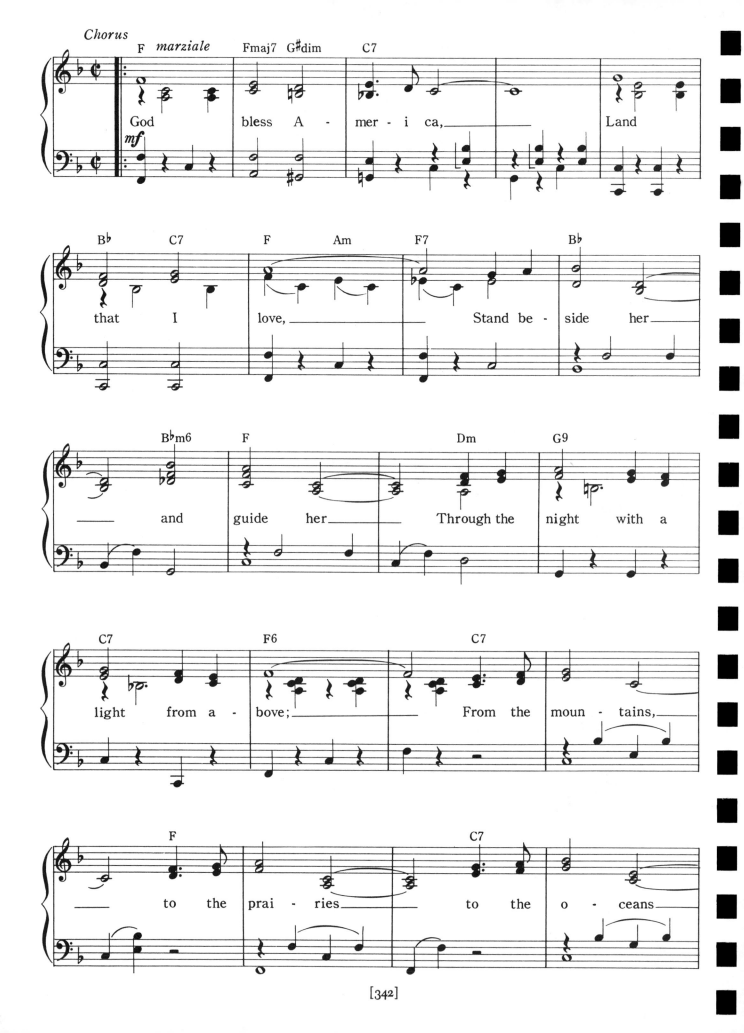

The Marines' Hymn

Words
Anonymous

Melody from
Jacques Offenbach's
"Geneviève de Brabant"

Lively march tempo

1. From the Halls of Mon - te - zu - ma To the shores of Tri - po - li, We fight our coun - try's bat - tles On the land as on the sea. First to

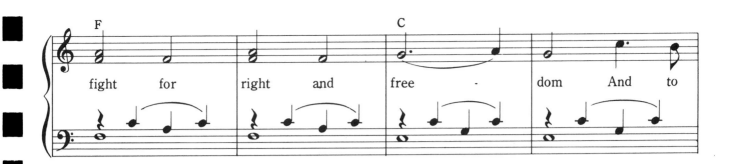

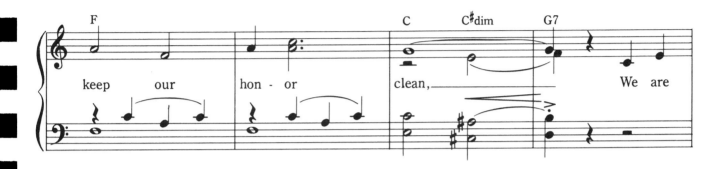

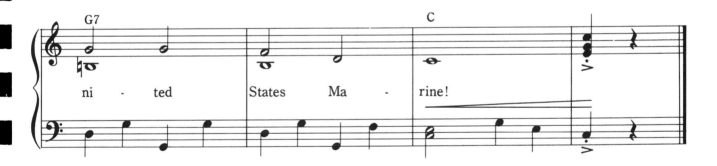

2. Our flag's unfurled to every breeze
   From dawn to setting sun.
   We have fought in every clime and place
   Where we could take a gun.
   In the snow of far-off Northern lands
   And in sunny Tropic scenes,
   You will find us always on the job –
   The United States Marines.

3. Here's health to you and to our Corps
   Which we are proud to serve.
   In many a strife we've fought for life
   And never lost our nerve.
   If the Army and the Navy
   Ever look on Heaven's scenes,
   They will find the streets are guarded
   By United States Marines.

The Caissons Go Rolling Along

Words and music by
Edmund L. Gruber

[346]

y, Call off your num-bers loud and strong! > > And where

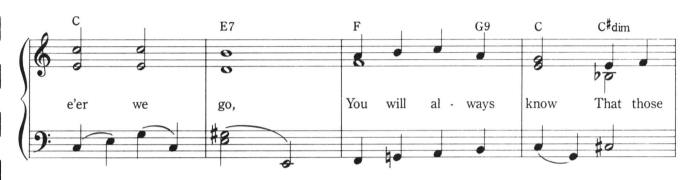

e'er we go, You will al-ways know That those

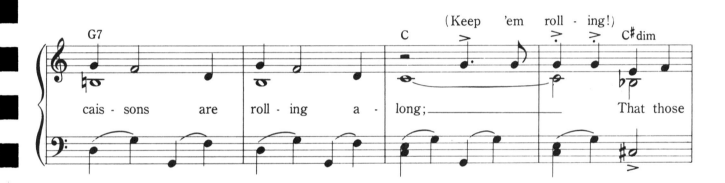

cais-sons are roll-ing a-long; (Keep 'em roll-ing!) > > > That those

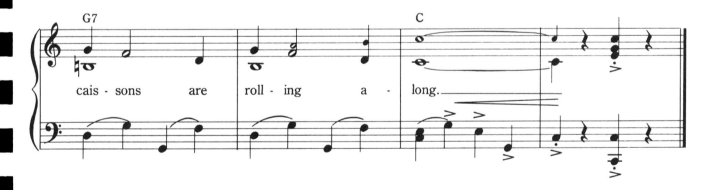

cais-sons are roll-ing a-long.

2. To the Front, day and night,
   Where the dough-boys dig and fight,
   And those caissons go rolling along.
   Our barrage will be there,
   Fired on the rocket's flare,
   Where those caissons go rolling along.   *Chorus*

June Is Bustin' Out All Over

from "Carousel"

Words by
Oscar Hammerstein 2nd

Music by
Richard Rodgers

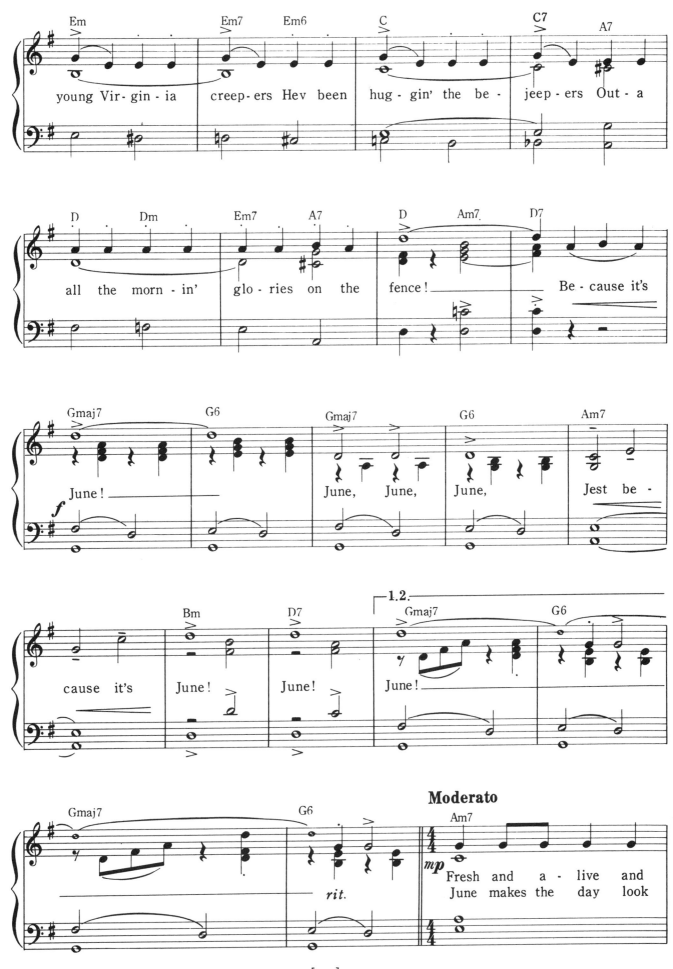

gay   and   young,   June   is   a   love   song   sweet-ly   sung.____
bright   and   new,   sails   gleam-in'   white   on   sun-lit   blue.____

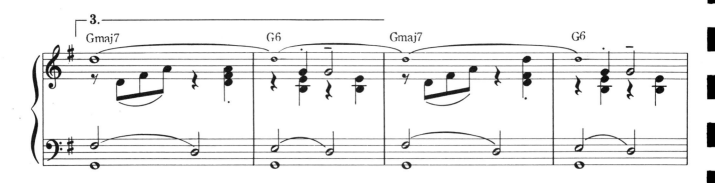

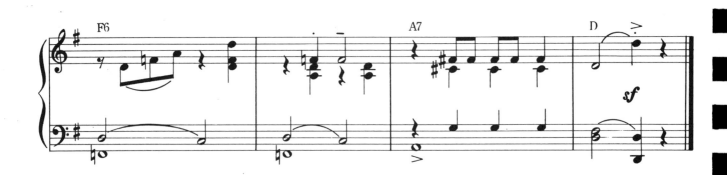

2nd Refrain

June is bustin' out all over!
The saplin's are bustin' out with sap!
Love has found my brother, junior,
And my sister's even lunier!
And my ma is gettin' kittenish with pap!

June is bustin' out all over!
To ladies the men are payin' court.
Lotsa ships are kept at anchor
Jest because the Captains hanker
Fer a comfort they ken only get in port!

Because it's June! June, June, June,
Jest because it's June! June! June!

3rd Refrain

June is bustin' out all over!
The ocean is full of Jacks and Jills.
With her little tail a swishin'
Every lady fish is wishin'
That a male would come and grab her by the gills!

June is bustin' out all over!
The sheep aren't sleepin' any more!
All the rams that chase the ewe sheep
Are determined there'll be new sheep
And the ewe sheep aren't even keepin' score!

On accounta it's June! June, June, June,
Jest because it's June! June! June!

Once In Love With Amy

from "Where's Charley?"

Words and music by
Frank Loesser

[355]

So In Love

from "Kiss Me, Kate"

Words and music by
Cole Porter

Steady, moderate tempo (*always with great warmth*)

1. Strange, dear, but true, dear, When I'm close to you, dear, The stars fill the sky, So in love with you am I, Ev-en with-out you, My arms fold a-bout you, You know

[357]

Careless Love

Folk Blues

Moderately slow

1. Love, oh love, oh care-less love. Love, oh love, oh care-less love. Love, oh love, oh care-less love, you see what care-less love has done.

2. Oh, it's broke this heart of mine,
   Oh, it's broke this heart of mine,
   Oh, it's broke this heart of mine,
   It'll break that heart of yours sometime.

3. I love my mama and papa too,
   I love my mama and papa too,
   I love my mama and papa too,
   But I'd leave them both to go with you.

4. I cried last night and the night before,
   I cried last night and the night before,
   I cried last night and the night before,
   Gonna cry tonight and cry no more.

5. How I wish that train would come,
   How I wish that train would come,
   How I wish that train would come,
   And take me back where I come from.

When The Saints Come Marching In

Words and music of this version
by Edward C. Redding

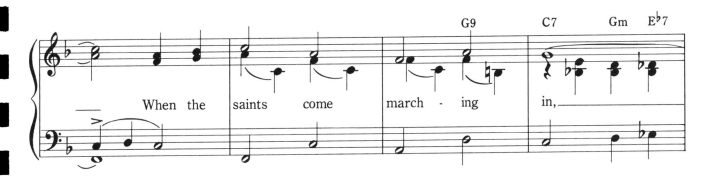

When the saints come march - ing in,

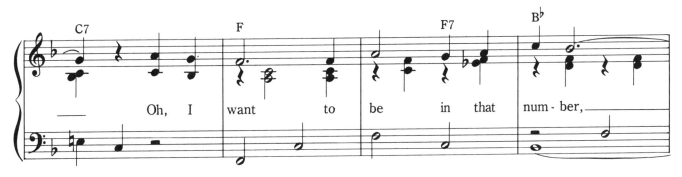

Oh, I want to be in that num - ber,

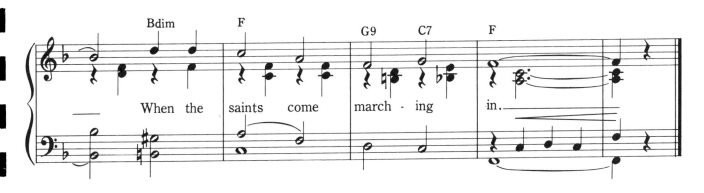

When the saints come march - ing in.

2. So I pray each day to heaven,
   For the strength to help me win;
   Want to be in that procession
   When the saints come marching in. *Chorus*

Extra choruses:

I want to join the heav'nly band,
Want to join the heav'nly band,
Want to hear the trumpets ablowing
When the saints come marching in.

I want to wear a happy smile,
Want to wear a happy smile,
Want to sing and shout "Hallelujah!"
When the saints come marching in.

I want to see those pearly gates,
Want to see those pearly gates,
Want to see those gates standing open,
When the saints come marching in.

On Top Of Old Smoky

Folk Tune

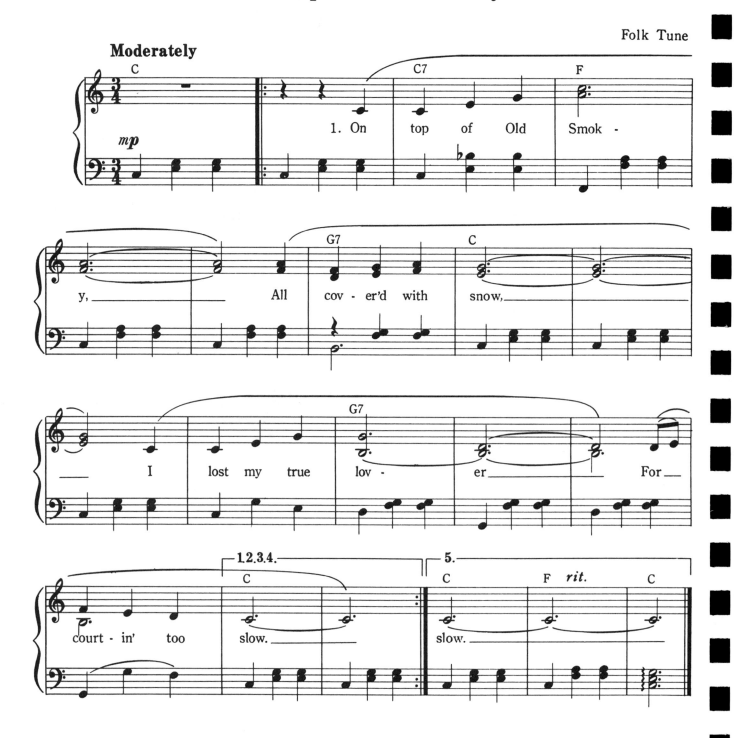

2. Now courtin's a pleasure
   But partin' is grief,
   A false hearted lover
   Is worse than a thief.

3. A thief will just rob you
   And take what you have,
   But a false hearted lover
   Will send you to your grave.

4. They'll hug you and kiss you
   And tell you more lies,
   Than cross-ties on the railroad
   Or stars in the skies.

5. On top of Old Smoky,
   All covered with snow,
   I lost my true lover
   For courtin' too slow.

Down In The Valley

Folk Song

With an easy, gentle flow

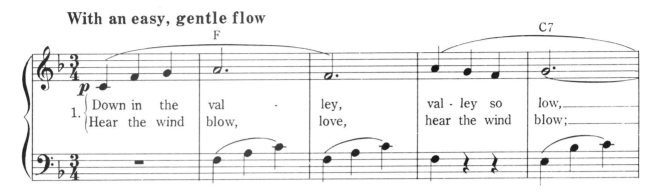

1. Down in the valley, valley so low,
   Hear the wind blow, hear the wind blow;

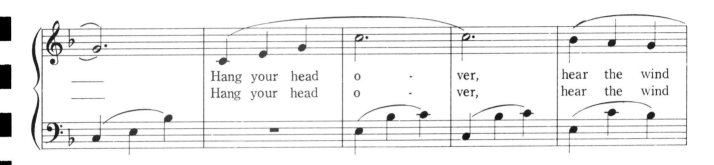

Hang your head over, hear the wind
Hang your head over, hear the wind

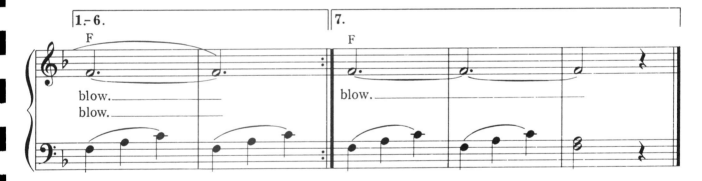

1.-6. blow.
blow.

7. blow.

2. Roses love sunshine, violets love dew;
   Angels in Heaven know I love you.
   Know I love you, dear, know I love you;
   Angels in Heaven know I love you.

3. If you don't love me, love whom you please;
   Throw your arms 'round me, give my heart ease.
   Give my heart ease, love, give my heart ease;
   Throw your arms 'round me, give my heart ease.

4. Build me a castle, forty feet high;
   So I can see him as he rides by.
   As he rides by, love, as he rides by;
   So I can see him as he rides by.

5. Writing this letter, containing three lines,
   Answer my question, "Will you be mine?"
   Will you be mine, dear, will you be mine?"
   Answer my question, "Will you be mine?"

6. Write me a letter, send it by mail;
   Send it in care of Birmingham jail.
   Birmingham jail, love, Birmingham jail;
   Send it in care of Birmingham jail.

7. Down in the valley, valley so low,
   Hang your head over, hear the wind blow.
   Hear the wind blow, love, hear the wind blow;
   Hang your head over, hear the wind blow.

Paper Of Pins

Moderately

Folk Tune

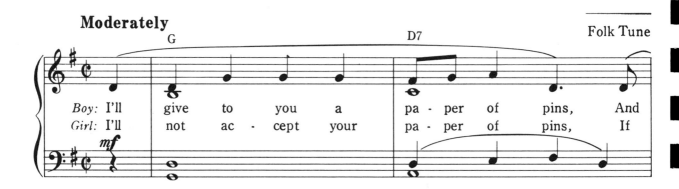

Boy: I'll give to you a pa-per of pins, And
Girl: I'll not ac-cept your pa-per of pins, If

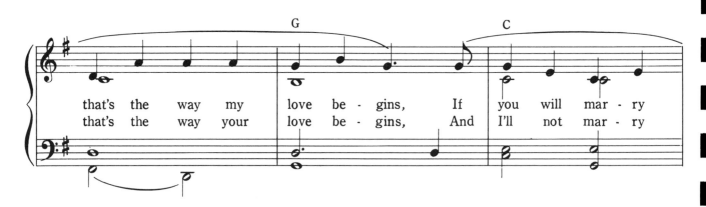

that's the way my love be-gins, If you will mar-ry
that's the way your love be-gins, And I'll not mar-ry

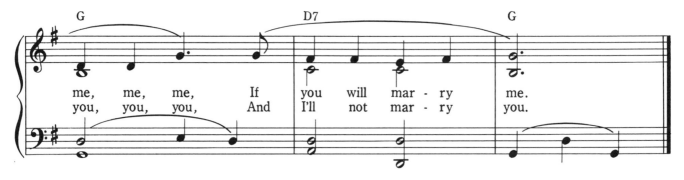

me, me, me, If you will mar-ry me.
you, you, you, And I'll not mar-ry you.

2. I'll give to you a dress of red,
Stitched all around with a golden thread,
If you will marry me, me, me,
If you will marry me.

I'll not accept your dress of red,
Stitched all around with a golden thread,
And I'll not marry you, you, you,
And I'll not marry you.

3. I'll give to you the keys to my chest
And all the money that I possess,
If you will marry me, me, me,
If you will marry me.

Oh, yes, I'll take the keys to your chest
And all the money that you possess,
And I will marry you, you, you,
And I will marry you.

4. Now, you love coffee and I love tea,
You love my money, but you don't love me,
And I'll not marry you, you, you,
And I'll not marry you.

Oh, then I'll be a withered old maid
And take my stool and sit in the shade,
If you'll not marry me, me, me,
If you'll not marry me.

Tom Dooley

Moderately

Folk Ballad

Verse 2: 'Bout this time tomorrow,
Reckon where I'll be?
Down in some lonesome valley,
A-hangin' from a white oak tree.

Chorus: Hang down your head, Tom Dooley,
Hang down your head and cry,
Hang down your head, Tom Dooley,
Poor boy, you're bound to die.

Seventy Six Trombones

from "The Music Man"

Words and music by
Meredith Willson

There were more than a thou - sand reeds spring - ing up like weeds, There were horns of ev - 'ry shape and kind. There were cop - per bot - tom tym - pa - ni in horse pla - toons, Thun - der - ing, thun - der - ing all a - long the way. Dou-ble bell eu - pho - ni - ums and big bas-soons, Each bas-soon hav-ing his big fat say. There were fif - ty mount-ed can - non in the

bat - ter - y,_____ Thun-der-ing, thun-der-ing, loud-er than be - fore.

Clar - i - nets of ev - 'ry size and trum-pet-ers who'd im - pro-vise a full oc - tave

high - er than the score._____

He's Got The Whole World In His Hands

Spiritual

With spirit

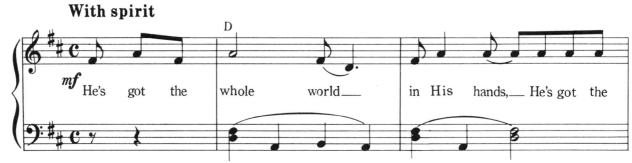

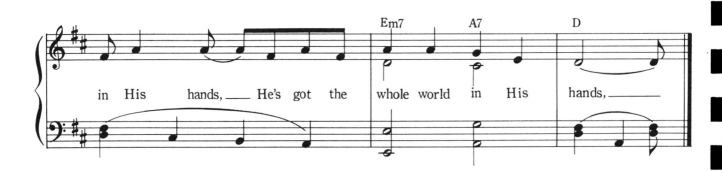

2.   He's got the wind and the rain in His hands,
He's got the wind and the rain in His hands,
He's got the wind and the rain in His hands,
He's got the whole world in His hands.

3.   He's got the tiny little baby in His hands,
He's got the tiny little baby in His hands,
He's got the tiny little baby in His hands,
He's got the whole world in His hands.

4.   He's got you and me in His hands,
He's got you and me in His hands,
He's got you and me in His hands,
He's got the whole world in His hands.

Michael, Row The Boat Ashore

Spiritual

With a moderately broad beat

2. Brother, lend a helping hand, Hallelujah!
   Brother, lend a helping hand, Hallelujah!

3. Sister, help to trim the sail, Hallelujah!
   Sister, help to trim the sail, Hallelujah!

4. Jordan's River is deep and wide, Hallelujah!
   Meet my mother on the other side, Hallelujah!

5. Jordan's River is chilly cold, Hallelujah!
   Kills the body but not the soul, Hallelujah!

6. Trumpet sound the jubilee, Hallelujah!
   Trumpet sound the jubilee, Hallelujah!

7. Michael, row the boat ashore, Hallelujah!
   Michael, row the boat ashore, Hallelujah!

The Riddle Song

(I Gave My Love A Cherry)

Folk Tune

2. How can there be a cherry without a stone?
   How can there be a chicken without a bone?
   How can there be a ring that has no end?
   How can there be a baby with no cryin'?

3. A cherry when it's bloomin', it has no stone;
   A chicken when it's pippin', it has no bone;
   A ring when it's rollin', it has no end;
   A baby when it's sleepin', there's no cryin'.

Wabash Cannonball

Traditional Railroad Song

Moderately lively

1. From the great Atlantic Ocean, To the wide Pacific shore; From the queen of flowing mountains To the southland by the shore, She's mighty tall and handsome, And quite well-known by all; She's the mighty combination of the Wabash Cannonball.

2.   Listen to the jingle,   Hear the mighty rush of the engine,
     The rumble and the roar,   Hear that lonesome hobo call,
     As she glides along the woodland,   You're trav'ling through the jungles
     Through the hills and by the shore,   On the Wabash Cannonball.

We Shall Overcome

Traditional Spiritual Song

2. We shall walk in peace,
   We shall walk in peace,
   We shall walk in peace some day.
   Oh, deep in my heart
   I do believe
   We shall walk in peace some day.

3. We shall build a new world,
   We shall build a new world,
   We shall build a new world some day.
   Oh, deep in my heart
   I do believe
   We shall build a new world some day.

Wildwood Flower

Folk Song

2. Oh, he taught me to love him, he promised to love,
   And to cherish me always all others above.
   I woke from my dream and my idol was clay,
   All my passion for loving had vanished away.

3. I will dance, I will sing and my life shall be gay,
   I will banish this weeping, drive troubles away.
   I will live yet to see him regret this dark hour
   When he won and neglected this frail wildwood flower.

Scarborough Fair

English-American Folk Song

[376]

2. Tell her to make me a cambric shirt,
   Parsley, sage, rosemary and thyme;
   Without any seam or fine needlework,
   And then she'll be a true love of mine.

3. Tell her to wash it in yonder dry well,
   Parsley, sage, rosemary and thyme;
   Where water ne'er sprung, nor drop of rain fell,
   And then she'll be a true love of mine.

4. Oh, will you find me an acre of land,
   Parsley, sage, rosemary and thyme;
   Between the sea foam and the sea sand
   Or never be a true lover of mine.

5. Oh, will you plough it with a lamb's horn,
   Parsley, sage, rosemary and thyme;
   And sow it all over with one peppercorn,
   Or never be a true lover of mine.

6. Oh, will you reap it with a sickle of leather,
   Parsley, sage, rosemary and thyme;
   And tie it all up with a peacock's feather,
   Or never be a true lover of mine.

7. And when you have done and finished your work,
   Parsley, sage, rosemary and thyme;
   Then come to me for your cambric shirt,
   And you shall be a true love of mine.

The Impossible Dream

from "Man of La Mancha"

Lyric by
Joe Darion

Music by
Mitch Leigh

Moderate, steady motion

To dream _____ the im-pos-si-ble dream, _____ to

fight _____ the un-beat-a-ble foe, _____ To

bear _____ with un-bear-a-ble sor-row, _____ to

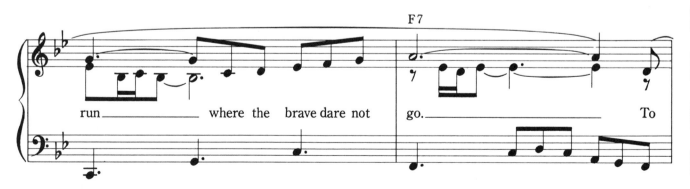

run _____ where the brave dare not go. _____ To

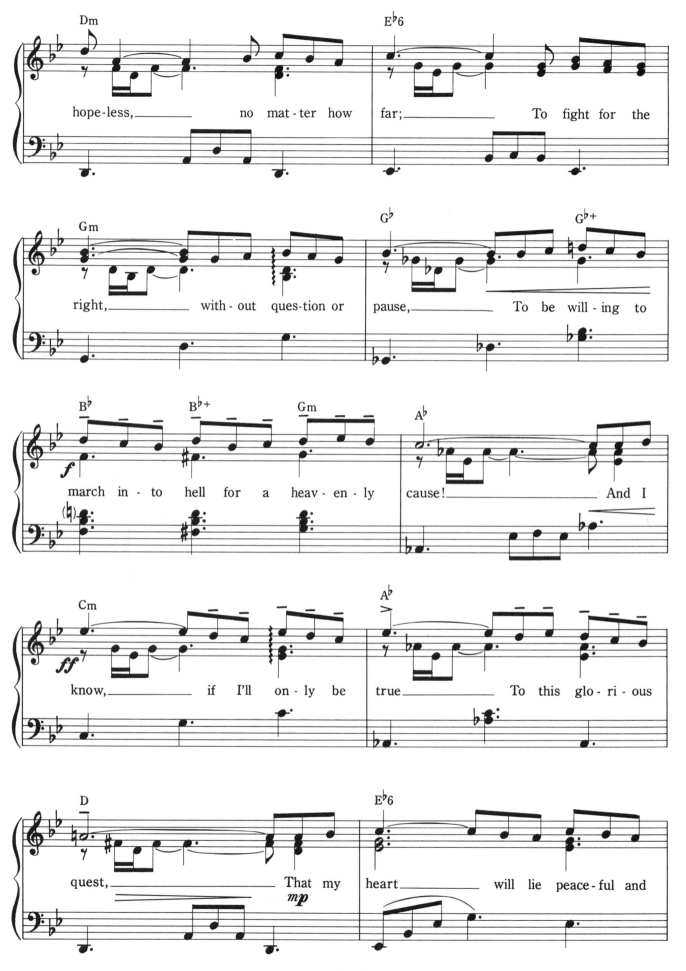

calm,_____ When I'm laid to my rest, *dim.* And the

world_____ will be bet - ter for this;_____ That one

man,_____ scorned and cov-ered with scars,_____ Still____

strove_____ with his last ounce of cour-age,_____ To

reach____ the un-reach-a - ble stars.

NOTES ON THE SONGS

ACRES OF CLAMS (see OLD ROSIN THE BEAU)

AFTER THE BALL One of the most successful songs of all time. It was introduced in a musical extravaganza, *A Trip to Chinatown,* in 1892; the following year John Philip Sousa and his band played it daily at the Chicago World's Fair. Through the years it sold more than five million copies and made a fortune for its author, who, only a year or two before he wrote it, had a shingle hanging outside his modest Milwaukee abode advertising: "Prof. Charles K. Harris—Banjoist and Songwriter —Songs Written to Order."

ALL HAIL THE POWER OF JESUS' NAME (see CORONATION)

ALL THE THINGS YOU ARE A beautiful example of Jerome Kern's songwriting art, with words by Oscar Hammerstein II. It was written in 1939 for the show *Very Warm for May.* In contrast to the immediate and lasting appeal of the song, the show itself was a complete failure.

AMAZING GRACE This hymn, as popular today as ever, goes back to camp-meeting days and beyond. The melody is of folk origin; the words are by John Newton, who gave up his stormy life as a British Navy deserter and slave-ship captain to study the Scriptures and become a minister of the Gospel.

AMERICA This melody is identical to "God Save the King," the British national anthem. It is an old English air of undetermined origin; the tune appeared in its present form in 1744. The words "My country 'tis of thee . . ." were written by the Rev. Samuel Francis Smith for a children's celebration held in a Boston church on July 4, 1832.

A PERFECT DAY Probably the finest lyric ballad of Carrie Jacobs Bond, the First Lady of Amer-

ican Song, who also wrote "I Love You Truly" and "Just A-Wearyin' for You." Published in 1910, this is one of those never-fading, nostalgic little gems which continue to delight generations of Americans by evoking sentiments of a gracious past with a natural, uncontrived flow of simple words and melody.

AT A GEORGIA CAMP MEETING Featured with great success by John Philip Sousa and his band, both here and in Europe, this song was written and published by Frederick Allen Mills (Kerry Mills) in 1897. Mills, a concert violinist and teacher, was also, somewhat incongruously, one of the earliest successful composers of cakewalk and ragtime.

AT DAWNING Published in 1906 with music by Charles Wakefield Cadman, whose works were often influenced by melodies of the American Indian. "As widely known and as welcome as the miracle of morning is this song of rapturous melody and tender sentiment," read a contemporary, and still pertinent, advertisement.

AULD LANG SYNE A very old Scottish air to which Robert Burns wrote second and third stanzas. It was imported into America in the 1790s and since then has been the theme song for New Year's Eve celebrations and other convivial social gatherings.

AURA LEE Written in 1861, this lovely melody has been best loved in various lyric settings. As "Aura Lee" it became very popular in the 1880s with college glee clubs and barbershop quartets. With the words "Army Blue" it became a song of the U. S. Military Academy at West Point. In the 1950s an entirely new set of words, "Love Me Tender," made it again a popular success.

BABY MINE A quite unique and truly charming little song of the year 1878 which somehow succeeds in combining the moods of a lullaby and a tender love song.

BAND PLAYED ON, THE This famous waltz tune about Casey and the strawberry blonde was written in 1895 by a young actor, John F. Palmer. Unable to have the song published, he sold it to Charles B. Ward, a vaudevillian singer-songwriter, who made a few changes and published it himself. Ward succeeded, through a promotional campaign in the New York *World,* in making the song a lasting success.

BARB'RA ALLEN An exquisite folk ballad, more than three centuries old, which exists in innumerable versions. It came from the British Isles, was known all through Colonial America, and has maintained its popularity to the present time.

BATTLE HYMN OF THE REPUBLIC This splendid, rousing marching song, the American "Marseillaise," was originally a camp-meeting hymn with words, "Oh brothers, will you meet us on Canaan's happy shore?" Later it became "John Brown's Body Lies A-moldering in the Grave." The words "Mine eyes have seen the glory of the com ing of the Lord . . ." were written by Julia Ward Howe, the wife of a government official, in 1861. She sold her poem to the *Atlantic Monthly* for a payment of five dollars. The magazine printed it under the title "Battle Hymn of the Republic." There is hardly another national song which compares with it in spirit and fervor.

BEAUTIFUL DREAMER The original edition of 1864 carries the note that this was "the last song ever written by Stephen C. Foster, composed but a few days previous to his death." In fact, Foster had written the song at least two years earlier and the engraved plates were, for some unexplained reason, gathering dust on the publisher's shelf at the time of Foster's death, when it was rushed into print to capitalize on the sad, but well-publicized event. It is unquestionably the finest song of Foster's last years.

BECAUSE Although not written for the popular market, this song has been widely known and loved since its publication in 1902. The work of two English writers, Edward Teschemacher and Guy d'Hardelot (pseudonym for Helen Guy), its prominent status in the repertory of wedding songs easily rivals that of "Oh Promise Me" and "I Love You Truly." It also continues to be a favorite program piece for vocalists of every description from crooners to opera singers.

BECAUSE YOU'RE YOU The ever-popular duet song from Victor Herbert's 1906 operetta hit *The Red Mill.* The words are by Henry Blossom.

BIG SUNFLOWER, THE An unusually appealing song of the minstrel repertory, made popular in the 1860s by Billy Emerson, the most celebrated blackface performer of the period.

BILL BAILEY, WON'T YOU PLEASE COME HOME This, one of the most durable and popular of all ragtime songs, was written in 1902 by Hughie Cannon, an amiable Tin Pan Alley personality. The story of the famous B&O brakeman and his lady love, set to the jaunty syncopated tune, instantly captivated not only this country, but Europe too, and intrigued even George Bernard Shaw.

BIRD IN A GILDED CAGE This heart-wrenching prototype of lachrymose balladry was written in 1900 by Arthur J. Lamb (words) and Harry Von Tilzer (music). In the original version the relationship between the heroine and the rich old man was somewhat unsettled. At Von Tilzer's request, one line in the song was revised to read: "She married for wealth, not for love." Respectability thus firmly established, tears could flow unrestrained.

BLOW THE MAN DOWN One of the most popular of sea chanteys, dating from the early years of the nineteenth century. The melody has been essentially unchanged through many lyric versions.

BLUE TAIL FLY, THE Originally a favorite minstrel tune of the 1840s attributed to Dan Emmett, writer of "Dixie" and "Old Dan Tucker." It is, however, of unquestionable folk origin. Widely known throughout the nineteenth century, it actually has increased in popularity during the past few decades.

BOLL WEEVIL SONG, THE It was around 1900 that vast hordes of these destructive little black insects invaded Texas from Mexico. In a few years they ate their way through all the cotton-growing states, "jes lookin' for a home," and outwitting every human effort to stop them. This song, relating the plight of farmers and sharecroppers in a half-pathetic, half-humorous manner, is of Negro origin.

BONNIE BLUE FLAG, THE With "Dixie," the most popular song of the Confederacy. The words were written in 1861 by an English-born vaudevillian, Harry McCarthy, to the melody of an old Irish song, "The Irish Jaunting Car."

BUFFALO GALS Published in 1844 under the title "Lubly Fan," written by Cool White, one of the first blackface minstrels. It was extremely popular with minstrel troupes, and the title was changed according to the locality where it was sung: "New York Gals," "Charleston Gals," "Lou'siana Gals"; finally, and permanently, "Buffalo Gals." In 1944, with some minor changes, it reached the hit parade under the title "Dance with a Dolly."

BULLY SONG, THE Tamed version of a rowdy St. Louis waterfront ballad; introduced and made famous in 1895 by blonde, buxom and boisterous May Irwin, as leading lady of the show *The Widow Jones*. This is one of the first hit songs in the ragtime idiom.

BUNKER HILL One of our first patriotic songs. It was written in the year of the battle, 1775, by Andrew Law, composer of anthems and essayist on music. The poem, originally titled "The American Hero," is by Nathaniel Niles.

BY THE WATERS OF MINNETONKA This song, published in 1914, is based on an Indian folk theme. Its composer, Thurlow Lieurance, spent many years among American Indians, studying their music.

CAISSONS GO ROLLING ALONG, THE An army officer, Edmund L. Gruber, wrote this song for the U. S. Field Artillery while stationed in the Philippines in 1908. In 1918, through John Philip Sousa's colorful band arrangement, it became a favorite service song and it reached the peak of popularity during World War II. In spite of all the changes and advances in military hardware, the caissons will evidently never become obsolete in the hearts of song-loving Americans.

CAPE ANN A very old, charming folk tune of English origin, which was widely sung in early New England. It was featured, and made popular nationwide, in the 1840s by the singing Hutchinson Family.

CAPTAIN JINKS This rollicking comedy tune by two English writers became very popular in post-Civil War days and has been periodically revived on the stage. The nonsensical lyrics, wedded to a jaunty marching tune, have never lost their appeal.

CARELESS LOVE One of the earliest folk blues, originating in the southern mountains, this song has been known in numerous versions. The form included in this volume is the most widely known through performances in nearly all popular styles, jazz, hillbilly, blues.

CARRY ME BACK TO OLD VIRGINNY By James Bland, the first successful Negro songwriter. Born in New York and educated in Washington, D.C., he left Howard University with a "banjo under his arm" to join a minstrel troupe, and in a few years became a celebrated music-hall performer both here and in Europe. He wrote nearly seven hundred songs, several of which are still known and loved today. "Carry Me Back . . ." was declared the official state song of Virginia in 1940.

CHAMPAGNE CHARLIE Popular singer-comedian George Leybourne, who wrote the words of this 1868 hit (and also of "The Man on the Flying Trapeze"), used to perform the song with a bottle of champagne in his hand and, after the last line, "Come and join me in the spree," often treated the entire audience to free glasses of the bubbling nectar.

CHESTER This patriotic anthem and marching tune of the Revolutionary Army came from the pen of William Billings, one of the first native American writers of songs.

CINDY Perhaps the happiest, hand-clapping, foot-stamping dance tune in our folklore. It originated in the southern mountain regions around the time of Thomas Jefferson and was carried everywhere by country fiddlers, banjo pickers and black-face minstrels. Much later, the radio and phonograph helped to maintain its popularity.

CLEMENTINE For some strange reason, the macabre story of Clementine, the miner's daughter with shoes number nine who "fell into the foaming brine," has been a continual source of vocal merriment since the 1880s. The authorship of this ever-popular sing-along tune is uncertain; the credit often given to Percy Montross is unsubstantiated.

CORONATION ("All Hail the Power of Jesus' Name") Music by Oliver Holden, with words by the Rev. James Perronet, first published in Holden's *Union Harmony* in 1793. Holden is said to have written the melody on the joyous occasion of the birth of his first child. This hymn has been loved and in constant use since its first appearance.

COWBOY'S LAMENT ("The Streets of Laredo") One of the most popular western songs, it has been known in many versions, the earliest of which can be traced to the British Isles.

DAISY BELL ("Bicycle Built for Two") Bicycling, including the riding of tandem bikes, became a national craze around 1890. This lilting, merry waltz tune was written in New York by Harry Dacre, who, as so often happened, was unable to find a publisher and approached singer Katie Lawrence to introduce it. This she did, in England, with resounding success, and within weeks "Daisy Bell" became known and loved on both sides of the Atlantic. She still looks sweet upon the seat of that tandem.

DARLING NELLY GRAY The sorrowful story related here has a factual background: a Negro slave girl, torn from her loved ones and sold, far from home, to a new master. This fine song was written in 1856 by Benjamin R. Hanby, whose father, an Ohio minister with strong abolitionist sympathies, helped escaping slaves and used his home as a station on the "Underground Railroad."

DIXIE The most popular war song of the Confederacy was written by a Northerner, Daniel Decatur Emmett, as a closing number ("walkaround") for the Bryant Minstrels. It was introduced in New York and shortly thereafter in New Orleans, where it was first printed as a broadside. It electrified audiences everywhere, North and South. It was played at the inauguration of Jefferson Davis, before Pickett's charge at Gettysburg, and, after Appomattox, Lincoln requested the band to play "Dixie" at the first public function he attended. The meaning of the word "Dixie" is still unsettled. It could refer to the region south of the Mason-Dixon Line, or, more possibly, to the worthless ten-dollar bills, issued in New Orleans, which were called "dixies" because of the French word *dix* (ten) printed on them.

DOWN IN THE VALLEY One of the most

widely known songs in the folk repertory; it originated in the southern Appalachians when the country was young. It is variously labeled a hillbilly song, a cowboy song, or just an all-purpose love ballad. In any case, whether performed on the guitar, the harmonica, the piano or on an electronic synthesizer, it always retains its quiet nostalgic appeal.

DRINK TO ME ONLY WITH THINE EYES The early popularity of this song is attested to by the fact that it was first published in America in a 1789 *Collection of Favorite Songs*. The words, Ben Jonson's poem "To Celia" (actually a near-literal translation of a classical Greek text), first saw print in 1616. The lovely melody has often been attributed to Mozart, without any substantive proof.

EMBRACEABLE YOU This beautiful amalgam of easy-flowing melody and charming words is one of the most often performed songs in the Gershwin catalogue. It was written for the 1930 show *Girl Crazy*, in which Ethel Merman and Ginger Rogers made their debuts.

ENRAPTURED I GAZE By Francis Hopkinson, musician, poet, lawyer, one of the signers of the Declaration of Independence, and—as he himself proudly claimed—"the first native of the United States who has produced a musical composition." Published in 1788 as part of a *Set of Eight Songs*, dedicated to George Washington.

ERIE CANAL, THE The famous "ditch," connecting the Great Lakes with the Atlantic, was opened in 1825 and was soon teeming with horse-and mule-drawn barges. The "canawlers" relieved the monotony of the slow 425-mile trip between Albany and Buffalo with frequent brawls and lusty singing. This, the best-known song of the extensive canal lore, dates from the second half of the nineteenth century.

FLOWERS THAT BLOOM IN THE SPRING, THE Although Queen Victoria thought that the plot of *The Mikado* was "rather silly," this operetta, introduced in 1885 in both London and New York, became one of the most popular theater pieces ever written. "The Flowers that Bloom in the Spring," and the entire wonderful Gilbert and Sullivan *oeuvre*, will never wilt.

FOR HE'S A JOLLY GOOD FELLOW The melody of this merry tune of conviviality, also known as "We Won't Go Home till Morning" and "The Bear Went over the Mountain," is a very old one and was taken from a popular eighteenth-century French nursery tune, *"Marlbrook s'en va-t-en guerre."* The song's often maintained connection with the Duke of Marlborough is rather tenuous.

FOR ME AND MY GAL   A noteworthy song on several counts—in addition to its indestructible popularity. Written in 1917 in a period of stylistic transition, it successfully combines the joyous, relaxed, let's-all-sing-together quality of earlier song hits with certain unmistakable traits and accents of the coming jazz age.

FRANKIE AND JOHNNY   Carl Sandburg termed this the American gutter song classic. Hundreds of versions of it are extant; in some variants Frankie's unfortunate victim is named Albert. The song's origin is obscure; words and melody of this modern version date from not later than the 1880s. The theme itself, the jealous rage of a woman scorned, is of course much older and goes back to ancient balladry.

FROGGIE WENT A-COURTIN'   Burl Ives calls this "one of the oldest and most popular narrative animal songs for children in the English language." It was first printed in England in 1611, under the title "A Most Strange Weddinge of the Froge and the Mouse." It probably came over with the Pilgrims and later migrated to the Blue Ridge and southern Appalachian regions.

GAILY THE TROUBADOUR   A popular sentimental serenade of the 1820s by Thomas Haynes Bayly, who also wrote "Long, Long Ago."

GET ON BOARD, LITTLE CHILDREN (see GOSPEL TRAIN)

GIRL I LEFT BEHIND ME, THE   This lively traditional fife tune, imported from England as "Brighton Camp," was known in America as early as the seventeenth century, and became generally popular during the Revolution.

GIVE MY REGARDS TO BROADWAY   The famous New York thoroughfare has been the subject of many songs, but none of them is held in greater affection by the American people than this inimitable paean to the Great White Way. A hit song—

together with "Yankee Doodle Boy"—from the 1904 show *Little Johnny Jones*, book, music and lyrics by George M. Cohan.

GLOW WORM   European import of the early 1900s by German composer Paul Lincke. It became a hit as an interpolated production number in the show *The Girl Behind the Counter.* Anna Pavlova also used the melody for her *Empire Gavotte* presentation. With or without words, it has always been an immensely popular piece.

GOD BLESS AMERICA   Words and music by Irving Berlin. This song, introduced on Armistice Day, 1938, by singer Kate Smith, quickly achieved the status of a national song. The author assigned all income from the song to the Boy and Girl Scouts of America.

GOSPEL TRAIN, THE ("Get on Board, Little Children")   A lively spiritual, expressing the comforting and exalting thought that "the fare is cheap . . . all can go . . . and ride to Heaven at last."

GRANDFATHER'S CLOCK   Words and music by Henry C. Work, the writer of numerous all-time favorite songs. Dating from 1876, this was one of Work's most successful sentimental ballads. A well-written and effective song, which never has failed to impress audiences in the theater or gathered around the piano in the parlor.

GREENSLEEVES   An English folk song, centuries old, which was brought to these shores by the Pilgrims and was sung throughout the Colonial period. Its popularity has never abated and has actually increased in our time, reaching the status of a best-seller in the 1950s. With the words "What Child Is This?" it is also a beloved Christmas carol.

HAIL, COLUMBIA   Originally written by Philip Phile as an instrumental piece, "The President's March," honoring George Washington. The words were added in 1798 by Joseph Hopkinson, son of Francis Hopkinson, the first American writer of songs. It was introduced at a Philadelphia concert attended by President John Adams and his entire cabinet, and was received with thunderous acclaim. For more than a century this stirring national song rivaled the status of "The Star Spangled Banner" as our national anthem.

HELLO, MA BABY   One of the first "telephone"

songs and a big ragtime-cakewalk hit of the year 1899, by Joseph E. Howard, a legendary show-business personality who, during his long and active career, performed in all media from vaudeville to television. He wrote this song in collaboration with his second wife, Ida Emerson. Joe Howard married eight times and—by his own account—spent the considerable fortune he earned on "wine, women and alimony."

HE'S GOT THE WHOLE WORD IN HIS HANDS This deeply expressive Negro spiritual, known in various versions for several generations, was often featured on concert programs of Marian Anderson and Roland Hayes. The song became a commercial hit during the 1950s through numerous best-seller recordings.

HINKY DINKY, PARLAY-VOO (see MADE-MOISELLE FROM ARMENTIÈRES)

HOME ON THE RANGE This famous Western song, known in one form or another for at least a century, attained its great nationwide popularity during the 1930s after having been labeled one of President Franklin D. Roosevelt's favorites. There has been a great deal of doubt, controversy and even court litigation about its origin. At various times an Arizona couple, a Kansas country doctor and a Colorado prospector claimed, or were given credit for, authorship. There can be little doubt, however, that the song grew from the fertile soil of American folklore.

HOME, SWEET HOME This, one of the most popular sentimental ballads of all time, is a joint English-American product. The words are by John Howard Payne, actor, playwright, U.S. diplomat abroad; and the music is by Sir Henry Bishop, renowned English musician and conductor of the London Philharmonic Society. Originally, the song was part of a now long-forgotten opera, *Clari, or the Maid of Milan,* introduced in 1823. Its popularity spread rapidly on both sides of the Atlantic. "Surely there is something strange in the fact," wrote Payne in a letter, "that it should have been my lot to cause so many people in the world to boast of the delights of home, when I never had a home of my own."

HOT TIME IN THE OLD TOWN, A (see THERE'LL BE A HOT TIME)

HO! WESTWARD HO! Most songs of the westward expansion and the California gold rush were folk-based. This tune was an exception. It was written around 1850 by a Boston singer, songwriter and man-about-town, Ossian Dodge, who, in addition to his musical gifts, obviously had a flair for publicity even in those serene pre-Tin Pan Alley days. At an auction he purchased a ticket for $625 to attend the famous Jenny Lind's first Boston concert, and thereby created a nationwide sensation. Of course, it's impossible to know whether this was a *bona fide* purchase or just a promotion stunt engineered by the concert's impresario, P. T. Barnum.

HUNTERS OF KENTUCKY, THE This virile, good-humored tune about the exploits of the Kentucky riflemen under Andrew Jackson at the battle of New Orleans, became Old Hickory's campaign song for the presidency and was very popular during his tenure, 1829–37. The words were written by Samuel Woodworth, author of "The Old Oaken Bucket," to the traditional melody "Miss Bailey's Ghost."

HUSH LITTLE BABY This best-loved American folk lullaby dates from pioneer days.

I CAN'T GIVE YOU ANYTHING BUT LOVE Words by Dorothy Fields and music by Jimmy McHugh, from the show *Blackbirds of 1928.* One of the most popular songs of the 1920s and known since then through a steady stream of arrangements and recordings, in all styles of the popular idiom.

IDA, SWEET AS APPLE CIDER Hit song of the year 1903, introduced by its lyricist, Eddie Leonard, one of the last of the blackface minstrels. Eddie's sagging career as a song-and-dance man received a powerful boost through the song's popularity. He and numberless other famous and obscure vaudevillians performed it for years and pushed the song into the magic circle of more-than-a-million sheet-music sellers. Ida is still sweet and does not show her age.

I LOVE LIFE ". . . so I want to live—And drink of life's fullness, take all it can give." For the past half century a multitude of professional and would-be vocalists have tried to soar to fame with the jaunty strains of this tuneful Epicurean credo. Composer Mana-Zucca, a gifted lady of many musical accomplishments, started her career as a child piano prodigy and wrote many works, some even in the larger forms. Her best-known opus remains "I Love Life," a melody of sterling durability and a surefire vehicle for easy vocalizing.

I LOVE YOU TRULY Carrie Jacobs Bond, the writer of this song, a great lady of extraordinary gifts and indomitable spirit, overcame a series of personal misfortunes to become the most successful female songwriter this country has ever known. She not only wrote the words and music of her songs, she also published, performed and promoted them, and even designed the sheet-music covers. "I Love You Truly" first appeared in 1900 and in a few short years had sold more than a million copies.

IMPOSSIBLE DREAM, THE The ballad of Don Quixote from the musical play *Man of La Mancha.* Written in 1965, the show, with the song, became a worldwide success, and has been translated into twenty-two languages.

IN THE GLOAMING This tender love song, almost classic in its melodic simplicity and fine construction, was imported from England in the late 1870s.

IN THE GOOD OLD SUMMERTIME Two stage performers—George Evans, a minstrel, and Ren Shields, a comedian—wrote this song in 1902. Several publishers refused it, fearing that it would have only a seasonal appeal. A singer-actress, Blanche Ring, came to the rescue and introduced the song in a musical comedy, *The Defender,* and launched it on its long life of year-round popularity.

I'VE BEEN WORKING ON THE RAILROAD One of the oldest and most durable of railroad songs. Some opinions trace its ancestry to a Louisiana "Levee Song" of Negro lore; others believe that the melody is an old hymn adapted by the predominantly Irish work gangs while building the rail lines west of the Mississippi. The additions "Dinah, won't you blow your horn" and "Someone's in the kitchen with Dinah" are of much later vintage. Another variant is "The Eyes of Texas Are Upon You."

I'VE GOT THE WORLD ON A STRING Featured for decades in motion pictures, on radio shows and on innumerable recordings, this song was originally written for a nightclub review, the 1932 *Cotton Club Parade,* by Harold Arlen (music) and Ted Koehler (words). A fine example of

Arlen's songwriting art, it has actually gained in popularity through the years.

JEANIE WITH THE LIGHT BROWN HAIR The general assumption is that Stephen Foster had his wife in mind when he wrote this song. Although his marriage to Jane McDowell, daughter of a Pittsburgh physician, was not a very happy one, the loneliness during one of their periodic separations may well have inspired the line "I dream of Jeanie . . ." It is strange that this, one of Foster's most popular songs, was only moderately successful for many years following its publication in 1854.

JINGLE BELLS In the age of superhighways and jet travel, the simple pleasures of a sleigh ride seem far removed indeed. Nothing evokes these nearly forgotten winter days better than the merry jingle of this Yuletime classic. It was published in 1857 with the title "The One Horse Open Sleigh."

JUMP JIM CROW One of the earliest and most popular of blackface minstrel songs which, in 1828, introduced Negro-style singing and dancing to the stage. It is credited to actor-singer Thomas D. Rice, who is said to have heard it from a Negro worker. Originally inoffensive in meaning and intent, it was only much later that the character in this humorous dialect song became synonymous with racial segregation. (See also page 52)

JUNE IS BUSTIN' OUT ALL OVER This exuberantly tuneful and lively ode to summer by Richard Rodgers and Oscar Hammerstein II is from *Carousel,* a 1945 musical adaptation of Ferenc Molnar's *Liliom.*

KINGDOM COMING ("Year of Jubilo") One of Henry C. Work's best-known songs of the Civil War period. Work, an ardent abolitionist and intense Union partisan, was one of the most successful songwriters of the nineteenth century.

KISS ME AGAIN Hit song of the 1905 Victor Herbert operetta *Mlle. Modiste,* which became closely identified with the show's primadonna, Fritzi Scheff. This famous waltz is actually only the third segment of an extended solo number entitled "If I Were on the Stage," in which the heroine demonstrates her versatility in portraying various characters. As a shy country maid she sings a simple gavotte; as a Queen she delivers a stately polonaise, and in a "strong romantic role . . . a dreamy, sensuous waltz," which, of course, is "Kiss Me Again."

KISS ME QUICK AND GO A lively, flirtatious song of 1856, which represents a marked and welcome contrast to the tearful, sentimental ballads in vogue during that period.

LASS OF RICHMOND HILL, THE A charming song, in the Scottish folk idiom, which was very popular here in the 1790s and has retained its appeal. It was written by James Hook, a very successful and prolific English composer of the period.

LAST WEEK I TOOK A WIFE This favorite comedy song of the 1820s was featured with great success by a Mr. Twaite in the "grand pantomime" *The Forty Thieves.*

LIBERTY SONG, THE Published in 1768, this is believed to be our first patriotic song. The melody is that of a famous English air, "Hearts of Oak" by William Boyce, to which John Dickinson, a Delaware lawyer and member of the First Continental Congress, wrote the stirring words, "Come join hand in hand, brave Americans all. . . ."

LI'L LIZA JANE The lively syncopations and strophic construction of this old American tune indicate roots in early minstrelsy.

LILLY DALE The parlors, the ballrooms and the concert halls of the 1850s were filled with the strains of this, one of the best and most popular of heart-wrenching ballads, in which the untimely demise of a young maiden is mourned with doleful stanzas and a tear-filled refrain.

LISTEN TO THE MOCKING BIRD This song, published in 1855 as a "Sentimental Ethiopian Ballad," attained phenomenal popularity both here and in Europe. For decades the authorship was attributed solely to "Alice Hawthorne," a pseudonym for Septimus Winner, a prolific composer and publisher, of Philadelphia. In fact, only the words and the musical arrangement are by Winner; the melody was written by a black guitar-playing professional whistler (and occasional barber), Richard Milburn, whose name, with the proper credit, does appear on the original edition of the song.

LITTLE BROWN JUG Without question the best and merriest of American drinking songs. It is credited to Joseph E. Winner, younger brother of songwriter Septimus Winner ("Whispering Hope," "Listen to the Mocking Bird"), and was published in 1869. It is perhaps understandable that the author—in view of the gathering temperance forces —chose to use the pseudonym R. A. Eastburn on the printed copy.

LONG, LONG AGO A popular classic, expressing in a simple and durable form the ever-present nostalgia for the golden memories of the past. With words and music by Thomas Haynes Bayly, poet and songwriter, it was published in 1843.

LONG TAIL BLUE One of the very first blackface minstrel songs, popularized by the "Celebrated American Buffo Singer" George Washington Dixon in the late 1820s. The title of the tune refers to the long swallowtail coat, a characteristic stage costume of the "burnt cork" period.

LOOK DOWN THAT LONESOME ROAD This folk ballad beautifully blends various elements of Negro lore. The words are in the spiritual vein, while the melody, the "beat" and the harmonic context lean toward the blues.

LOVE'S OLD SWEET SONG The fine nostalgic refrain "Just a song at twilight, when the lights are low . . ." has been held in the affection of the American people since 1884, when it was imported from England. The melody is by a versatile Irish composer, James Lyman Molloy, who was also a distinguished member of the bar; the lyrics were written by the English poet G. Clifton Bingham. Both words and music represent the highest standards in the popular-song idiom of the nineteenth century.

MADEMOISELLE FROM ARMENTIÈRES One of the most popular songs to come out of World War I. Its origin is unsettled; there have been several claims of authorship, but the lilt and character of the tune strongly indicate roots in French folklore. Most of the endless humorous, and often unprintable, verses reflect the collective inspiration of the American doughboys.

MAN ON THE FLYING TRAPEZE, THE Originally published in 1868, without writer credits, under the title "The Flying Trapeze," this is the work of two Englishmen, George Leybourne and

Alfred Lee, who also wrote another hit of that year, "Champagne Charlie." In its early days "The Flying Trapeze" was performed mostly by singing circus clowns; later it became a mainstay in the repertory of famous vaudevillian Tony Pastor, and from then its wide popularity was firmly established. Through the years the song has been featured by many star performers in numerous versions, all of which furnish a zesty vehicle for vocal conviviality.

MAPLE LEAF RAG, THE   The most popular and one of the finest of instrumental rags was written in 1899 by Scott Joplin, an extraordinarily gifted Negro pianist and composer. He named the piece after the Maple Leaf Club in Sedalia, Missouri, where he was playing at the time. The great success of this piano rag prompted the publication of a vocal version, which came out in 1903, with the unusually clever lyrics of Sidney Brown.

MARINES' HYMN, THE   The words of this favorite service song were unquestionably inspired by the inscription on the flag of the Marine Corps, which, after the Mexican War of 1846–48, read, "From the shores of Tripoli to the halls of Montezuma." The tune is based on the "Gendarme Duet" from Offenbach's 1867 operetta *Geneviève de Brabant*. It is not certain when the song, in its present form, emerged, but it has been growing in popularity since its first publication in 1918, and was on the lips of all uniformed men during World War II.

MARY'S A GRAND OLD NAME   One of George M. Cohan's all-time hits, sung in the 1906 musical *Forty-five Minutes from Broadway*. Cohan also wrote the libretto of the show, which launched the careers of two star performers, Fay Templeton and Victor Moore.

MICHAEL, ROW THE BOAT ASHORE   This song, from the Georgia Sea Islands, off the Atlantic coast of the southern United States, is an interesting amalgam of two song idioms—the Negro spiritual and the sea chantey. It first appeared in a collection, *Slave Songs of the United States*, published in 1867. Nearly dormant for almost a century, it was rediscovered and attained best-seller status through many recordings in the early 1960s.

MIGHTY LAK' A ROSE   Ethelbert Nevin, a truly gifted composer and important contributor to the American heritage of beloved melodies ("The Rosary," "Narcissus") wrote this charming song in 1901, just a few months before his death. The words are by Frank L. Stanton, journalist and poet, who wrote a daily column for *The Atlanta Constitution* for nearly forty years. For every one of his columns he produced a poem, often in Negro dialect; this soft, tender lyric, perfectly matched with Nevin's enduring melody, is one of them.

MULLIGAN GUARD, THE   This famous satirical song sketch, introduced in 1873 and featured for many years by Harrigan and Hart, poked fun at the pseudomilitary organizations of post-Civil War years, whose members loved to parade in ornate military uniforms. The song was so successful and the satire so devastating that the clubs of the would-be soldiers soon disbanded. The tune's popularity spread as far as India, where, by Kipling's account, it became a favorite marching song of the British troops.

MY FAITH LOOKS UP TO THEE   Still one of the best-loved hymns of American Protestant congregations, this song was composed by Lowell Mason, "the Father of American church music," and first published in 1832, in a collection, *Spiritual Songs for Social Worship*.

MY GAL SAL   A line in this ever-popular song hit aptly describes its writer: "A heart that was mellow, an all 'round good fellow" was Paul Dresser, one of the most successful songwriters of his time, who was also a music publisher and brother of the novelist Theodore Dreiser. This song was written in 1905, at a time when Dresser was in strained financial circumstances, largely because of his trusting, sentimental nature and excessive generosity. He died just a few months before "Sal" scaled the heights of Tin Pan Alley success.

MY HEART STOOD STILL   This first great ballad hit to emerge from the legendary collaboration of Richard Rodgers and Lorenz Hart is from the 1927 musical *A Connecticut Yankee*, an adaptation of Mark Twain's satirical romance relating the imaginary adventures of a nineteenth-century Yankee in King Arthur's court.

MY LONG TAIL BLUE (see LONG TAIL BLUE)

MY OLD KENTUCKY HOME   It is believed that Foster was inspired to write this song by the serene and picturesque countryside at Bardstown, Kentucky, while visiting some relatives there in the summer of 1852. His manuscript sketches, however, indicate that there was an earlier version of the song, probably influenced by the great success of Harriet Beecher Stowe's *Uncle Tom's Cabin,* which began with the lines, "Oh goodnight, goodnight poor Uncle Tom, grieve not for your old Kentucky home." Although Foster always sang about the Negro with affectionate sympathy and deep understanding, there was never any abolitionist sentiment in his family; for this reason, he may have discarded this first version in favor of the later one, which became famous through the Christy Minstrels and was made the official song of Kentucky in 1928.

MY WILD IRISH ROSE   One of the best-loved Irish songs of all time, written in 1898 by singer-matinee idol Chauncey Olcott and introduced by him in the show *A Romance of Athlone.*

NIGHT AND DAY   When Cole Porter's publisher first heard this song, he was concerned that harmonically it might be too sophisticated for popular consumption. In theory he was right, but the song belied all predictions and became the greatest success of Porter's fabulous career. Fred Astaire introduced it in the 1932 musical comedy *Gay Divorcee.*

NOBODY KNOWS THE TROUBLE I'VE SEEN
One of the best-known spirituals and one of the most beautiful songs to emerge from the desperation and deep faith of an oppressed people.

OH PROMISE ME   Published as a concert song in 1889, this love ballad attracted little attention until a year later when composer Reginald de Koven added it—as an afterthought—to the score of his operetta *Robin Hood.* The show prospered, the song became a best-seller, and for many decades numberless bonds of holy matrimony have been tied against a background of its romantic strains.

OH! SUSANNA   One of the two Foster songs (the other is "Old Folks at Home") which are sung in nearly all languages of the globe. First published in 1848, the tune became popular very quickly through minstrel shows and was, in many different versions, the favorite of the forty-niners on their westward rush for gold. The overwhelming

success of the song established Foster as the most important songwriter of his time.

OLD COLONY TIMES   This merry song originated in the early 1800s when "good old Colony times" were already receding into a mist of nostalgia. It was popular throughout the nineteenth century and is still a very fine tune for community singing.

OLD DAN TUCKER   A tuneful bit of Americana which is noteworthy on several grounds. It is one of the earliest and most popular of blackface minstrel songs, its syncopated chorus contains the seeds of ragtime, and it has been a favorite "play-party" and square dance tune since its first publication in 1843. Daniel Decatur Emmett, who also wrote "Dixie," is credited with authorship.

OLD FOLKS AT HOME   Foster never saw the Swanee River. When he set out to write a song for the Christy Minstrels, all he had in mind was to write a nostalgic tune about a home near a southern stream. He first thought of the "Yazoo," then of the "Pedee River," but neither of these pleased him. His brother, on being asked for advice, suggested that they consult an atlas, in which they found the "Swanee." "That's it, that's it exactly!" exclaimed Stephen, and the little Florida river became known the world over.

OLD HUNDREDTH   This hymn of praise and thanksgiving was brought to the New World on the *Mayflower.* It is one of the oldest songs, still in constant use, in the English language. The melody, probably by Louis Bourgeois, first appeared in 1551 in the *Genevan Psalter.* A metrical version of the one hundredth Psalm ("All people that on earth do dwell . . .") was added ten years later. The words "Praise God from whom all blessings flow . . ."—the Doxology of Protestant churches—dates from the seventeenth century.

OL' MAN RIVER   From the score of *Show Boat,* which opened in 1927, and is a landmark of originality, artistry and native color in the annals of American musical theater. "Ol' Man River" is so well known and loved that it can be considered a part of our folk heritage. Jerome Kern's beautifully conceived melody soars to a breathtaking climax, and the touching, idiomatic words are Oscar Hammerstein II at his best.

OLD OAKEN BUCKET, THE The words and music of this song, written separately in the 1820s, were combined and became very popular about a century ago, with some help from the temperance movement. The image of "the moss-covered bucket that hung in the well" was thought to extol the homely virtue of drinking only fresh, clean, wholesome water.

OLD ROSIN THE BEAU ("Acres of Clams") First published anonymously in 1835, this song has maintained consistent popularity through numerous entirely different lyric versions. "Old Rosin"—as Sigmund Spaeth described it—"remains the prototype of all the songs about genial tipplers, whose popularity reaches a climax when they are about to be buried." The tune, with different words, was used in the presidential campaigns of James K. Polk, Abraham Lincoln and Horace Greeley. Finally, as "Acres of Clams," it was a favorite tune of prospectors during gold-rush days. In 1889, it became the official song of Washington State.

OLD ZIP COON (see TURKEY IN THE STRAW)

ONCE IN LOVE WITH AMY Words and music by Frank Loesser, from the score of *Where's Charley?*, a musical adaptation of the venerable English farce *Charley's Aunt*. This charming love song became a hit through the inimitable "slow and easy soft-shoe" rendition of the show's star, Ray Bolger. The instantaneous appeal of the song was demonstrated—and a bit of theatrical history made—when audiences immediately picked it up and sang along with the performer all through the show's long run.

ON THE BANKS OF THE WABASH, FAR AWAY The simple, folklike strains of this song must have been a sincere, heartfelt expression of its writer, Paul Dresser, who was born in Terre Haute, Indiana, on the banks of the Wabash. His younger brother, novelist Theodore Dreiser, wrote that Paul's songs "set forth with amazing accuracy the moods, the reactions, the aspirations of this very successful and very humble man." Published in 1899, the song sold a million copies of sheet music within a year. In 1913 it became the official state song of Indiana.

ON TOP OF OLD SMOKY A lovely "lonely tune" of the southern Appalachians, with roots in the song lore of the British Isles. It was widely known in pioneer days and traveled wherever the wagons rolled. Some older variants of the tune ("Little Mohee," "The Wagoner's Lad") are also still remembered. A strong revival of interest in folk songs produced several hit recordings of "Old Smoky" during the early 1950s.

OVER THE HILLS AND FAR AWAY This song was featured in *The Beggar's Opera*, the greatest hit of the eighteenth-century theater, and also, in various versions, in numerous other successful stage presentations played all over Colonial America (*The Recruiting Officer, The Devil To Pay*, etc.). An altogether fresh and zesty tune, which, in spite of its unmistakable baroque ancestry, does not in the least show its age.

PAPER OF PINS An old, popular and durable courting song, singing game and "play-party" tune. A perennial and timeless boy-and-girl dialogue for vocalizers of all ages.

PETER GRAY A lively, humorous folk tune which was in the repertory of many blackface minstrels. It is still often featured by folk singers today.

POOR WAYFARING STRANGER This beautiful religious soliloquy of a lonely balladeer "trav-'ling through this world of woe" originated in the early camp meetings of the southern mountain regions. It is one of the gems of American folklore.

POP! GOES THE WEASEL Children's play tune that originated in England centuries ago and may have been brought over by the Pilgrims. It was widely known in Colonial America, but its first publication occurred only in 1853. It is still popular, with innumerable nonsensical stanzas. Some scholars believe that the title has nothing to do with a quick, bursting sound involving an animal. In old English slang, "pop" meant to pawn something, and "weasels" were the tools of a trade.

PRAYER OF THANKSGIVING ("We Gather Together") This song of praise was written in the Netherlands in 1597 to celebrate that country's victory over Spain. The first Dutch settlers brought it to New Amsterdam and it eventually became America's hymn for Thanksgiving Day. The words beginning "We gather together" were written by Dr. Theodore Baker in 1894.

RED RIVER VALLEY A genuine folk song's becoming a commercial hit and best-seller is a frequent occurrence; the reverse, however, very seldom happens. This song is such a rarity. It started as "In the Bright Mohawk Valley," a popular song of the 1890s about New York State. It was picked up by folk singers and, within a relatively short period, adapted, polished and refined into an authentic western piece. "A lazy little tune," as Alan Lomax put it, "that drifts straight into your heart like smoke from a lonely cabin, rising and disappearing in the prairie sky."

RIDDLE SONG, THE Folklores of all nations abound in riddle songs. This one, the most popular in the English language, is very old, and, in various forms, was known in Elizabethan times. The early settlers took it to the mountains of Kentucky, from where it spread in all directions. The great folk-song revival during the years following World War II gave it new dimensions of popularity.

ROCK OF AGES The words of this famous hymn, a passionate expression of evangelical faith, by English clergyman Augustus M. Toplady, pre-date the melody by about a half century and first appeared in 1774. The tune, written by Thomas Hastings, one of America's most distinguished hymnodists, was published, with Toplady's words, in 1832. "No other hymn . . . has laid so broad and firm a grasp upon the English-speaking world," said a Victorian authority.

ROSALIE, THE PRAIRIE FLOWER Favorite sentimental ballad of the 1850s, popularized by the famous Christy Minstrels. The author's name appearing on the original edition was G. F. Wurzel, a pseudonym for George Frederick Root. ("Wurzel" is the German word for "root.") It is said that Root, who became one of the most successful songwriters of the Civil War period, had asked his publisher for an outright payment of one hundred dollars for the song, which was refused as excessive. He had to settle for a modest royalty contract, which eventually earned him more than three thousand dollars, a tremendous harvest for a writer in those days.

ROSARY, THE This American classic has proven conclusively that a song of high artistic integrity can also become a huge commercial success. Published in 1898, the sentimental religiosity of Robert Cameron Rogers' poem, with Ethelbert Nevin's inventive musical setting, had such a wide appeal that copies of the song sold in the millions, topping the sales of most Tin Pan Alley hits.

SAINT LOUIS BLUES W. C. Handy's classic lament-in-rhythm, about that St. Louis woman grieving for her faithless man, is the most popular and most imitated blues song ever written. This is not only a unique, best-loved American song, but also an important musical-historical document which crystallized a popular art form, the blues, and contributed greatly to the flowering of jazz.

SALLY IN OUR ALLEY The original version, both words and music, were by Henry Carey, famous English composer and playwright, who had it published in a 1726 collection of his songs "To please my friends, to mortify my enemies, to get money and reputation." Later the melody was superseded by another traditional English tune, "What Though I Am a Country Lass," and it is in this form that the song became very popular in eighteenth-century America.

SCARBOROUGH FAIR A very old folk song brought to the New World by the early English and Scottish settlers. Known in many variants, of which the one quoted in this volume climbed to the top of popularity charts during the late 1960s.

SEVENTY SIX TROMBONES One of the best and most popular marching tunes of our time, written by Meredith Willson for the 1957 Broadway hit The Music Man.

SHE'LL BE COMIN' ROUND THE MOUNTAIN An old spiritual, "When the Chariot Comes," was the ancestor of this popular "railroadin'" tune. The track-laying gangs adopted it, added a new set of repetitious verses and gave the whole thing a happy hillbilly twist. An indispensable entry in any good community songfest.

SHENANDOAH The story of a trader who wooed the daughter of an Indian chief, Shenandoah. An exquisite, romantic chant of the Seven Seas, American in origin, and probably born inland, somewhere along the wide Missouri, when the fur-laden boats of the *voyageurs* plied the rolling river.

SHORT'NIN' BREAD A twentieth-century version of a merry old Negro plantation tune, with echoes of minstrelsy and a touch of Tin Pan Alley veneer. Radio and recordings helped to establish its permanent popularity.

SIDEWALKS OF NEW YORK, THE   Also known as "East Side, West Side," this lilting waltz tune was written in 1894 by vaudevillian Charles B. Lawler and hat salesman James W. Blake. It soon attained nationwide popularity and eventually also became the unofficial theme song of New York City. In 1928 it accompanied Alfred E. Smith throughout his presidential campaign, and the New York World's Fair of 1939 made good use of the "boys and girls together" phrase as an automobile horn signal.

SILVER THREADS AMONG THE GOLD   Eben E. Rexford, the editor of a Wisconsin farm weekly, occasionally printed his own little poems in the paper to fill in empty spaces. In 1873 one of these verses caught the eye of songwriter Hart P. Danks, who bought it for three dollars and proceeded to write this, one of the favorite sentimental ballads of all time.

SO IN LOVE   Cole Porter, whose distinguished career as composer-lyricist spanned nearly a half century, reached the peak of his creative powers with the score of *Kiss Me, Kate*, a 1948 adaptation of Shakespeare's *The Taming of the Shrew*. "So in Love" from this show is a rare phenomenon: an artfully conceived dramatic love song which quickly reached the top of popularity charts and became a "standard" in its own time.

SOMETIMES I FEEL LIKE A MOTHERLESS CHILD   A spiritual of striking beauty and expressive power, singing about the loneliness and despair of a "true believer—a long way from home."

SPRINGFIELD MOUNTAIN   There are numerous variants of this, one of America's earliest and best-loved folk ballads, about a youth bitten by a "pesky sarpent" and his girl who tried to save him, but who also died of the "pizen." Originally it was probably meant as a sincere lament, but it soon acquired humorous overtones and is now best known and enjoyed in this comic version.

STAR DUST   This phenomenally successful song was written by Hoagy Carmichael, in 1929, as a piano solo in a pseudo-ragtime style. A year later, with the tempo relaxed and the beat mellowed,

a fine lyric by Mitchell Parish was added. During its remarkable tenure of undiminished popularity, it has been recorded more than any other American song.

STAR SPANGLED BANNER, THE   The melody of our national anthem was borrowed from an English song of merriment and conviviality, titled "To Anacreon in Heaven," and was well-known in America long before Francis Scott Key's inspiring words were added in 1814. The young Baltimore lawyer wrote his poem during the British naval bombardment of Fort McHenry, while he was on board one of the enemy ships, as an emissary to obtain the release of a friend. When the fierce shelling ceased and dawn came, he was elated to see that "our flag was still there." The song became popular immediately and was soon recognized as our national anthem; an act of Congress made this official in 1931.

STREETS OF LAREDO, THE   (see COWBOY'S LAMENT)

SWEET BETSY FROM PIKE   Betsy and her lover, Ike, two hearty and rugged forty-niners, traveled the long road from Pike County, Missouri, to California and survived to sing about it. The many grueling adventures they experienced are recorded in this splendid folk tune with spice, zest and humor.

SWEET GENEVIEVE   George Cooper, a close friend and occasional collaborator of Stephen Foster, wrote the words of this song in 1869, after the death of his young wife, Genevieve. In financial distress, he sold his poem outright (an all-too-familiar story in those days) for the sum of five dollars to composer Henry Tucker, whose fine melody proved to be a perfect match for the poem's nostalgic outpouring. Known around the world for more than a century, it is still a strong favorite of all lovers of close harmony.

SWEET IS THE BUDDING SPRING OF LOVE   A two-and-a-half-century-old, and still delightful, whimsical love ballad from *Flora, or Hob in the Well*, one of the first musical shows presented on the American stage. Written by one of the principal players in the original cast of *The Beggar's Opera*, it was first played here in Charlestown, now Charleston, S.C., in 1735, and remained popular with colonial audiences throughout the eighteenth century.

SWEETEST STORY EVER TOLD, THE Who is R. M. Stults? The name certainly would not spark recognition today even among musical connoisseurs. Mr. Stults, an erudite musician, wrote many vocal and instrumental pieces around the turn of the century, including this very popular and still appealing love song. The familiar strains of this dainty gavotte—"Tell me, do you love me?" —were plunked out on countless parlor pianos and warbled across the footlights by a multitude of vaudeville crooners of the 1890s.

SWING LOW SWEET CHARIOT The yearning for "home," the cry for spiritual and physical salvation, are expressed with timeless beauty and simplicity in this song. The Fisk Jubilee Singers featured it on their programs and delighted audiences both here and in Europe.

TA-RA-RA BOOM-DER-É Henry J. Sayers, an impresario for a theatrical road company known as *The Tuxedo Girls,* heard this song in 1891 in a notorious St. Louis cabaret. He laundered the words somewhat, included a not too subtle "plug" for his show ("A sweet Tuxedo girl you see . . ."), and left the naughtily repetitious refrain unchanged. The song became a worldwide success through the presentation of Lottie Collins, a celebrated music-hall performer of the 1890s.

TEA FOR TWO The indestructible hit song by Irving Caesar and Vincent Youmans, from the show *No, No, Nanette,* which opened in 1924 and enjoyed an equally successful long-run Broadway revival nearly half a century later. The song's popularity never flagged, and the characteristic lilt of the melody has been easily adapted to all styles of our ever-changing popular idiom: jazz, swing, mambo, rock. Most people, however, still enjoy it best with the original, easygoing "soft-shoe" beat, with a bit of intimate harmonizing on the phrase, "We will raise a family, a boy for you, a girl for me."

TENTING ON THE OLD CAMP GROUND (see TENTING TONIGHT)

TENTING TONIGHT War-weariness and longing for home are expressed in simple, unpretentious and lasting terms in this Civil War ballad. "Many are the hearts that are weary tonight, wishing for the war to cease," sings the chorus. It is not surprising that the song was popular in both North and South.

THERE IS A TAVERN IN THE TOWN In its present form this song was first published anonymously in 1883, but it is unquestionably much older. In its early days the song's popularity was largely restricted to colleges and their glee clubs, but the bright and easy-to-harmonize tune was destined for much wider success. It is still favored as an ideal piece for community singing.

THERE'LL BE A HOT TIME Although there is no consensus as to its origin, the overwhelming evidence suggests that this rambunctious tune was written by two minstrel performers, singer Joe Hayden (words) and band leader Theodore A. Metz (music). It was popular on the minstrel stages and also in many less dignified waterfront establishments before it became the favorite chant of Teddy Roosevelt's Rough Riders, who sang it so often that our Spanish adversaries thought it must be our national anthem.

THERE'S MUSIC IN THE AIR George F. Root, composer of "Tramp! Tramp! Tramp!," "The Battle Cry of Freedom" and "Just Before the Battle, Mother," also wrote many popular ballads and hymns in the years preceding the Civil War. This gentle air, published in 1854 and considered by many to be his best work, has words by Fanny Crosby, blind poet and author of numerous widely known hymns.

TOM DOOLEY The words of this folk ballad relate a factual account of a crime committed by an embittered Confederate veteran, Tom Dula, who, in a rage of jealousy, or seeking revenge, killed his sweetheart, Laura Foster. He was hanged in Wilkes County, North Carolina, in the spring of 1868. The story of Tom Dula (later changed to Tom Dooley for easier singing) inspired this song, of which numerous variants circulated in the Great Smokies for many decades. The present version became very popular in the early 1950s through recordings by several folk singers and singing groups.

TOYLAND From one of Victor Herbert's most successful operettas, *Babes in Toyland* (1903). This score also contained the famous "March of the Toys." This great and versatile composer was a prodigious worker, a most genial man and an epicure. It is said that in his studio he had a small washtub filled with ice, in which lay a large assortment of fine bottled beverages. He drew sips of inspiration from these bottles to fit the mood of the piece on which he was working at the time. One can easily connect a heady Tokay with "Gypsy Love Song" and a good champagne with "Kiss Me Again," but one wonders whether "Toyland" did not pose a problem.

TRAMP! TRAMP! TRAMP! ("The Prisoner's Hope") Words and music of this memorable Union marching song were written in 1863 by George F. Root, an eminently successful composer of the Civil War years. Because of its extreme popularity it crossed the battle lines and was adopted, with some lyric changes, by the Confederate troops.

TURKEY IN THE STRAW The classic all-American square-dance tune. It is a folk version of an early minstrel song, "Old Zip Coon," published anonymously in 1834. There are innumerable verses attached to this melody, which is probably of Irish origin.

UNDER THE BAMBOO TREE This imperishable reminder of the tuneful ragtime era was written in 1902 by one of the first successful black songwriting teams, Robert Cole and J. Rosamond Johnson. Cole, who studied dramatics at Atlanta University, and Johnson, a graduate of the New England Conservatory of Music, joined forces in New York to perform in vaudeville and also turned out a long list of popular tunes. Tin Pan Alley legend has it that this song was conceived as a syncopated adaptation of the spiritual "Nobody Knows the Trouble I've Seen," which—on musical grounds at least—is rather far-fetched.

WABASH CANNONBALL The "jingle, the rumble and the roar" of this mythical supertrain, called The Wabash Cannonball, may have inspired a lonely hobo to create this hillbilly classic. It is a relatively recent entry in the rich catalogue of railroad songs.

WAIT FOR THE WAGON The eternal game of courting had often taken place on pleasant twosome rides on whatever conveyance was the novelty or the favorite of the day. All this was duly recorded in song: Daisy on the bicycle built for two, Lucille in the merry Oldsmobile, Josephine in the flying machine. A half century earlier, "dear Phyllis" had to be satisfied with more modest means of transportation; she was urged to "wait for the wagon and we'll all take a ride." We can be sure—as the popularity of this song amply attests—that the outing was not less romantic.

WAIT TILL THE SUN SHINES, NELLIE Composer Harry Von Tilzer maintained throughout his life that, among the two thousand songs he wrote, this was and remained his favorite. It is easy to see why—even disregarding the fact that it made a fortune for both him and for lyricist Andrew B. Sterling. The fine melody, the lively two-step beat, the perfect fit of words and music, all contributed to give the tune its irresistible spontaneity and appeal. It was published in 1905.

WALKING FOR THAT CAKE Another Harrigan and Hart success of 1877, advertised as an "Exquisite Picture of Negro Life and Customs." This was one of the first published cakewalk songs and anticipated the later fad by at least twenty years. The tune itself, in spite of its characteristic strutting tempo and occasional syncopations, is still closer to a quadrille than to cakewalk.

WE SHALL OVERCOME A most inspiring and deeply moving song of the civil rights movement. The melody is that of an old spiritual; the words —dozens of improvised stanzas—are the creations of many people, mostly union workers of the coal mines and tobacco fields. It attained its nationwide status as a song of freedom, brotherhood and dignity during the protest marches of the 1960s.

WHEN JOHNNY COMES MARCHING HOME As long as wars persist, this robust tune, with its surefire homecoming celebration lyric, will not lose its appeal. Written in 1863 by Patrick S. Gilmore, official bandmaster of the Union Army, it became increasingly popular in the postwar decades and inspired countless arrangements and adaptations in all conceivable styles from minstrel parodies to symphonic variations. The melody, Gilmore's credit notwithstanding, bears definite earmarks of Irish folklore, but the claim that it derived from a touching antiwar ballad, "Johnny, I Hardly Knew Ye" (in which a girl meets her maimed sweetheart returning from war), is unsubstantiated, and, most probably, the reverse is true.

WHEN THE SAINTS COME MARCHING IN One of the rousing, hand-clapping spirituals which lent itself ideally to the expression of high-pitched revivalist fervor. It was also a favorite marching tune of Negro brass bands which, around the turn of the century, proliferated in the cities of the South, especially in New Orleans. These bands were much in demand for rallies and funerals; a band, on its way to the cemetery, would play a sedate "Nearer My God to Thee," and return with an exuberant "Dixieland" rendition of the "Saints." This is one of our earliest authentic jazz numbers.

WHEN YOU AND I WERE YOUNG, MAGGIE A Canadian schoolteacher, George W. Johnson, wrote these words as a loving tribute to the memory of his wife, Maggie, who died in the first year of their marriage. The melody is by an English musician, James A. Butterfield, who lived in Chicago at the time. It was published by the composer himself, in 1866, and became popular all over the world.

WHILE STROLLING THROUGH THE PARK Originally titled "The Fountain in the Park," this song was introduced at Tony Pastor's vaudeville emporium in 1884, and soon became a great favorite, not only as a tune, but also as a soft-shoe dance routine. The song is credited to a mysterious Ed Hailey, of whom no record whatever is available, and dedicated to Robert A. Keiser, a well-known songwriter of the time. The general assumption is that, in fact, Keiser is the author.

WILDWOOD FLOWER This wild flower which for a long time grew discreetly in the shady groves of our song heritage, burst into full bloom of popularity in the 1960s. So far, scholarly research has not been able to trace its exact origin. Some believe that the pseudo-archaic flavor of the lyric may derive from classic Greek or Elizabethan sources. The melody, simple and most appealing, defies musical classification. A delightful hybrid, this song, a great favorite of our generation and destined to continue blooming for many seasons.

WOMEN ALL TELL ME, THE This noble ancestor of the "Little Brown Jug" must have been popular in Colonial America, as it appears in many song collections of the period, including the widely used *Convivial Songster*. It was first published in England; words and music are anonymous.

WONDROUS LOVE The early nineteenth-century camp meetings needed religious songs which were simple enough to be learned quickly by large assemblies; often folk tunes were matched with newly written spiritual texts. This one, one of our most beautiful folk hymns, has words by Alex Means, a Methodist minister, and the melody is an adaptation of "Captain Kidd," an old ballad about the legendary British pirate.

WOODMAN, SPARE THAT TREE A song of phenomenal popularity, published in 1837, which initiated a long trend of sentimental balladry. It was composed by Henry Russell, an English-born pianist, songwriter and singer, who spent several successful years in America. By all accounts, he was a master showman who "was an expert at wheedling audiences out of applause." The motive behind this song was not ecological, of course, but purely sentimental ("My heart strings round thee cling, close as thy bark, old friend").

YANKEE DOODLE This infectiously merry tune, which was so important during the Revolutionary War, is of undetermined origin. Some think that a British Army surgeon, stationed in Albany, composed it to poke fun at the Yankee troops. Others believe that it is a New World version of the old English nursery rhyme "Lucy Locket"; at least a half dozen other European countries are also claimants. In all probability, it is a native American song, written in the 1750s, which became known quickly in many versions and countless parodies. It is the embodiment of the "Spirit of '76" and has enjoyed continuous popularity for two centuries.

YANKEE DOODLE BOY, THE George Michael Cohan, the one and only and original "Yankee Doodle Dandy—born on the fourth of July," burst upon Broadway in 1904, at the age of twenty-six, in the show *Little Johnny Jones*. He wrote book, music and lyrics for this, one of the first truly American musical comedies; he also directed it and played the leading role. "Yankee Doodle Boy" was one of the hit songs of the show, and time has not dimmed its star-spangled exuberance and luster.

YEAR OF JUBILO (see KINGDOM COMING)

YELLOW ROSE OF TEXAS, THE This rousing tune about the light-skinned Negro girl of Texas who "beats the belles of Tennessee," was first published in 1853—the author identified only as "J.K." —and was probably intended for the minstrel stage. During the Civil War it was a popular marching song of the Confederate troops, and during the postwar decades it kept spirits high on U.S. cavalry outposts, on the cowboy trails and at many social gatherings. In 1955, numerous hit recordings re-established it as a favorite "sing-along" piece.

YOU NAUGHTY, NAUGHTY MEN Hit song of the epoch-making musical extravaganza *The Black Crook,* which opened in 1866 at Niblo's Garden in New York. A lavish production, this show—for the first time in American theatrical history—featured a chorus of young ladies in brief skirts and pink tights. It created a sensation and a raging controversy. "Nothing in any other Christian country . . . has approached the indecent and demoralizing exhibition," commented an editorial. This song also represented something new in an era which thrived on sentimentality and nostalgia; for the first time a set of cleverly constructed lyric stanzas mounted an effective and witty attack on male hypocrisy. "Of love you get us dreaming, And when with hope we're teeming, We find you are but scheming, Oh you naughty, naughty men"—are not only novel and daring lines for their time, but also point the way straight to Lorenz Hart and Cole Porter. (See also page 122)

YOU'RE IN THE ARMY NOW The doughboys of World War I were initiated with this brief, good-natured and rather explicit vocal greeting of what lay ahead. The melody obviously derived from, or imitated, a trumpet call, as it employs only the three characteristic tones of a horn signal.

INDEX OF TITLES

INDEX OF FIRST LINES

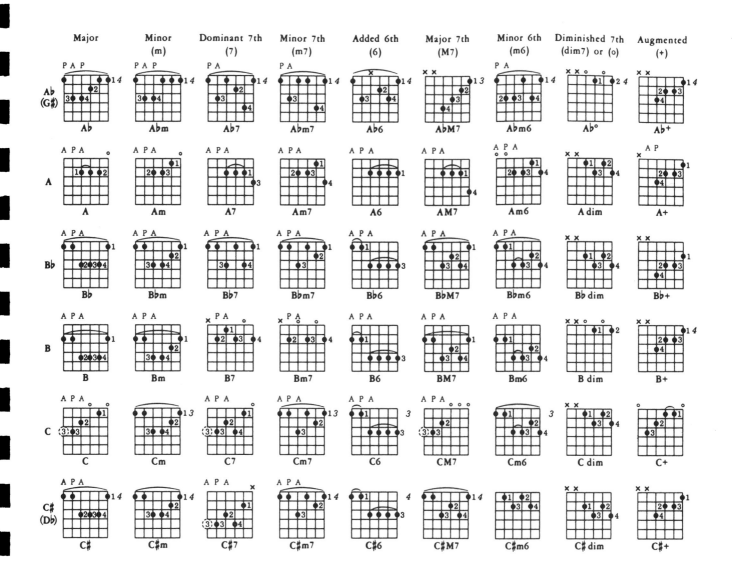

BASIC GUITAR CHORDS

Key to symbols employed in this chart:

P = Primary Bass String
A = Alternate Bass String
x = String Not To Be Played
o = Open String To Be Played

③ = Finger May Be Moved
For Alternate Bass

⌒ = Barre

Note:

The numbers immediately to the right of
some of the diagrams indicate the fret at
which the chord is to begin.

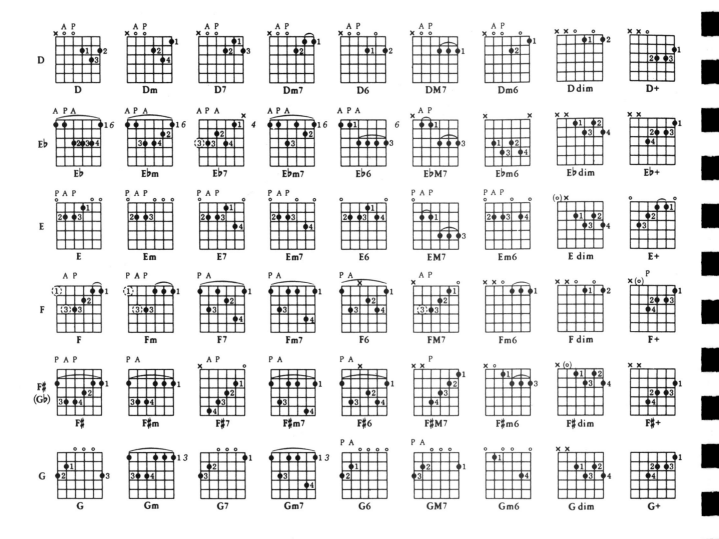